W9-CEU-049

NOV 6 '78

THE PHILOSOPHY OF LEIBNIZ
and the Modern World

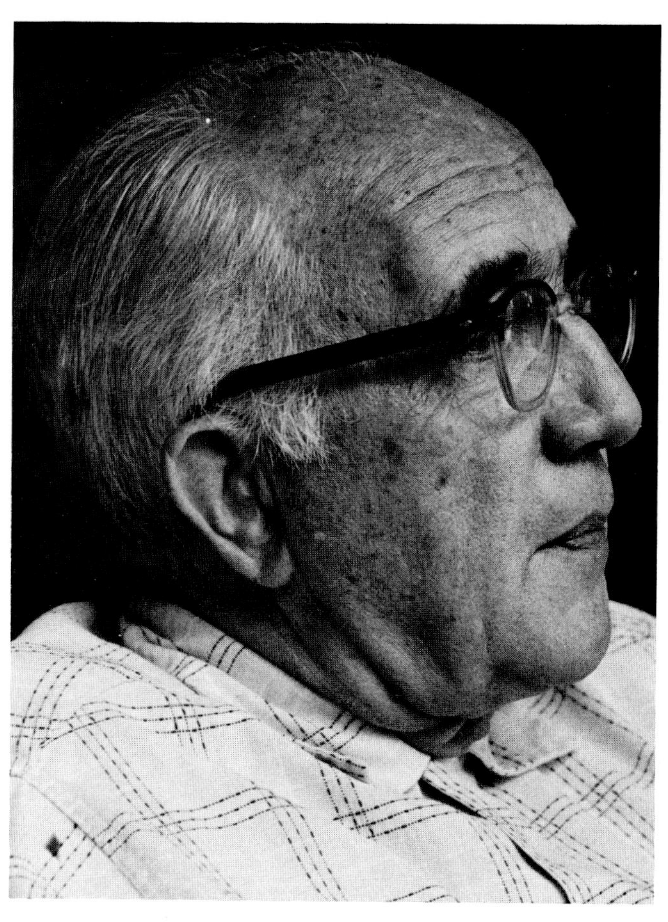

LEROY E. LOEMKER
Photograph by Kay Leclerc

GOTTFRIED WILHELM LEIBNIZ
Copy of a portrait by an unknown master in late autumn 1711.
Courtesy of Library of the Land of Lower Saxony, Hanover, Germany

THE PHILOSOPHY OF

LEIBNIZ

and the Modern World

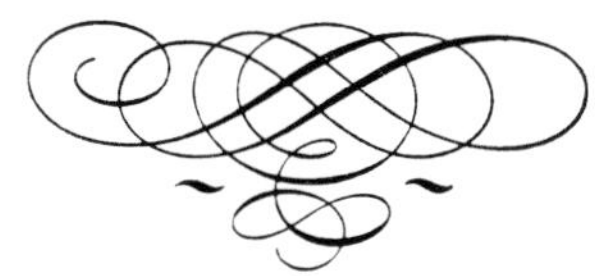

Edited by

IVOR LECLERC

1973
Vanderbilt University Press
Nashville

Library of Congress Cataloguing-in-Publication Data

Leclerc, Ivor, comp., 1915–
The philosophy of Leibniz and the modern world.

Ten papers by L. E. Loemker, and four other papers (by M. Čapek, I. Leclerc, N. Rescher, and N. L. Wilson) which were read at a special meeting of the Georgia Philosophical Society in 1966.
Includes bibliographical references.
1. Leibniz, Gottfried Wilhelm, Freiherr von, 1646–1716. I. Loemker, Leroy E. II. Title.
B2598.L4 193 72–1346
ISBN 0–8265–1181–3

Printed in the United States of America by
Heritage Printers, Inc.
Charlotte, North Carolina

Contents

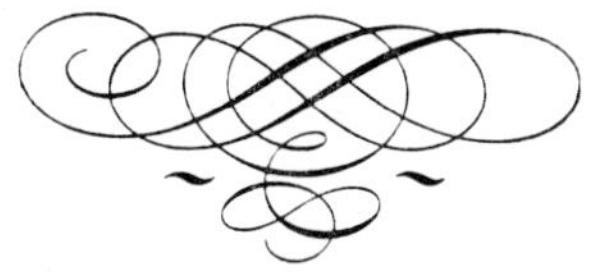

PART III: *Historical Studies*

Abbreviations

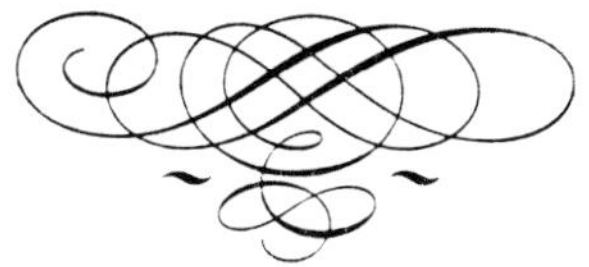

Editions of Leibniz's writings from which quotations are made with some frequency will be referred to in footnotes by the following abbreviations:

Academy Ed.	*Gottfried Wilhelm Leibniz: Sämtliche Schriften und Briefe,* edited by the Preussische Akademie der Wissenschaften, after 1945 the Deutschen Akademie der Wissenschaften (Berlin: Akademie-Verlag, 1923–).
Couturat	*Opuscules et fragments inédits de Leibniz,* edited by Louis Couturat (Paris: F. Alkan, 1903; Hildesheim: Georg Olms, 1961).
Dutens	*Gothofredi Guillelmi Leibnitii. . . . Opera Omnia,* edited by Louis Dutens (Geneva: Fratres de Tournes, 1768).
Jagodinsky	*Leibnitiana elementa philosophiae arcanae de summa rerum,* edited by Ivan Jagodinsky (Kazan, 1913).
Gerhardt	*Die philosophischen Schriften von Gottfried Wilhelm Leibniz,* edited by C. I. Gerhardt, 7 vols. (Berlin: Wiedmann, 1875–90; unchanged reprint, Hildesheim: Georg Olms, 1965).
Gerhardt Math.	*Leibnizens mathematische Schriften,* edited by C. I. Gerhardt, 7 vols. (Berlin: A. Asher; Halle: H. W. Schmidt, 1949–63; unchanged reprint, Hildesheim: Georg Olms, 1961).
Grua	*G. W. Leibniz: Textes inedits d'apres les manuscrits de la Bibliotheque provinciale de Hanoure,* edited by Gaston Grua (Paris: Presses Universitaires de France, 1948).

Guhrauer	*Leibniz' Deutsche Schriften*, edited by G. E. Guhrauer (Berlin: Veit, 1838–40; unchanged reprint, Hildesheim: Georg Olms, 1966).
Loemker	*Leibniz: Philosophical Papers and Letters*, translated and with an introduction by Leroy E. Loemker, revised edition in 1 vol. (Dordrecht, Holland: D. Reidel Publishing Company, 1969).

Preface

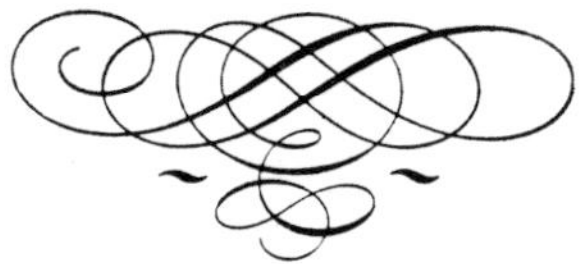

ALFRED NORTH WHITEHEAD, some three decades ago, made the comment that "there is a book to be written and its title should be, 'The Mind of Leibniz'."[1] That the book still remains to be written is not surprising, because of the sheer magnitude of the task. That becomes clear from the first essay in this volume, in which Professor Leroy E. Loemker, the foremost Leibniz scholar in America, has briefly surveyed the breadth, scope, variety, and depth of the lifework of Leibniz. From this survey it is also evident that there is room for a good many other books on Leibniz, especially at the present time when the particular significance of Leibniz for our day is becoming increasingly appreciated.

There has indeed recently been occurring a revival of interest in Leibniz's thought. A mark, but not the beginning, of this is the International Leibniz Congress held in Hanover, Germany, in November 1966, which celebrated the two hundred and fiftieth anniversary of the death of Leibniz. At the Congress an International Leibniz Society (the Gottfried-Wilhelm-Leibniz-Gesellschaft) was founded and has since flourished, holding a number of meetings each year for the reading and discussion of philosophical papers. The Society also publishes a journal, *Studia Leibniziana,* and special supplementary volumes. Further, the Society is connected with the Leibniz-Archiv in Hanover, which continues the monumental task of preparing the complete edition of Leibniz's writings, a vast amount of which still lie

1. A. N. Whitehead, *Modes of Thought* (Cambridge: The University Press; New York: The Macmillan Company, 1938), p. 4.

unpublished in the archives. A complete index to the Gerhardt editions of Leibniz's writings is now under preparation under the editorship of Professor Gottfried Martin of Bonn University.

The main intent and justification for this volume is to bring together a number of papers on Leibniz by Professor Loemker—papers published over a number of years and scattered in various journals. Other essays included in the work are papers which were read at a special meeting of the Georgia Philosophical Society held at Emory University in April 1966 in commemoration of the two hundred and fiftieth anniversary of the death of Leibniz.

Many of Professor Loemker's papers were written at a time when interest in Leibniz was much smaller than it is now, which alone is a good reason for their republication. Further, however, the understanding of Leibniz to be gained from these papers is greater when they are taken together than when they are read separately over a period of time. Although his publications have not been numerous, they have established Professor Loemker's reputation internationally, as indicated by the fact that it was he who was invited by the German journal *Philosophische Rundschau* to write for them the survey of the postwar literature on Leibniz.[2]

Professor Loemker's major contribution, to date, especially so far as the English-speaking world is concerned, is his two-volume translation of an extensive selection of Leibniz's writings entitled *Leibniz: Philosophical Papers and Letters*,[3] with a long introduction on "Leibniz as Philosopher." That this, the only translation of Leibniz in English which comes anywhere near adequacy in extent even for graduate work in philosophy, let alone for scholarship, should have gone out of print and should not have found another American publisher can hardly be viewed as to the credit of this country. Fortunately, a second edition of the book, revised and in one volume, has appeared, brought out in 1969 under the imprint of the D. Reidel Publishing Company of Dordrecht, Holland.

For many years a considerable part of Professor Loemker's

2. *Philosophische Rundschau*, 13. Jahrgang, Heft 2, 1965, pp. 81–111.
3. Chicago: The University of Chicago Press, 1956.

philosophical effort has been devoted to a book on Leibniz's philosophical development. Its appearance is eagerly awaited. Meanwhile, another of his books, entitled *Struggle for Synthesis,* is in the process of being published by Harvard University Press. The book—a mellow, erudite product of a lifetime of study and reflection on the age of Leibniz, the seventeenth century, in the wide range of its significance for the present-day world—examines the conflict between freedom and order in that vital period, tracing the complicated interweaving of thought and action across the spectrum of human life and experience and contributing considerably to the illumination of the inheritance with which we today have to come to terms.

So far I have stressed the fact that Leibniz's particular relevance to the present day is steadily coming to be appreciated. It is appropriate in the preface to this volume also to elaborate somewhat on a few of the reasons for Leibniz's special relevance. Why should he, more than the other great figures of that "Century of Genius,"[4] be of so particular an importance to us today? After all, did not thinkers like Galileo, Descartes, and Newton have a much more profound effect on subsequent developments?

That they did must certainly be acknowledged. But it is precisely in this connection that Leibniz is of such pertinence to the present day. For Leibniz, more penetratingly than his contemporaries, understood the philosophical foundations of the science of nature which had been effectively launched by Galileo and had reached maturity in Newton's *Philosophiae Naturalis Principia Mathematica.* In the seventeenth and eighteenth centuries, the question of the philosophical foundations was a very live issue, but Kant's *Die Metaphysischen Anfangsgründe der Naturwissenschaften* (1786) was the last great work on the topic. The combined consequences of the immense success of the Newtonian scheme in physical science, on the one hand, and of Kantian philosophy, on the other, was the turning away of the interest of philosophers to other fields. The philosophical conception of material atomism gained complete ascendency over all rivals

4. The title of Chapter 3 of A. N. Whitehead's *Science and the Modern World* (Cambridge: The University Press; New York: The Macmillan Company, 1927).

and became entrenched firmly in physical science; and by an interpretation of Newton, space and time were accepted as having the status of some kind of independent existents.

But twentieth-century developments in the science of nature have undermined the concepts accepted as fundamental during the previous two centuries. Slowly still, but inevitably, the recognition is growing that the entire issue of the philosophical foundations of natural science will have to be opened up again; the whole range of problems will have to be examined anew. In other words, there will have to occur in the near future the kind of fundamental rethinking which was necessitated in the seventeenth century and which the philosophical endeavor of that time represented. We are still standing very much at the beginning of the process of rethinking; with some notable exceptions, very little of it has yet been attempted, and indeed even the realization of its necessity is still not very widespread.

It is in this situation that Leibniz is of particular relevance to us, in a number of respects. One of these arises from the very difference between his time and ours. The inquiry into the philosophical foundations has during the last two centuries languished to the point that the understanding of the problems at issue has been largely lost. Leibniz, by contrast, stood in a very live tradition of that fundamental inquiry; thus a study of Leibniz today assists enormously toward the recovery of that understanding.

But of equal significance is Leibniz's own positive contribution to that inquiry, the import of which to the present situation is immense. In his time, his positive contribution came to be quickly eclipsed by the Newtonian development. Now, more than two and a half centuries later, his thought might come to have a more profound influence than it had then.

I should like to express my gratitude to the Reverend Edward C. Connelly for his painstaking and extensive assistance in preparing this book for the press and for the proofreading.

I should like also to express my gratitude for a grant from the Research Committee of Emory University toward the printing costs of the book.

Atlanta, Georgia
July 1970

IVOR LECLERC

Acknowledgments

I wish to thank the following for their kind permission to reprint in this volume those of the papers which had previously been published:

The *Journal of the History of Ideas,* for the following four essays by Leroy E. Loemker: "Leibniz's Judgments of Fact," VII, No. 4 (1946); "A Note on the Origin and Problem of Leibniz's *Discourse* of 1686," VIII, No. 4 (1947); "Boyle and Leibniz," XVI, No. 1 (1955); and "Leibniz and the Herborn Encyclopedists," XXII, No. 3 (1961), copyright © 1946, 1947, 1955, and 1961 by the *Journal of the History of Ideas.*

The *Kant-Studien,* for "Leibniz and the Limits of Empiricism," by Leroy E. Loemker, 56. Jahrgang, Heft 3–4, 1966.

The Open Court Publishing Company, for "On Substance and Process in Leibniz," by Leroy E. Loemker, from *Process and Divinity: The Hartshorne Festschrift,* edited by William C. Reese and Eugene Freeman, copyright © 1964 by the Open Court Publishing Company.

The *Philosophical Review,* for "Leibniz's Doctrine of Ideas," by Leroy E. Loemker, 55 (1946), copyright © 1946 by the *Philosophical Review.*

Franz Steiner Verlag GmbH, for "Das ethische Anliegen des Leibnizschen Systems," by Leroy E. Loemker, from *Studia Leibniziana Supplementa* IV (1969); and "Logische Schwierigkeiten der Leibnizsche Metaphysik," by Nicolas Rescher, from *Studia Leibniziana Supplementa* I (1968).

Verlag Anton Hain K.G., for "Leibniz's Conception of Philosophical Method," by Leroy E. Loemker, from *Zeitschrift fur Philosophische Forschung,* Band XX, Heft 3 and 4, 1966.

I. L.

THE PHILOSOPHY OF LEIBNIZ
and the Modern World

1

Leibniz and Our Time

Leroy E. Loemker

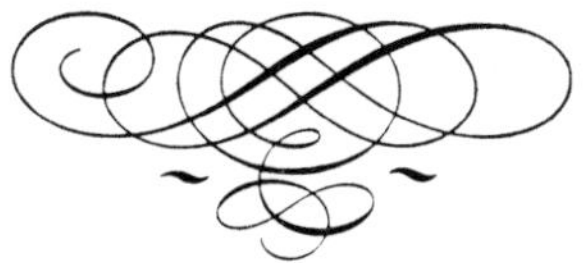

Can one draw out Leviathan with a fishhook? The magnitude of Leibniz's intellectual vision, the prophetic depth of his mathematical, linguistic, and philosophical perceptions, and the grandeur of his great syntheses—of individual particularity with universal harmony, of the widest possible range of scientific and historical facts with a systematic philosophical whole, and (most of all) of this philosophical system with a comprehensive program of projects for the peace of Europe and the resolution of its cultural tensions—all of these place him beyond the angling of lesser thinkers who have sought to interpret him and beyond the critical barbs of those who have probed for gaps and inadequacies in his thought. Even to try to weigh the enduring influence of a mind so comprehensive, original, and adventuresome is difficult.

The age in which Leibniz lived was in many ways alien to ours, in no way more so than in the faith in reason to which its best minds clung, and in their quest for unity and harmony in human affairs. In a culture in which specialization is encouraged to the point that our children write "research papers" in the third grade and become junior scientists in high school, it is not easy —though it might be wholesome to try—to achieve something of the comprehension and universality of his mind.

In its strife and disorder, on the other hand, his age is, perhaps more than any other, like our own. Leibniz was born in 1646 in the provincial university city of Leipzig, two years before the end of the Thirty Years' War, which for three decades had laid waste to Northern Europe and decimated its population. With the cessation of war began an unhappy peace of exhaustion. In the seven decades of Leibniz's life, Europe experienced very few years of peace. Old institutions and adjustments had failed, new powers had been released, and divided allegiances perpetuated conflict. The two swords upon which European order had once been built had long since lost what unifying power they once may have had: the Papacy through Reformation and schism, the Holy Roman Empire through disintegration and the rise of new independent nations, its two remaining parts in constant danger —Austria, from the Turks, who twice reached the gates of Vienna, and both Austria and Spain from Louis XIV of France. Dissent and deviation could be overcome, it seemed, only through violence. Rulers of states, however large or small, no longer derived their right to rule from ancient Roman families, but from God; but Charles I, by divine right King of England and Scotland, was executed by order of the English Parliament. Calvinist Holland was known as the liberal refuge of the oppressed. Even the Jews from Spain had found refuge there, and when Huguenots and Jansenists were persecuted in France, it was in Holland that they found freedom. Yet Holland executed or imprisoned its own religious dissenters, and Catholics persecuted in England had to find refuge in France. Early in the century, the gentle Cardinal Spee, after having heard the last confessions of several hundred women burned for witchcraft, wrote the *Cautio Criminalis* to express his conviction that all were innocent of the charge and to urge a cessation of the murders.

New discoveries and new ventures threatened what stability remained. Petty principalities still operated on the basis of laws which mixed memories of Roman justice with old tribal traditions, but the new strong nations were already sweeping old boundaries aside. Exploration, missionary zeal, and trade were discovering strange new cultures both to the East and to the West. Under its greatest Czar, Peter I, barbaric Russia was struggling toward

Europeanization; beyond it, China was proving to the Jesuit missionaries a source of new science, new tastes, and new wisdom. New wealth flowed from Africa and the Americas. Conquest and colonization outmatched missionary zeal in capturing these new worlds now exposed to Europe's blessings and miseries alike.

There is much evidence to show that Leibniz did not consider himself a philosopher, even though he was always conscious of formulating a new system of thought to provide understanding and moral support for the projects which he proposed for the peace of Europe. Philosophers were regarded as Schoolmen, members of Universities, and, like Descartes and Spinoza, Leibniz viewed thought as inseparable from practice, and practice as inevitably demanding action for reform, whether in individual life or in the common world. It was with reason that he chose as his life motto *Theoria et Praxis*—theory and practice—a slogan as fitting to our own pragmatic age as to his more speculative one. He always insisted that logic serve knowledge and action, that theory be applicable to good causes, and that metaphysics rest upon ethical principles.

Accordingly, after completing a baccalaureate in the liberal arts and two advanced degrees in jurisprudence, Leibniz declined an invitation to continue in a brilliantly begun academic career, and at twenty-one accepted service at the court of the Prince Elector of Mainz, Bishop John Philipp of Schönborn. For five years he labored at the recodification of the legal codes and served as a consultant and propagandist for the political goals of his patron. It was in these years that Leibniz formulated most of his projects: for the advancement of scientific knowledge, the establishment of scientific societies, for consolidating the political power of the lesser states in the Empire, for the reunification of Christianity, and for shifting the attention of France from her campaigns in Europe to Egypt and the Levant. This last plan took him to the great city of Paris. There, in four years, he mastered the French language, advanced in mathematics from Euclid to the discovery of the calculus, began a series of logical studies which two centuries later were to inspire the founders of modern logic, and reached a fuller understanding of the scientific and philosophic achievements of the times.

Failing to attain a secure appointment at the French court, Leibniz then accepted the invitation of John Frederick of Hanover to become Court Counsellor and librarian. With obvious reluctance, he made his way from Paris by way of London and the Low Countries to the city where he was to spend the remaining forty years of his life, constantly seeking appointments more commensurate with his abilities and visions—first in Paris, then in Vienna, and after the Hanoverian succession to the British throne, in London; but always he fell short of success.

Leibniz's life can be summarized briefly in two parts. The first three decades were a period of education and free and energetic adventure in perfecting a system of thought, in mastering the intellectual and cultural tradition, and in establishing contacts with European leaders in many fields. The last four decades, from 1676 to 1716, were a period of fuller definition and reinterpretation of his mature thought in response to much misunderstanding and criticism. This also was a period of growing distraction and frustration because of the demands of the three rulers whom he served in the petty but ambitious duchies of Hanover, Wolfenbüttel, and Brunswick.

For forty years, Leibniz's life was torn between his unceasing work toward the advancement of science and the peace and well-being of Europe, and the intrigues and compromises required of him by the ambitions of his masters. He was librarian and collector of coins; landscape designer and engineer, laboring for years on projects to rid the Harz silver mines, the basis of Hanoverian currency, of the water which threatened them. His engineering skill planned the water displays of the great garden of Herrenhausen for the delight of the court. He was jurist-politician, rendering historical and judicial opinions in favor of, and stinging satires against opponents of, the interests of the House of Hanover. He was a diplomat, successfully arguing for Hanoverian admission to the Electorate of the Empire and for Hanoverian succession to the English throne. He collected historical documents to establish the line of Brunswick, back beyond Henry the Lion, the great leader of the Guelphs who defied the Emperor Frederick II, to a marriage with the House of Este; and, finally, he was the historian of the House of Brunswick itself.

His letters complained increasingly of this tension between the official and the essential in his life. In 1695, he wrote:

> How extremely distracted I am cannot be described. I dig up various things from the archives, examine ancient documents, conquer unpublished manuscripts. From these I strive to throw light on the history of Brunswick. I receive and send letters in great number. I have indeed so many things in mathematics, so many thoughts in philosophy, so many other literary observations which I do not wish to have perish, that I am often bewildered as to where to begin.[1]

When his last master, the Duke Elector George Louis, became George I and the Hanoverian court moved to London, Leibniz was ordered to remain behind to complete the arduous task of the history, a labor which he had carried only as far as the eleventh century when he died in 1716—forgotten by his court, but acclaimed by all Europe as one of its greatest geniuses.

Leibniz's imagination was always disciplined by reason, yet he never allowed the greatness of his projects to be scaled down to the measure of his rules for a method. His enthusiastic hopes for the future of both the telescope and the microscope are symbolic of the wide latitude and the minute detail in which he worked out his plans for his age. Most of his proposals are not yet achieved, yet all are still alive in the hopes of men. The term *geopolitics* first appeared in the definitions which he gathered together for a universal encyclopedia. And such places as Vietnam, Korea, China, and the France of Charles de Gaulle are reminders of the pertinence of this idea of a world order in which geographical determinants are considered. We are reminded of Leibniz's designs for ordered consolidations of power, knowledge, law, and faith, first in Europe, and later, after his correspondence with Jesuit missionaries in China and three meetings with Peter the Great, in the Eurasian land mass, with a modern Russia mediating between East and West. It might have been! Leibniz's life was a long effort to awaken in princes, nobles, and scholars the vision of such a harmony of learning and faith and to enlist them in the subordinate projects which it entailed. To these ends he wrote most of his philosophical, political, and scien-

1. Gerhardt, IV:431*n* (Leibniz to Placcius).

tific treatises, and thousands of letters. His proposals encompassed the codification and unification of law in splintered Europe, the reunification of the Christian churches. He proposed the urgent but orderly effort to fulfill the dream of Francis Bacon and many others for the advancement of science by securing subsidies from the princes, by promoting new societies and journals to encourage co-operative research, by perfecting its physical and mathematical tools, by devising a universal language and a science of symbols, and, above all, by a new *philosophia perennis,* which, when it was understood, should end disagreement and serve men of good will with the motive, the unity of insight, and the moral grounds to achieve these ends. These are goals still urged by many, and distrusted by others, in our own troubled times.

Also instructive are the more detailed labors—they might be called by-products—of the life of this universal mind who was at once courtier, historian, scientist, mathematician, bibliographer, philosopher, theologian, and Latin stylist. It has been said that he participated creatively in every field but the artistic; yet he composed masques for the court at Herrenhausen; his epigrams on such events as the new bombs which Vauban had unleashed on Europe were quoted widely; he devised moderately risqué rhymes and couplets to titillate the sensibility of the Electress Sophia; his epithelamia for the weddings of royalty and his epicedia on the occasions of their deaths are still cited as models of modern Latin style; and his German devotional hymn to Christ on the Cross still appears in some German hymnals. Leibniz foresaw the importance of calculation in new fields, invented the algorithms of the calculus, determinants, a nonquantitative geometry, the dynamics of force. He spent much of his earnings to invent a modern calculating machine which did not, however, make use, as do the greater calculators of our day, of the binary number system whose virtues he understood. He was an early initiate into the alchemical arts. When he learned the secret of making phosphorous from its discoverer, he at once proposed its manufacture on a large scale at military posts, for use as a weapon of war. So inclusive was his genius and so complicated his life that each detail of his biography takes on a unique intellectual flavor when one contemplates it. His work included innovations in library design and organization, the first modern collections of historical documents, refutations of historical slanders such as the account of the Popess Johannah, innovations in windmill design, satires that helped arouse Europe against the great Sun King, and efforts for the advancement of medicine which are still hidden in a pile of folio manuscripts in the Hanover Archives. The details of his labors still outreach the patient scholarship engaged in editing the papers which he left behind.

As a philosopher, he had no school of followers, though he received and answered criticisms from many excellent thinkers. But then, as a philosopher, he was a stern critic of all followers; he tolerated no intellectual sectarianism, but sought only that philosophy which should reject all errors while retaining and unifying all truth in other philosophies. Yet, like his other projects, his philosophy too remained incomplete—a hypothesis, he called it in his later decades—though it grew in the fifty years of his active career from the wide-ranging, unassimilated eclecticism of his university years to that high degree of harmony regulated by universal principles which found expression in his later letters and summaries.

In the end, however, it is probably in this philosophy itself that Leibniz's greatest heritage to us is found. Except for the shorter popular versions of his thought, written to satisfy noble supporters, and the much imitated defense of God in his *Theodicy*, Leibniz's thought was largely ignored in the popularizing, pragmatically oriented "Age of Reason" of the eighteenth century. It remained for the mathematicians and logicians of the nineteenth century to recover his innovations of logical theory, and to the physical discoveries of our own century to confirm, against Newtonian absolutes and atomistic materialisms, his reduction of matter to force ordered by law, his relational interpretation of space and time, and his theories about the interdependence of truths of reason and truths of fact. If the restoration of science to its proper place in a humanistic and moral culture is our chief problem, Leibniz, who sought the common principles underlying the realms of nature and of grace, is our man. If our main task is the establishment of a world order to which knowledge and faith both may contribute and in which means and ends are commensurate, Leibniz's combination of thought and practice deserve our study. Our concern about the predicament of modern man as an individual has sent our thinkers back to Descartes rather than to Leibniz. But Leibniz supplements Descartes in a most important respect; Leibniz's man is an active center drawing into himself the various orders of other spirits and other beings through perception, and urged forward purposefully by appetite to participate in the total order of monads and God. Leibniz portrays a social universe of which the harmonizing principle is the love of the wise man, that is, justice, and in which love of fellow man is identical with love of God.

In short, Leibniz, more clearly than others in his century, saw the process by which the individual is formed by the order about him, not causally, but through his own active responsive growth. Yet he also saw the importance of the individual as an independent component of the objective social order; it is man's commitment to harmony, to the fulfillment of mechanism and law in common purpose, that transforms his inclination into moral will and gives the assurance of peace and order.

Without the particular achievements of Leibniz in mathematics, the physical sciences, and the study of logic and language, we should be much the poorer. His theory of physical force has been greatly elaborated and vividly demonstrated. His theory of good and evil is rightly neglected, and his conception of man's motives seems to most too intellectualistic. But his very failures and ambiguities enable philosophers of every persuasion to call him an intellectual kinsman. It is his vision and his commitment to intelligent action—*theoria et praxis*—that binds us to him most of all.

I

Investigations

2

Leibniz's Judgments of Fact

Leroy E. Loemker

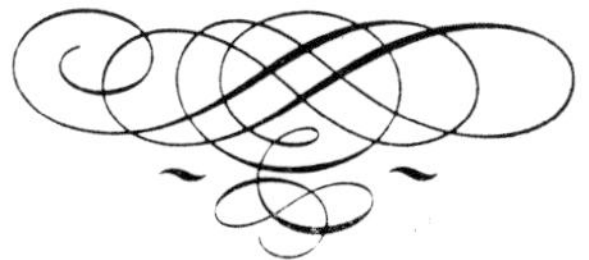

"[There are] three classes of philosophers," George Simmel wrote in his journal; "the first hear only the heart-beat of things, the second that of universals, the third of persons—and a fourth," he added, "the professors of philosophy, who hear only the voice of the literature." Leibniz is great, among other reasons, because of his creative efforts to combine all four interests, but this same fact has also left him at the mercy of his critics, who are more one-sided. Even more than usual, his interpreters have insisted on taking his thought on their own terms rather than his; and though the prominence and brilliance of the minds who have re-threaded their way through the labyrinth of his work bear witness to his stature, each has insisted upon closing all entrances but one, and then has insisted that his own discovered path is the only way through the maze. This is a severe historical fate for one who had not only a universal mind but a universal purpose, one who was always concerned with convincing many rather than with completely satisfying a few, one who never found leisure enough, in fifty years, to bring into a single unified focus

This paper was read at the meeting in commemoration of the tercentenary of Leibniz held by the Fullerton Club at Bryn Mawr College, May 11, 1946, and was subsequently published in the *Journal of the History of Ideas* VII (October 1946): 397–410.

the structure of meaning and existence upon which he believed the special perspectives which he had discovered in so many fields must converge. The exclusive particularity of the critics has therefore repeated itself again and again in the same pattern: first, each approaches Leibniz from what he chooses to regard as an adequate perspective; then he reconstructs his thought as it should be disclosed from this perspective; and, finally, he rejects those parts which do not in fact conform to the pattern he has worked out.

Certainly if such exclusive particularity can do justice to so universal a mind, those who seek the door through his logic do so with the greatest reason, for Leibniz did propose a strict method of analysis and synthesis and, unlike some logicians, sought actually to apply it in his investigations. The three great interpretations undertaken from the logical side, unfortunately, have so confused method with logical theory as to do violence to Leibniz's own opinions.[1] They assume "that all sound philosophy," in Bertrand Russell's words, "should begin with an analysis of propositions,"[2] whereas Leibniz himself frequently asserted that the knowledge of existence must begin with two facts: "That we think [in Descartes's broad sense of the term] . . . and that there is a great variety in our thoughts."[3] The purpose of this paper is to correct the critics and to examine some of the conditions involved in Leibniz's application of logic to his pluralistic and temporalistic metaphysics of existence.

The brilliant historical and systematic analysis by Louis Couturat of Leibniz's logical studies ends by neglecting entirely the relevance of logic for existence. Couturat does argue, in his introduction, that Leibniz sought to establish a panlogistic metaphysics purely on the basis of his logic. Couturat's chief evidence

1. Ernst Cassirer, *Leibniz' System in seinen wissenschaftlichen Grundlagen* (Marburg: N. G. Elwert, 1902; second edition unchanged, Hildesheim: Georg Olms, 1962); Louis Couturat, *La Logique de Leibniz d'après des documents inédits* (Paris: Felix Alcan, 1901; second edition unchanged, Hildesheim: Georg Olms, 1961). Bertrand Russell, *A Critical Exposition of the Philosophy of Leibniz,* second edition (London: Allen and Unwin, 1937).

2. Russell, *Philosophy of Leibniz,* p. 8.

3. Gerhardt, I:370; Loemker, p. 152.

is the widely discussed *Primae Veritates*,[4] which he himself dates in the years prior to "the little discourse on metaphysics" of 1686, and in which Leibniz uses an analytic theory of the proposition to support his notion of the individual. But as Leibniz fully recognized, this work cannot establish a panlogism, and even less a metaphysics of plurality and change, for it professes to be only a derivation of his fundamental principles from the laws of identity and reason. Only Couturat's erroneous inclination to consider definition and demonstration as purely analytic processes would support his interpretation that Leibniz here proposed a complete metaphysical analysis; as the method of deduction had been described to Hermann Conring somewhat earlier, it was one of progressive synthesis since the definitions which are introduced in minor premises bring fundamental principles into specific application in various special realms of meaning.[5] It is not surprising, therefore, that Couturat claims no determinative metaphysical role for the great incomplete body of Leibniz's logic itself, but treats it as the science of the structure of meaning, his chief criticism being that Leibniz's loyalty to Aristotle conflicted with his own efforts to develop a broad and unhampered logic of symbols and relations.

By this restraint Couturat was able to put into their proper subordinate places certain doctrines of Leibniz which others have magnified. He recognized that the logical calculus is inseparable from the universal characteristic, or science of symbols and formulas, since ratiocination is itself inseparable from representation, and that it is, in fact, only a special case of this more general science, restricted to the relation of compounding and dividing terms, and to the processes of equating and substituting identities. The result is that, though the proposition is the fundamental unit of thought, it is not the fundamental unit of meaning. As Leibniz said, implication exists to establish true propositions, true propositions exist to establish consistent notions. Propositions

4. Couturat, *Opuscules et Fragments inédits de Leibniz*, pp. 518–523. See also Couturat, *La Logique de Leibniz*, p. x, and "Sur la Métaphysique de Leibniz," *Revue de Métaphysique et de Morale* 10 (1902): 1–25.

5. Gerhardt, I:194 f.; Loemker, pp. 186 f.

are reductive processes to serve the analysis and synthesis of structures of meaning. And however universally Leibniz may have stated his principle that in every true affirmative proposition the predicate is included in the subject, expressly or virtually, this must be regarded as an abstraction from a more concrete theory of the proposition in which the composite subject is equivalent to the product of its predicates and can be substituted for them. Finally, Couturat recognized the inconsistency in Leibniz's treatment of negative propositions; considering them merely a denial of the relevancy of an affirmative proposition for reality, Leibniz was inclined to neglect them. Yet Leibniz also held that the incompatibility of ideas is a factor in creation since existence is separated from total possibility by a wide gulf of determinateness and nonexistence. Couturat's studies therefore tend to emphasize the relation of logic to human judgment rather than to metaphysics.

Of the second great criticism from the viewpoint of logic, Russell's, the opposite is true. Granting that the five premises from which he reconstructs Leibniz's philosophy were really Leibniz's primary principles—which they were not—Bertrand Russell's systematic analysis is as compelling as his historical appraisals are unconvincing. Assuming that Leibniz's basic logical principle is that of the inclusion, connotatively understood, of the predicate in the subject in every proposition, he argues that Leibniz built upon this a good, esoteric metaphysics, which he suppressed because the subject-predicate form of proposition cannot express relations between substances or modifications of the same substance, and he contends that the principle therefore led logically to a monism like Spinoza's.[6] On the other hand, according to Russell, Leibniz had a popular theological philosophy to which he restricted his later thinking, and this he freely published for the edification of the courtly patrons and noble friends upon whom he depended for patronage and favor.

The strong antipathy which Russell feels toward Leibniz's theological opinions and purposes seems to have blinded him, at this

6. Russell, *Philosophy of Leibniz*, pp. 5, 202; cf. Russell, *A History of Western Philosophy* (New York: Simon and Schuster, 1959), pp. 593, 595.

point, to the entire cultural climate and to the unity of Leibniz's scientific, philosophical, logical, and political plans for the alteration of that climate. Thus the so-called "Discourse on Metaphysics," the work which he regards as "the best account [Leibniz] ever wrote of [his system],"[7] because it uses the argument from the nature of propositions to the existence of individuals, is at the same time the most theological of Leibniz's shorter expositions of his thought. It contrasts rather sharply in this respect with the more mature *Monadology* and *Principles of Nature and of Grace*, which begin by establishing the grounds for individuality instead of dealing with the problem of God's grace, to which the controversy between Antoine Arnauld and Malebranche had drawn Leibniz's attention before he wrote the earlier immature work. The record is clear that Leibniz was kept from printing many of his works, either because he himself was unsatisfied with them or because the critics to whom he first submitted his drafts could not understand them or found difficulties in them. To say that he published only for the edification of nobles and princes neglects the wide range of his published writings and the outlets he used for them. The *Acta Eruditorum*, for example, and the liberal refugee journals in Holland hardly served to flatter courtly circles.

It is true, as Leibniz himself once admitted to Christiaan Huygens, that he "tried always to accommodate [his] manner of speech to popular usage, *salva veritate*."[8] But he tried also to consider the diversity of his readers, and he developed several terminological sets, the translation from any one of which to any other could be carried out, though not always without sacrifice in distinctness and adequacy. "There are two kinds of readers to whom I want to explain my principles," Leibniz said in the preface to a mathematical paper, "namely the tyro and the doctor." But there were, in fact, more kinds than two, all essential to his grandiose plans; and his own conception of the analogical and isomorphic structures of meaning supported his hope that the language of mathematics and theology, of com-

7. Russell, *Philosophy of Leibniz*, p. 7.
8. Gerhardt Math., II:193 f. (Leibniz to Huygens, September 4/14, 1694).

mon sense and Scholasticism (whether medieval or Cartesian), would serve together to unfold parallel patterns of the same ultimate structure of being. That theology and logic distinguish the two philosophies of Leibniz, as Russell holds, is sufficiently refuted by the obvious fact that Leibniz intended his logical studies to serve as introductions to two much greater intellectual projects toward a united Europe: the universal encyclopedia and his great apologetic work, the *Catholic Demonstrations.*

Russell's particular refutation of the argument of the "good philosophy" is also too narrow in its premises. It is true that Leibniz repeatedly stated his conviction that the predicate is included in the subject, connotatively, in every true affirmative proposition, and that his exploratory logical studies aimed, but never succeeded, in relating this principle to many other things which he said about propositions. It is also true that for a few years, from 1679 to 1687, the years ending in the correspondence with "the great Arnauld," Leibniz proposed what he called an "argument" from this logical principle to his theory of individual substance. It was not an argument, however, but the arbitrary imposition of a logical doctrine upon a metaphysical one. It is not prominent in the writings of his later years, but it belongs to a time when he had just given up the effort to ground his union of essence and existence by means of the ontological argument, and before his dynamism had become explicit and his analysis of individuality complete. For the time being, Leibniz seems to have believed that this old Aristotelian-Scholastic theory of the proposition could be equated with the pluralistic but ambiguous Scholastic metaphysical doctrine that *modificationes sunt suppositorum,* which he usually quotes at the same time. He seems to have believed further that the more completely the method of analysis is applied to the reduction of propositions, whether universal and necessary or particular and contingent, the closer it will lead to complete or self-contained propositions whose subject is a determinate or complete concept, and whose predicates contain all of its essential and existential contents.[9] The logical completeness of the complex notion would

9. Cf. Couturat, p. 403.

assure its self-sufficiency, and the mutual restriction of many such complete notions would make inevitable the fulfillment of its predicates in temporal succession. This so-called argument is then generally held to have been buttressed by another Scholastic maxim, which Leibniz never abandoned, to the effect that "there are no purely extrinsic denominations," which is understood to mean that there are no external relations, in one or more of the many possible senses of that doctrine.

A brief examination suffices to show, however, that Leibniz did not base his theory of the individual upon so abstract an argument. It is true that he always regarded logical completeness or determinacy as essential to metaphysical substantiality. This became very obvious in the correspondence with Burcher de Volder when the latter attempted, on purely logical grounds and in anticipation of neo-realism, to make every essence and modification of Leibniz's substances into a substance; Leibniz refuted him on the very ground that such a purely logical analysis could not explain time and change.[10] Yet even in the early period of the *Discourse,* Leibniz must have admitted that there are complete notions that do not represent substances. In the *General Inquisitions* of the same period (1686), a work in which he carried his logical analysis of metaphysics as far as he ever succeeded in doing, "the sword" is a complete notion, and it is made no more complete by the addition of an oblique relationship, "the sword of Evander."[11] But neither of these logically complete terms is a substance in the metaphysical sense. The very examples, in fact, which Leibniz offered to Antoine Arnauld in support of his argument refute it, for the Adam whose "individual concept has involved that he should have so many children" (April 12, 1686) and the Alexander whose "individual notion" includes "for instance, that he will conquer Darius and Porus" and even "whether he died a natural death or by poisoning," do not involve single, metaphysical individuals but a great many.[12] It was not a single monad, however complex, which died

10. Cf. Gerhardt, II:226; Loemker, p. 525 (Leibniz to de Volder, July 6, 1701).

11. Couturat, p. 357.

12. Gerhardt, II:15, 22, *et passim.*

of poison or which begat the children of earth but a harmonious interdependent series of a great many, which are capable, therefore, of further logical analysis and of many different syntheses.

Nor did Leibniz ever make a persistent effort to establish the possibility of a progression, by analysis and synthesis, from universal and particular propositions to a complete singular one, as his theory of the proposition would demand. It is true that he held that in both cases the stages would be infinite and therefore beyond the powers of creatures. But he was unable to show even the logical possibility of such an analysis. The *General Inquisitions* make it clear that the fundamental principle of subject-predicate inclusion is to be applied to most propositions only in a most qualified sense. It applies only to affirmative propositions, and it applies to particular propositions only virtually, or in the sense that some genus can be found to which the particular subject belongs and in which the predicate is contained. And it applies only to notions related *in recto,* that is, already involved in the relationship of identity of subject and total predicate. Leibniz makes only the most tentative efforts to reduce oblique relations, and relations represented rhetorically by the particles, to that of contained and container, but these very efforts show that he considered such analysis to be reductive of the complex relationships of being and existence rather than determinative of them. There are many kinds of relations in existence beyond that of the propositional form into which he sought to compress them in his calculus.

The fact seems to be that the further Leibniz tried to expand his logical principles into a symbolic treatment of all kinds of relations, the less conclusive they were for his metaphysics, and the greater became the abstraction of the symbolic structures from a determinate order of existence. When he affirms that "there are no purely extrinsic denominations," he is affirming neither that all relations are internal nor that individuals are completely isolated from the world, but that the representations or symbolic expressions of external relations are built upon the analysis of internal mental qualities and symbols, the *materia prima* of the knowing mind.

Whatever his theory of the proposition may mean, Leibniz did in fact recognize the validity of relational propositions, in the realm both of possibility and of existence. He quoted John Locke with approval to the effect that the largest field of our knowledge is the knowledge of relations, and he pointed out, further, that his own system was developed by an analysis which discovers intermediate terms between the grosser relations in which experience begins.[13] An earlier example of such a gross relational proposition will serve to recall both the principles according to which he held that judgments of fact are to be analyzed and synthesized and the relation of his theory of predicate-subject inclusion to this process. From the class of propositions dealing with essence and possibility alone, he distinguishes

> an entirely different kind, existential or contingent judgments whose truth can be understood *a priori* only by an infinite mind, and cannot be proved by any analysis. Such are the propositions which are true at a particular time, and express not merely what belongs to the possibility of a thing, but also what really exists, or what would exist under certain conditions. For example, that I am living now, or that the sun is shining. For if I say that the sun is shining at this hour in our hemisphere, because its motion has been such until the present, so that assuming the continuity of this motion, this truth follows certainly . . . yet this assumption that its motion was the same earlier is a contingent truth whose basis must be sought in its turn, and can be given only from a perfect insight into all parts of the universe.[14]

"The sun is now shining in our hemisphere," like every other judgment of fact and unlike every judgment of merely logical necessity, participates in two dimensions of being, and analysis and synthesis may proceed in each of these two dimensions. The first is the dimension of existence, which is bound to the continuity of time and space and in which the relations are between the immediately apprehended particular qualities and symbols of the perceiving mind. Here the logical reference is denotative. The second dimension is that of essence or of logical possibility, where the reference is connotative; it is this dimension of meaning that is the proper locus of Leibniz's logic of the proposition,

13. *Nouveaux Essais*, bk. IV, chap. 3, sec. 18.
14. Couturat, pp. 18 f.

and of the general logic of analysis and combination to which it belongs.

The fullest development of this view is to be found in the correspondence with de Volder (1699–1706), where Leibniz makes clear the distinction among the predicates of every complete subject, between changing modifications and timeless essences, yet points out the dependence of essences upon existing events, so that every modification—that is, every momentary quality representative of an external order—may be considered in its essential dimension as a single term or a combination of terms. On January 21, 1704, he writes:

> You do not distinguish between universal and particular natures. From universal natures there follow eternal consequences; from particular natures there follow also temporal ones, unless you think that temporal things have no cause.[15]

That the sun is shining implies that the essence of sun includes that of shining, in one case at least; thus existence includes possibility. Such transition from existential to essential interpretation is possible, moreover, at any stage in the infinite temporal, spatial and causal analysis of which existence is capable; thus a structure of abstractness and of universality becomes increasingly available in the dimension of essence as the analysis of existence proceeds. Facts can thus be analyzed existentially in terms of the events upon which they depend in occurrence and essentially in terms of their possible composition out of simpler essences; in theological language, the mind has the power to "represent not only the world but also God in the world."[16]

The abstract principles of these two orders of analysis and synthesis are ultimately the same, but those of the existential analysis are more determinate. The analysis of existence is causal, and the principle of causality is the law of sufficient reason applied in the forms of spatial and temporal relation—that is, of simultaneity and succession. (This, of course, is an anticipation of Kant's schematism of the categories.) Similarly, the equivalence

15. Gerhardt, II:263; cf. Loemker, p. 534.

16. Gerhardt, VII:452; Loemker, p. 473 (Leibniz to des Billettes, 1696). God is "the region of ideas" or essences.

of forces in dynamics is a temporalized form of the law of identity. Causal analysis, therefore, may begin with any one of an infinite number of perceived facts of existence and may analyze it into its relations to significant antecedent and simultaneous states, as long as these are functionally related to it by the general harmony or congruence of existence. Leibniz believes that such causal analysis-synthesis, if our intellects were infinite, could pass from indistinct, phenomenal entities through the various formulas or structures of dependence until it arrives at the ultimate equations of functional dependence—the laws of the individual series, or monads. Since man cannot escape the blurred perceptions and sensuous limitations of his symbols—which are necessary to stop the continuous flow of events, as it were, and to hold the functional relations in suspense so that they may be analyzed—such ultimate analysis is humanly impossible.

But at every stage in this existential analysis, there is also possible an essential one if the transformation be made from event or passing quality to permanent meaning. To do this is always to sacrifice the complete determinateness of existence and to pass to the order of logical possibility and consistency, or, in such formal fields as mathematics, to logical necessity. This shift is necessary in order to pass from mere recurrence to true universalization; at certain stages of causal interpretation, therefore, one may use the principles of identity, contradiction, and sufficient reason to formulate universal natural laws. These "subordinate maxims," as Leibniz calls them in the *Discourse* (his favorite examples being the laws of optics and the law of the conservation of force) are in another dimension of meaning from the laws of the individual series; yet every individual law could, by an infinite mind, be transformed into essential laws or combinations of essences. For example, the law determining a human individual could be resolved into abstract but universal psychological rules (such as those of the association of ideas formulated in the *New Method for Teaching and Learning Jurisprudence*, 1667). From these laws a denotative application can be made, in turn, to particular facts of existence—and Leibniz believed, further, that the concrete law of the individual is the combination of an adequate number of these abstract laws. The logical calculus—and with it the theory of subject-predicate inclusion—seems to be restricted entirely to this essential dimension. Except for a perfect mind, therefore, such a logic can never be entirely determinative of existence, for logical necessity constitutes existential possibility and no more; to move from existence to logic always involves a sacrifice in determinateness.

There remains, however, the problem of the law of the individual series or the individual concept. On what logical grounds could Leibniz affirm such laws and regard them as the essential source of the continuous series of events which constitute an individual substance? The ultimate reason for this doctrine must be sought in his dogmatic identification of the simple notions to which essences can be analyzed with the perfections of God. His only *a priori* proof of individuality is inseparable from the ontological argument, which he had already abandoned by 1679. This was an attempt to prove not only the existence of God, but individual existence as well, for it began not merely with the idea of God but with the simple notions of the logical calculus, each one of which was assumed to be a simple perfection of God; to prove his existence becomes a matter of proving these perfections compatible. But as in mathematics a variable can be determined completely by enough functional conditions, so God too determines a combination of essences or simple notions so completely that they will coincide with the series of events in which the completest possible analysis and synthesis of existence results. Thus there is a logical identity between a completely determined combination of essences as subjects and a serially complete order of temporal events or modifications as predicates—the law of the individual series.

This argument failed, however, when Leibniz discovered the gulf of negation and inconsistency which separates existence from logical possibility—a discovery which, his early criticisms of Spinoza and Descartes show, was made on moral grounds; it would be an evil world in which every possibility must ultimately attain existence.[17] With this failure to weld together "the old

17. Gerhardt, IV:281, 283 f.; Loemker, pp. 272–273.

way of ideas" with a logic of existence, the keystone to his "system" is gone, though his faith in it remains. It is in this faith that the dogmatism of his thought must be found. Henceforth his argument for individual substances must be *a posteriori*; the "new way of ideas" can no longer be derived from the old, though he still seeks to develop it within the framework of the old.

The third point of reference for Leibniz's judgments of existence thus comes into prominence. The two dimensions of an existential proposition have been described as if they rested upon a theory of direct realism. But they do not; both the temporal relations of existing events and the combination of eternal meanings are in terms of the qualitative and symbolic content of the perceiving mind. Ratiocination, or the construction of symbolic formulas, whether in mechanics or in the logical calculus, is inseparable from representation. From his earliest years Leibniz was a phenomenalist, and propositions are never to be divorced from the qualitative content, the *materia prima* of the thinking mind. Indeed, it is this very symbolic quality of the proposition that makes possible the application of logic to continuously changing events; they must be held suspended in "momentary memory," as it were, in order to be analyzed. From this point of view, causality must be viewed as a merely abstract and descriptive synthesis of two observed occurrences which are really in functional dependence—the more distinctly grasped perception being taken for the cause, as Leibniz explained to Arnauld, and the less distinctly perceived, as the effect. Now, too, natural laws cannot be considered as the subordinate maxims of God, but of man. Thus there emerges a further restriction upon Leibniz's general theory of the proposition. A completely analyzed proposition now states the equivalence of a symbolic formula with the structure of analyzed experience which it represents; and affirmative propositions, in which the predicate is included in the subject, may be considered merely methodological devices for passing from symbols to the complex structure of meaning and so of carrying further the analysis and synthesis, the judgment and invention. In addition to their existential and essential dimensions, therefore, in which propositions follow the coercive structure of reality, they also have a pragmatic function in making the formulas of science more adequate and in unfolding the complex patterns of symbolic analogies which bind the various sciences together. The dependence of propositions upon the symbolizing mind-monad is necessary to fit Leibniz's logic to continuous temporal change. No other view will suffice to establish individuality, for it is only the momentary but cumulative memory of this representing and reasoning mind which makes it possible to arrest the flux of existence for the purpose of analyzing its organization, and it is that same memory which attests the enduring nature of individual substance. Essence is therefore no longer constitutive of existence but is instrumental to its analysis and correction, and the role of propositions is to reveal and reduce the structure of existence to its possibilities.

With the failure of Leibniz's logical construction of his metaphysics, it is the empirical, or, to use a currently popular label, the phenomenological, pattern of his philosophy which comes into prominence. We may venture the opinion that his critics have not generally appreciated the magnitude of the change in emphasis which Leibniz's thought underwent in the 1690s as the result of his dynamic physical notions and of the critical discussions evoked by his first hesitant publication of the *New System*, nearly a decade after he wrote the *Discourse*. It is not too much to say that questions of essence are now subordinated to the investigation of well-ordered phenomena and their essential and existential structures. As Professor Arthur O. Lovejoy has shown, the great chain of being is almost broken in the interest of time and progress. The most complete derivation of logical relations from individual substance is in the Leibniz-de Volder correspondence; but even in discussion with the Scholastic Bartholomew des Bosses, Leibniz's argument abandons the problem of relating essence and existence to concern itself with an analysis of bodies and minds and to penetrate to a formula for their harmonious common activity. His system is repeatedly called a hypothesis, though, as he writes to Lady Damaris Masham, it is the best of all available hypotheses and therefore has the presumption of truth.[18] Both Leibniz's mathematical analogies and

18. Gerhardt, III:353.

his ultimate logical resolution have failed to establish an ultimate unity, and his philosophy appears more and more as the derivation of formulas in various fields of experience and their projection, by the discovery of analogous or isomorphic structures, into what he sought to establish as a single and harmonious order of being. But it is the noetic or "reflective" grasp of the mind's structure itself, with its unity of vitality and form, of active representation with passive content, that provides the analogy by which the grasped qualities and structures of the physical, mathematical, logical, and moral realms may be combined.

Yet Leibniz goes beyond phenomenology in refusing to restrict being to the qualitative and symbolic forms of experience or to the general principles which analysis reveals within them. The real is the corrective and regulative ideal in experience—not an entirely other, independent of perception, but an incompletely grasped order of possibility involved in the various levels and forms of well-founded phenomena. Individuals are the requirement of existence rather than of essence, for our experiences are not only well-founded, but are representations, increasingly uniform as analysis and synthesis proceeds, of a reality that is itself only implied, but on which the scientific, moral, and religious possibilities of existence rest.

Leibniz's thought thus maintains a position midway between a nominalism in which logic is only indirectly relevant for existence and there is no universal basis for men's thought and plans, and a logical universalism in which the distinction between existence and possibility itself vanishes. In terms of the cultural conflicts of his own century, he sought, for honorable men (the *homines honestatis* about which the literature of the century abounds), a basis for avoiding the "two sects of naturalism," absolutistic quietism, on the one hand, and the libertinism which he feared threatened a European revolution, on the other. Both logically and in terms of moral, if not cultural, purpose, Leibniz stood at Spinoza's side. Both sought to harmonize intellectual and moral needs; both emphasized, therefore, the ultimate unity of the scientific and the religious attitude, and both sought a logic adequate to combine them. But Spinoza proceeded to identify the two, so that the intellectual love of God is both scientific integration and religious devotion, its result both universal scientism and a religion of renunciation. The very ethical motive of Leibniz's philosophy demanded a subordination of the scientific investigation of existence to man's penetration into that harmonious order of values available in common, which depends on the disparity between existence and the realm of possible perfection, not yet achieved. The progress of Leibniz's own thought was toward libertinage, but his demand for a source of universal meaning and univeral compulsion held him to a logic of existence and one of possibility as well, with a gulf imperfectly bridged by human thought, but spanned by the creative powers of man's spirit. His own age rejected the universal; out of the victory of the libertine and his divisive projects have grown the crises of our own times. But goodwill still requires, not merely warm feelings, but the perception of possible harmonies that are universal, yet capable of determinate existence. And to complete our inadequate perceptions and build these harmonies *in actu* demands, as Leibniz well saw, the perfection of common symbols, common law, and a common faith.

3

Leibniz's Doctrine of Ideas

Leroy E. Loemker

THE LONG-STANDING project of a complete critical edition of Leibniz's works is still far from completed. Until such an edition provides the basis for a careful chronological study of his thought, discussions of his consistency such as have recently been revived will be confused because of the failure to consider when, why, and for whom particular works were written. But the full productive power of some of his central concepts can be put in historical and critical perspective on the basis of existing materials, and the effort to do so throws some light upon those connections in his thought which are most obscure. Particularly important is his doctrine of ideas, for he finds in this doctrine not only the basis for the theoretical unity of his philosophy, but also the warrant for its practical effectiveness in solving the moral conflict which so disturbed him in the culture of his century.

Individualism, nationalism, and scientific universalism set the stage for the seventeenth century's crises and, therefore, for Leibniz's philosophical problem, which has been correctly stated as the metaphysical one of relating universalism and individualism.[1] His interest was obviously never in the individual inde-

This paper was first published in the *Philosophical Review* 55 (May 1946): 229–249.

1. D. Mahnke, *Leibnizens Synthese von Universalmathematik und In-*

pendent of all order but in the individual who is an instance or a fulfillment of universal order; in the *libertine* he saw the danger of European revolution,[2] while his own problem put in metaphysical terms the quandary of the *homme honnête*: how to achieve the honorable life, with its ideal of loyalty to a superior law, within the political and religious pluralism of the century on one hand and the universe of law revealed by the new sciences on the other. However adroit he may have been at power politics, his own convictions demanded a political and religious universalism which should provide an adequate social basis for using the new science and technology. The great projects among which, all his life, he dissipated his energies were to serve such a European universalism. These propects included the unification and systematization of law; the unity of the churches; the promotion of science and technology; and the development of such international agencies and instruments of science and learning as academies, journals, and a universal language, characteristic, and encyclopedia. True individualism was to be made possible through such universalism.

This interest also defined his metaphysical problem: he sought a theory of reality which is rational and simple and yet spacious enough to *harmonize*, to make *congruent*, or to reduce to mutual *consent* (these are the prominent Leibnizian terms) the varied interests which gave the century its distinction and to which he himself contributed so much. At the same time such a system of thought must provide both the unity and the motive of the true individual who finds his purposes and values in the universal order.

Only Platonism could provide both the universal order and the dynamism which he needed, and a pattern of Platonic thinking was ready at hand in the Augustinianism which the more liberal Protestant universities were using either to supplement

---

dividualmetaphysik (Halle: Niemeyer, 1925), treats this central problem, but with little reference to the cultural problems of the century.

2. On the moral nature of the European revolution, see *Nouveaux Essais*, bk. IV, chap. 16, sec. 4; Gerhardt, V:444.

Aristotle or to supplant him.[3] Once he accepted it, he never abandoned this "old way of ideas," and most of his later thought was given to the effort of adapting it to the new insights of the times—particularly to the "new way of ideas," which he feared as a part of the European revolution. In this effort the weaknesses but also the fruitfulness of the doctrine were made apparent, though they did not lead to any thorough modification of his opinions.[4]

I

Leibniz's first concern with the Platonic doctrine was more in applying than in clarifying it. He asserts dogmatically that the harmonious pattern of ideas provides an ontological assurance for an orderly, dynamic, perfect, and (later) progressive creation; he identifies it forthwith with the Aristotelian logic as taught in his day, combines with it his own interpretation of Hobbes's theory of *conatus* (which he seems from the start to have understood to be a mental process), and uses the result, specifically, to defend theological orthodoxy and to provide a logical basis for reordering the law. A few examples will show the metaphysical burden which the ideas are called upon to bear. They are taken from his theological and legal studies of the Mainz period, 1667–1672, and from a letter to Magnus Wedderkopf in 1671.

3. The immediate sources from which Leibniz derived this idea may never be traced; Leibniz read so much and cited so many authors whom he had not read that the problem of direct reference is hard to solve. Platonism was a part of the intellectual climate, the background alike of Kepler's new science, of Ramist as well as orthodox theology, and of the logical and educational reforms of Alsted and others. Erhard Weigel and John Bisterfeld have been noted as direct sources, but there must have been others. See W. Kabitz, *Die Philosophie des jungen Leibniz,* (Heidelberg: Carl Winters, 1909), pp. 6–14. As P. Miller has shown in *The New England Mind* (Cambridge: Harvard University, 1953), similar ideas underlay the Puritan world-view.

4. Most interpreters have misunderstood the role of ideas in Leibniz because of a tacit presumption of the "new way." Maine de Biran saw the importance of ideas in Leibniz's system (*Biographie Universelle,* XXIII, 604 f.), as have Ernst Cassirer, *Leibniz' System in seinen wissenschaftlichen*

The substance of things is an idea. Idea is the union of God and creatures, as action is the union of agent and patient. A point is at once common to two lines or secants. Most apt of all, an angle is at once both center and lines. N.B.: ideas are not in God except insofar as things are given outside of him. Thus a point is not a center without lines. . . . The ideas of God and the substances of things are the same in fact, different in relation, as are action and passion. And since the substances of things are the action of God upon species, we must inquire how it is possible that his action upon one species is numerically the same as his action upon another.[5]

In idea is contained ideally both passive and active power, both active and passive intellect. Insofar as passive intellect concurs there is matter in the idea, insofar as active intellect concurs, there is form.[6]

Thus the Platonic idea is the same as the substantial form of Aristotle.[7]

What then is the ultimate ground of the divine will? The divine intellect. . . . Of the divine intellect? The harmony of things. Of the harmony of things? Nothing. . . . This depends upon the essences of things or the idea of things. For the essences of things are numbers, as it were, and contain the possibility of beings; a possibility which God does not make but which exists, since these possibilities or ideas of things coincide with God himself.[8]

The divine mind consists of the ideas of all things. Since therefore there is one idea of thing A and another of thing B, it follows that there is one idea of the divine mind which concurs with thing A, another with thing B. It is elsewhere demonstrated by the example of a point that the parts do not make up the composition of the divine mind out of ideas.[9]

Grundlagen (Marburg: N. G. Elwert, 1902; second edition unchanged, Hildesheim: Georg Olms, 1962, pp. 119 f.), K. Eswein (*Philosophisches Jahrbuch der Görresgesellschaft* XLI (1928): 95 ff.), and H. Heimsoeth (*Die Methode der Erkenntnis*, II [Giessen: A. Töpelmann, 1912]), though some of these have been kept by their preconceptions from properly evaluating the metaphysical role of the ideas.

5. Academy Ed., VI, i:513 (1668). From a treatise on transubstantiation. Cf. Loemker, p. 119.

6. Academy Ed., VI, i:512; cf. Loemker, p. 118.

7. Academy Ed., VI, i:511; cf. Loemker, p. 118.

8. Academy Ed., II, i:117; cf. Loemker, p. 146. Leibniz to Magnus Wedderkopf, May 1671. Leibniz's first letter to Antoine Arnauld contains similar ideas.

9. Academy Ed., VI, i:511; cf. Loemker, p. 118.

Thus, years before he himself studied Plato in Paris, Leibniz chose this broadest possible metaphysical basis for his attempt at a philosophical synthesis and sought to derive from it all of the categories of his later thought.

Six aspects of Leibniz's maturer system may be pointed out:

1. Ideas are the perfect harmony of God's plan, and as such are the possibilities of a harmonious order of creation. They are at once mental and logical. As such, they assure the commensurability of logic and value, or, in Aristotelian terms, the coincidence of efficient and final with formal causality. The principle of sufficient reason is for Leibniz, therefore, a telic as well as a logical principle. Moreover, since all ideas are a unity in God's mind, every predicate *is in* its subject,[10] as part in whole, plurality in unity, purpose fulfilling plan.

2. Because of their perfection, too, the ideas have a drive or tendency toward existence, and so imply creation. In this sense ideas, being the potentiality of action, are operators, at least so far as God is concerned. Efficient causality flows from the perfection of form itself since a nontemporal order would be incomplete and imperfect.

> If God had no rational creatures in the world he would still have the same harmony, but alone and without echo; he would still have the same beauty, but without reflection, refraction, and multiplication. Hence the wisdom of God thrust forth (*exigo*) rational creatures, in which things may be multiplied. An individual mind is thus a kind of world in a mirror or lens, or in a single point of collected visual rays.[11]

The momentary aspect of this tendency, the conatus, is a differential of the intellect of God; it is temporal transition made necessary by the purposiveness of the ideas. In this sense ideas, which Leibniz later calls *vis primitiva*, become temporalized and actualized

10. This controversial doctrine Leibniz should have used only for propositions whose subject is God. He never held, as did F. H. Bradley, that the Absolute is the subject of all propositions, and he ought never to have taught that the principle is true of all propositions. The doctrine runs counter to his own work on a universal characteristic, and indeed to his theory of perception and scientific causality.

11. Academy Ed., VI, i:437. From the juristic studies, in which the harmony of the ideas is the basis of a psychology of values.

as *vis derivativa,* their particularity demanding existence as individual series of events.[12]

It is noteworthy here that, though Leibniz is never nearer to Spinoza's identification of the actual with the possible than at this time—when he knew Spinoza only by hearsay as a Cartesian—he is already concerned to escape monism (in the form of Averroism) by asserting the plurality of the ideas. On two of the great issues of Protestant Scholasticism—the scope of active intellect in the soul and the independence of soul from body—he inclines toward a Platonic solution, giving intellect dominance over will and desire and making soul a *substantia completa,* with its own matter as well as form. In view of the long controversy of Leibniz scholars on the relation of mind and body to the monad, it is important to note that Leibniz never permanently abandons the latter view. Soul, as the actualization of a pattern of ideas, has its own matter; *materia prima* is an aspect of spirit itself. Of course matter and body must not be confused in Leibniz.

3. But every idea also involves a polarity, its active force and its passive content being distinguishable in two ways: mutual correspondence along with some degree of resistance and symbolic reduction. Every individual, therefore, is a series of active-passive events corresponding to or reflecting (later, representing, expressing, perceiving) the other series, since all are actualizations of the ideas. The passive aspect of these sequences of existence is matter;[13] in soul it is sensory symbol and feeling. This differentiation into individuality, finiteness, and relative passivity is demanded by the fullness of the ideas; with it time, space, and causality (in the scientific sense) arise, time being the principle of serial order or succession, space that of simultaneous coexistence, and cau-

12. "To think harmony is to think with conatus" (Academy Ed., VI, i:484). Compare the later note (1677): "When God thinks and exercises his thought, the world is made" (Gerhardt, VII:191). Leibniz himself attributed the conatus doctrine to Weigel, rather than to Hobbes, Kepler, or Spinoza. For the identity of *vis primitiva* and ideas, see Cassirer, *Leibniz' System in seinen wissenschaftlichen Grundlagen,* pp. 299 f.

13. See Leibniz to Wedderkopf, May 1671 (Academy Ed., II, i:117; Loemker, p. 146).

sality the relation of active and passive factors in the mutual correspondence of the separate individuals.[14]

4. The universal harmony demands also that no two individual series of events should be alike. Mind series differ from body series by the addition of a more complex organization, that of memory and reflection.[15] Thus minds are creative mirrors which not only actualize the ideas but experience them. In physical motion conatus is "momentary" and merely transmissive because it lacks this higher organization; in mind it is permanently grasped in memory and self-awareness and so mirrors the ideas of God. Because of matter, of course, this mirroring is symbolic and imperfect; we see the ideas only unclearly, indistinctly, and incompletely, as we see a city from a particular perspective. Limitation is a necessary aspect of individuation. But the ideas provide the unconscious basis of our mental life,[16] which receives activity and reason of its own from God. Descartes's dualism is thus not ultimate, but Malebranche's passivism is also wrong.

5. It is the ideas, therefore, which make possible the whole range of man's experiences and social relations. The ideas are the basis of all science, particularly the complete science, the *universal characteristic*. Together with the complex order of creation which flows from them, they provide man with a range of experiences of various dimensions and with the logical principles for

14. Kabitz, *Die Philosophie des jungen Leibniz*, pp. 145–149, gives the first effort to interpret space, time, and causality within this metaphysical framework.

15. The important passage here is the seventeenth *Fundamentum Praedemonstrabile* in the *Theory of Abstract Motion*, 1671: "For what is conatus in a moment is the motion of a body in time. This opens the door to the true distinction between body and mind, which no one has explained heretofore. For every body is a momentary mind, or one lacking recollection [*recordatio*], because it does not retain its own conatus and the other contrary one together for longer than a moment. For two things are necessary . . . action and reaction, . . . Hence body lacks memory; it lacks the perception of its own actions and passions; it lacks thought" (Gerhardt, IV:230; Loemker, p. 141).

16. The theory of unconscious mental patterns and processes is implicit in Leibniz's earliest thought, though it appears explicitly only in 1678.

correcting and enlarging them. Social order, government and law, morality, and the vision of God are all perspectives of the universal harmony, variously mixed with passivity and finiteness, and all are subject to logical criticism.

6. The reason for this is that the divine harmony is the source of all human value. Man's experiences of beauty, truth, goodness, love, God, are experiences of harmony. Leibniz's value-theory reconciles hedonism with intuitionalism on the ground that pleasant feeling is merely the unclear perception of unimpeded and harmonious impulses originating in the ideas.

> Joy—harmony in a sentient being.[17]
>
> It seems that joy is also a certain perfection which follows when appetite is not impeded. When appetite is not impeded and the object is attained, there arises joy. . . . It follows therefore that there is joy in inanimate things too.[18]
>
> —to act unjustly, *i.e.*, disharmonically.[19]
>
> The beatific vision or intuition of God face to face is the contemplation of the universal harmony of things, because God or universal mind is nothing but the harmony of things or the principle of beauty in them.[20]

In social relations love is the highest expression of this harmony, though justice may exist on two less adequate levels also.

Thus the categories of Leibniz's maturer thought are implicit in his doctrine of ideas—*vis primitiva* and *derivativa,* active and passive power, and *materia prima.* Ideas are the cosmic possibilities of action, organization, individualization, purpose, and value. They constitute a dynamic order of being within which temporal change and spatial differentiation, matter and force, plurality and conflict, may be understood—perfectly only by him who possesses the first principles and can proceed analytically from them, imperfectly by him who must strive from imperfect experiences to

17. Academy Ed., II, i:98 (May 1671).

18. *Ibid.*, VI, i:61: Notes on J. Thomasius. Leibniz here cites Epicurus, Valla, Gassendi, and Hobbes as authorities for this hedonism.

19. *Ibid.*, VI, i:437. The threefold interpretation of justice in the *Nova Methodus*, part II, secs. 71–76, repeated in the preface to the *Codex Juris Gentium Diplomaticus* in 1693, rests on this same basis.

20. *Ibid.*, VI, i:499.

the clarity of the source.[21] But great mysteries remain. Why do ideas act? Why does action involve individuation? Is passivity involved in action in any but a merely verbal sense? Above all, on what grounds are activity, organization, and passivity transmitted to creatures themselves in the act of creation? And how can matter be reduced, ultimately, to the ideas?

Many of Leibniz's later papers struggle with these questions, and fall short of an answer.[22] Two grounds are constantly advanced by Leibniz himself, and no new ones are added: (1) *a priori,* ideas involve all of these concepts because they are perfect and imply a perfect world. But a world without individuals, change, passive content, would be less perfect because less full; (2) *a posteriori,* ideas involve all of these properties because reflection shows us that they do. It is this latter argument upon which Leibniz always calls for the support of his ontological one, and which reveals the empirical motive in his metaphysics, as distinct from his physics.

II

Leibniz's later thought involved no departures from this (except on subordinate points), but was merely a long effort to clarify, to refine, to give reasons, and to meet criticisms—a process in which his thought advances from the unformed eclecticism of the Mainz period to the carefully analyzed system to which he never gave adequate literary expression. By inclination he was impelled to find points of agreement with men of all schools. He developed distinct vocabularies and analogies for Scholastics, Cartesians, Academics, and the popular speech of his noble patrons and friends. For example, Leibniz uses ideas in the Cartesian sense in a letter to De Volder in 1699.[23] In the *Nouveaux Essais,* he

21. *The True Theologica Mystica,* ca. 1685–90, puts Leibniz's Platonism in the language of German mysticism (Guhrauer, I:410–413).

22. Two examples are the effort to explain matter in the *De Rerum Originatione Radicali* (1697) and the effort to prove the autonomous activity of individual created substances in the reply to John Christopher Sturm, *De Ipsa Natura* (1698). Neither can be considered as successful.

23. Gerhardt, II:171 f.; Loemker, pp. 517 f.

admits that ideas are, with qualifications, objects of the mind.[24] In each case, however, this function of the ideas is derivative, not basic. But his inclination to speak the language of those who adhered to the "new way" never led him to betray his Platonism. Ideas are always the possibilities of meaning, however distorted by symbols, of plurality, and of activity.

Some instances, from various periods, of the metaphysical nature of the ideas may be pointed out. Leibniz wrote, in the Paris notebook, 1675–76: "As a figure is in space, so an idea is in our mind. . . . Ideas are in our mind as differentiae of thoughts. Ideas are in God insofar as the most perfect being consists in the conjunction of all absolute forms or possible perfections in the same object."[25]

In the notes on Foucher's criticism of Malebranche, in 1676, he observed: "An idea is that in which one perception or thought differs from another by reason of an object. . . . Ideas can be taken in two ways: namely for the quality or form of thought, as velocity and direction are the form of motion, or for the immediate object or nearest perception. In the latter sense, the idea would not be a mode of being of our soul. And this is apparently the opinion of Plato and the author of the *Récherche*. For when the soul thinks of being, identity, thought, duration, it has a certain immediate object or proximate cause of its perception. In this way it may be that we see all things in God, and that the ideas or immediate objects are the attributes of God himself. The author is right in saying that thought is not the essence of the soul, for a thought is an act, and since one thought succeeds another, the essence of the soul must rather necessarily be that which remains permanent in this change. . . . The essence of substances consists in the primitive force of action, or in the law of the sequence of changes, as the nature of a series consists in its numbers."[26]

In "What is an Idea?" in 1678: "Thus the idea of things in us is nothing but the fact that God, the author alike of things and of mind, has impressed this power of thinking upon the mind so

24. Gerhardt, V:99, 128.
25. Jagodinsky, p. 126; Loemker, p. 163.
26. Felix Rabbe, *L'Abbé Simon Foucher* (Paris: Dijon, 1867), Appendix, xi.

that it can by its own operations produce what corresponds perfectly to the events which follow from things."[27]

In the *Discourse*, 1686: "As a matter of fact, our soul has the quality of representing to itself any nature or form when the occasion arises to think of it. And I believe that this quality of our soul, insofar as it expresses some nature, form, or essence, is properly the idea of the thing."[28]

In the *De Rerum Originatione Radicali*, 1697: "I reply that neither these essences nor the so-called eternal truths about them are fictions, but exist in a certain region of ideas, so to speak, namely in God himself, the source of all essence and of the existence of other beings."[29]

Thus ideas are not to be defined as names or signs, nor as contents or objects of the mind, nor, more specifically, as sensa or images or qualia of any kind, though all of these things are involved in the epistemological reactions included in the ideas.[30]

Names, symbols, or characters, to use the most distinctive Leibnizian terms, are arbitrary, though not entirely so. Ideas, on the other hand, are real. Otherwise there would be no distinction between nominal and real definitions, or essences.[31] To confuse sign with idea is the source of faulty analogy and empirical pseudo-reasoning.[32] Synthesis involves the process of interpreting symbols in order to reveal the ideas.

27. Gerhardt, VII:264; cf. Loemker, p. 208.

28. Gerhardt, IV:451; cf. Loemker, p. 320.

29. Gerhardt, VII:305; cf. Loemker, p. 488. See also Gerhardt, II:172 (1699); *ibid.*, VI:532 f. (1702); *ibid.*, VI:576 f. (1708); J. E. Erdmann, *Gothofredi Guillelmi Leibnitii Opera Philosophica quae extant*, 2 vols. (Berlin: G. Eichler, 1840; unchanged reprint, Aalen-Scientia, 1959) 445[b] (1707); Gerhardt, V:280 f.

30. Leibniz sometimes uses "ideas" interchangeably with "notions" and "essences," which they strictly are not. Cf. Couturat, pp. 243, 282; *Discourse*, sec. 8; Gerhardt, IV:426 (1684).

31. *Nouveaux Essais*, bk. III, *passim* (Gerhardt, V:280 f.; cf. Gerhardt, VI:262, vs. Spinoza, in 1678).

32 Jagodinsky, pp. 3, 4 f. (1676): "A distinction must be made between a progression by ideas and a progression by definitions or characters. All progression by definitions contains within it a progression by ideas. For I assume that he who speaks thinks."

Nor are ideas to be confused with thoughts. Thoughts are proportional to ideas but are not ideas, for ideas are present when thoughts are not.[33] Ideas are the possibility of thought.[34] They are not essentially related to thoughts as their objects, though they may indeed become the objects of thought, in reflection, and Leibniz often speaks of them in this connection.[35] The object of thought is always reality, or God and the fulguration of monads from him. Leibniz is always closer to Arnauld's representative realism than to Malebranche's Platonized Cartesianism in his theory of knowledge.

Neither are ideas essentially contents of mind.[36] Leibniz sometimes defends Malebranche's view against the empiricists that ideas are in God's mind, and sometimes, when pressed, puts them in ours. However, ideas are not mental content, but rather the order of mind itself. They are in the mind only as the statue's possibilities are in the veined marble.

Finally, ideas are not to be confused with sensations or sense-data.[37] Although his criticism of Locke involves terms such as *idées sensibles,* the context makes it clear that sense qualities, like more distinct symbols, are merely the passive poles of the perceptions or expressions of the universe which the ideas make possible. Sense is a confused quality by which we express reality in certain types of perception; it is due to the resistance which our imperfect nature offers to the complexity of the universe. Sense is therefore evidence of the reality of the world but gives us no distinct knowledge of it; it is datum for analysis.[38]

Therefore, when Leibniz says, "Idea, concept, cognition, consciousness, perception, etc., reduce to the same thing,"[39] he is not

33. Gerhardt, VI:592 (vs. Malebranche); Loemker, pp. 626–627; Gerhardt, V:108 (bk. II, chap. 1, sec. 23); *ibid.,* 99 sec. 1 (vs. Locke).

34. Gerhardt, V:279 (bk. III, chap. 3, secs. 2, 3). Cf. Jagodinsky, p. 126: "Ideas are in our minds as differentiae of thoughts."

35. Gerhardt, V:99 (bk. II, chap. 1, sec. 1); IV:424 (1684); Loemker, p. 292; IV:451 (1686); Loemker, p. 320.

36. Gerhardt, VII:263 (1678); Loemker, p. 207.

37. Jagodinsky, p. 4.

38. *Ibid.,* p. 11.

39. Gerhardt, I:131.

formulating an identity but a metaphysical reduction; all are aspects of the complex logical pattern which makes possible our knowledge of the universe, imperfectly externally, and more completely internally through reflection. Thus the polar structure of an idea is actualized in my knowledge, actively as thinking, passively as the sensory, affective, and symbolic content by which my thought expresses or represents the world. The ideas thus support a realistic theory of knowledge, in which the "new way" appears as an abstraction from the old.

III

To discuss Leibniz's further efforts to clarify his conception of ideas and to develop their role in his thought would involve all of the later analyses by which his system is amplified and altered. But his attempts to explain the process of individualization, beginning with the Paris period, serve to make clear the most conspicuous difficulties in his system. His argument is drawn from the mathematical notions of functionality, continuity, and symbolic expression, applied analogically to his previous ontological argument to explain *how* the fullness and perfection of the ideas demand the generation of many finite series, each reflecting the world according to its own point of view.

The functional notion has been shown to be essential to Leibniz's mathematics by 1673, though his use of the term in its present meaning comes later.[40] Just as a functional law implies a curve or a continuous series of values of a dependent variable, expressing one or more independently variable conditions, so the pattern of ideas, a perfect and complete universal functional law involving an infinite number of variables, can be resolved, by a mind great enough, into a distinct law for each variable in terms of all the rest. Thus each variable "expresses" the values of all the rest according to its individual law, and this law defines the nature of its dependence on the rest of the universe. Furthermore, successive values of an individual series or variable proceed from antecedent values according to a mode of variation (a differential)

40. D. Mahnke, "Die Entstehung des Functionsbegriffes," *Kantstudien* XXXI (1926): 426–428.

itself defined by the law of the individual. Any particular value, therefore, of an individual series depends upon two relationships, both of which follow from the law of the series: one, the temporal relationship of succession by which it is "the result of its previous state, so that the present is great with the future"; the other, the simultaneous relationship of reflecting the corresponding values of every other variable in the universe. The law of the series thus determines both the appetitive and the perceptual dimensions of the individual series,[41] the relations both of time and space. The law involves also, as an integral between any two temporal limits, the cumulative sum of its values, and the individual as totality may be understood thus to comprise all its possible states.[42] Every individual series is thus the direct result of the actualization of values implicit in its law and is therefore immediately connected with the ideas or with God, while it is functionally dependent upon, and expressive of, its own past and future values and the other individuals which constitute the existing world.

The psychological values of this theory is apparent: it supports Leibniz's intellectualistic theory of will, his unconscious perceptions, and the temporal continuity of mind in a functional interrelationship with its environment. Freed of its metaphysical origin, it offers interesting suggestions for psychological method, though the "individual concept" or "law of the individual series" would have to be considered synthetically and empirically.[43] For,

41. In this connection, Leibniz's revision notes, prepared between 1695 and 1709 for his early work on "A New Method of Teaching and Learning Jurisprudence," are enlightening. In Book I, sec. 33, of that work, he had named the qualities of mind which are perceived directly as *cogitatio* and *causalitas*. In his revision thirty years later, they become *perceptivitas* and *activitas* (Academy Ed., VI, i:286 and note; Loemker, p. 89).

42. As Leibniz came to rely more on a phenomenological and less on an *a priori* method, he interpreted the mathematical argument as an analogy. Cf. Leibniz to Nicholas Remond, February 11, 1715 (Gerhardt, III:635; Loemker, p. 658).

43. The doctrine appears in his papers at least by 1679, comes into the foreground of the metaphysics in the *Discourse* of 1686, and remains there until the correspondence with de Volder. Cf. *Discourse*, secs. 8, 9, 13 (Loemker, pp. 307–308, 310–311). For Leibniz's later use of this doctrine, see Gerhardt, IV:485 (1695); *ibid.*, 518, 522 f., 553 f. (vs. Bayle, 1702); Loemker,

as Arnauld's criticism should have shown, the mathematical notion of a law of the individual, which is a special solution of the law of universal harmony, fails to provide for a genuine pluralism and individualism. It does not explain the finiteness of human experience. It does involve the view that at any present moment I reflect the universe as a whole in a way determined by my past experiences and great with the future; but it does not involve, or even permit, the limitations of my "point of view" and the element of passivity, unclearness, resistance, or conflict by which Leibniz himself explains this finiteness. In the law of the individual, mathematically conceived, there is no reason why I should not reflect the universe as adequately as does God himself and, therefore, there is no explanation of empirical individuality at all. Leibniz did not, of course, recognize such a unity in any monads except spirits, in whom reflection or an internal sense supplies it.[44] But neither does he recognize this conscious unity as an adequate basis for individuality; self-awareness is by no means coextensive with self-knowledge. It is therefore not surprising that, though Leibniz never abandons the theory of an individual law, the mathematical argument for it becomes more clearly analogical in his later writings, while he depends increasingly on the metaphysical importance of reflection to establish individuality.[45] His mature conception of the individual can be understood as consistent only in relation to his gradual shift of emphasis from the *a priori* logical method and his increasing reliance upon a phenomenological scrutiny of the soul itself and its laws.[46]

A similar difficulty shows itself in the concept of scientific

---

pp. 458, 492–493, 495 f.; and the passages cited above in the *Nouveaux Essais*. The psychological uses of the concept seem to have been first suggested in the *De Affectionibus*, written in 1679 in the midst of fruitful studies in mathematical logic, published in Grua, II:512–537.

44. *Nouveaux Essais*, bk. II, chap. 27, sec. 9 (Gerhardt, V:219 f.).

45. Compare his gradual separation of mathematics and metaphysics. Reality is more than functional relatedness, as matter is more than extension.

46. Leibniz emphasizes the metaphysical importance of reflection from 1686 on, but especially so in the 1700s when the criticism of Bayle, Foucher, and de Volder have made his panlogism less stable. See *Discourse*, sec. 27 (Gerhardt, IV:452; Loemker, p. 320); see also Gerhardt, VI:488 f., 493, 501; *Monadology*, sec. 30.

causality which the doctrine of ideas makes possible and which is first formulated in the *Discourse* and the ensuing correspondence with Arnauld.[47] It is true that Leibniz's terminology is confused and that in some of his methodological studies the principle of sufficient reason includes not only the telelogical, creative function of the ideas (metaphysical causality), but the scientific concept as well.[48] This confusion he shared with Descartes, since its source was in the common tradition. But in 1686 scientific causality is interpreted functionally. The mathematical or quasi-mathematical dependence of an event in one monadic series upon other events in the same or other series is causal—a relatively more clear and distinct state, which determines a less clear and distinct one, the more clear being the cause and the latter the effect. Since God alone possesses adequate knowledge, he also possesses pure activity, which is proportional to the purity of the ideas and is thus the cause of all the rest. Thus all other events are predicates of God as subject; this Scholastic formula must be understood, however, in the sense not merely of logical subsumption, but of the specific and continuous values of a mathematical function.

When Leibniz denies interaction between the monads, therefore, he is not to be understood as rejecting all determining relatedness between them, but only causality as a real influence, in Suarez's sense. If causality means, as Leibniz holds, functional dependence, he establishes a causal connection between monads. His theory of causality leads also in the direction of more modern conceptions: causality is descriptive, pluralistic, and systemic, rather than linear. A cause is a more distinct whole determining a less distinct part. But in spite of these advantages, it must be admitted that the doctrine of ideas prevented Leibniz's breaking away from an inclusive logical determinism to develop a truly scientific view of causality, a failure which is illustrated by the ambiguity of the principle of sufficient reason itself.

47. Leibniz to Arnauld, 1686 (Gerhardt, II:57, 69; Loemker, pp. 337–338). Cf. *Monadology*, secs. 50–52 (Loemker, p. 648).

48. "On the Method of Arriving at a True Analysis of Bodies and the Causes of Natural Things," 1677 (Gerhardt, VII:265–269; Loemker, pp. 173–176).

A third application of the ideas, which reveals both the fruitfulness of the doctrine and its difficulties, is the realistic epistemology which is both based upon it and inconsistent with it. The mature formulation of Leibniz's theory of knowledge appears only in the early 1680s, after his study of the controversy between Malebranche and Arnauld over the representative nature of ideas. But his own opinions, developed while he was at Paris, were in direct connection with his first mathematical statements of the principle of continuity.[49] Ideas in their role of functional relations are the possibilities of knowledge, since knowledge is a special case of the present value of an individual "expressing" or "representing" the universe according to its law. Each such expression contains a character or sign which depends, however confusedly and indistinctly, on the characteristics of reality, and the law of continuity requires that there be a value in the characterizing series for every value in the series characterized. It is the task of the *characteristica generalis* or the universal language to develop a set of characters naturally responsive to the laws of logic, for the distinctive quality of a character is its usefulness in comprising a complex relationship in a unity which serves the purpose of predicting future experiences. Even the "empirical consecutions" or associations of the beasts have this symbolic correspondence with reality and thus imitate reason, but the adequacy of knowledge and its value for future fulfillment increase with the rational quality of the activity of perception. Perception in any case is thus the actualization of an idea, and it is frequently explicitly related to the ideas, as for example, in the "Quid Sit Idea?" (1678):

> The idea of things in us is nothing but the fact that God, the author alike of things and of mind, has impressed this power of thinking upon the mind,[50] so that it can by its own operations produce what corresponds perfectly to the events which follow from things.

49. Jagodinsky, pp. 3 f., "Quid Sit Idea?," 1678 (Gerhardt, VII:263–264; Loemker, pp. 207–208); Gerhardt, II:112 (1687); Loemker, p. 339; and throughout the correspondence with Arnauld. Many modern interpreters of Leibniz's theory of continuity overlook its essentially polar nature; continuity cannot be defined except in terms of at least two series.

50. Until 1686 Leibniz wavers between *cogitatio* and *perceptio* as the

Direct consequences of this theory of perception are the view that the soul is of infinite extent (which Leibniz carefully expounds in Section 27 of the *Discourse*), and the conception of *phenomena bene fundata*,[51] in which Leibniz's logistic, science, and epistemology are harmonized: for the various levels of the soul's perceptions, with varied degrees of the soul's participation and hence of indistinctness and inadequacy, are analogical patterns of God's own ideas and thoughts. Only through the perception of our own states can we perceive the ideas themselves; and in their most distinct apperception and least inadequate intuition, we come to understand the unity of the soul with God.

The crucial test of this theory of knowledge is the problem of error, and it is here that its defects become apparent. The failure of political and theological universals had convinced the *homme honnête* of the partiality and incompleteness of truth, but he seems to have found it hard to admit any forthright error, least of all his own. Leibniz was no exception. However confused and inadequate he may have recognized human knowledge to be, he held that it is within its limits true, since it is determined by the harmony of ideas. Error must therefore be either merely incomplete and confused truth, or a knowledge-claim not validated by any idea whatever. The latter seems to be Leibniz's conception. Error is venturing into the impossible; it is the use of symbols without reference to reality. It is assuming ideas when we have none. All error consists in this—we proceed by analogies about whose applicability to the matter at hand we have not been aroused.[52]

Nor is what Descartes, as I recall, said somewhere valid, to the effect that, when we speak of something with an understanding of what we say, we have an idea of the thing. For it often happens that we combine things that are incompatible, as for example when we think of the most rapid motion, a thing which is known to be impossible; and as a result

---

designation for this fundamental activity of the monads. After 1686 he uses perception fairly consistently.

51. Leibniz's phenomenalism is early in appearing (cf. Kabitz, *Die Philosophie des jungen Leibniz*, p. 140, from 1671) but it is related to his representative theory of perception only much later.

52. Jagodinsky, p. 3 (1676).

we have no idea, though we are conceded to speak of it with understanding. I have elsewhere explained that we often think only confusedly of what we are talking about, and that we are conscious of the existence of an idea on our mind only when we understand a thing and resolve it sufficiently.

I do not admit that errors are more dependent on the will than on the intellect. . . . The source of all errors is the same in kind as that which is observed as the basis of errors in mathematical calculations. It often happens through lack of attention or imperfect memory that we act unfittingly or fail to act fittingly, or we think we have done what we did not do, or have not done what we did do.[53]

The will does not enter into the cause of error, therefore, as Descartes had held, though a wrong will is the result of error. We err when we take a fragmentary or confused pattern of symbols for an idea, and we do this because of a weakness of memory or attention, not of will.

It must be admitted that though this conception of error provides a partly adequate criterion of truth—usefulness and coherence[54]—it does not adequately distinguish positive error from merely confused and inadequate truth. All error is of the type of Descartes's argument for the existence of God, based on valid inference but neglecting the question of possibility. Error is revealed in the inconsistency of our thinking because it does not adequately conform to real ideas, which are harmonious. Until he wrote the essay referred to in note 53, Leibniz did not distinguish between mere unfounded appearances, such as dreams and fantasies, and forthright error.

But the real difficulty is the possibility of error even in this sense. Error, even as confused truth or as ungrounded thinking, is compatible with the doctrine of ideas only if the source of limitation and imperfection is explained, which it is not. How it is possible for an individual, whose perceptions are first defined as expressions and actualizations of the harmony of ideas, to perceive a pattern of symbols which correspond to no ideas at all,

53. Gerhardt, IV:360, 361 (1692); cf. Loemker, pp. 387–388.

54. For the criterion of truth, see "On the Method of Distinguishing Real from Imaginary Phenomena" (Gerhardt, VII:319–322; Loemker, pp. 363–365).

Leibniz cannot explain. To admit such a possibility is to free the individual from the rigid intellectual determinism which the ideas impose upon him.

Leibniz never explicitly abandons this intellectualism, but traces of a tendency to break the rigid chain of being appear early in his thought. The first of these is his distinction between possibility and compossibility, which parallels that between necessary and contingent truths, metaphysical and mechanical laws, and absolute and hypothetical determinism. It is in criticism of Spinoza, in 1678, that he first asserts that not all possibilities are actualized and that therefore, though all ideas demand (*exigo*) existence, God does not permit all to be actualized;[55] of the many possibilities, only that one pattern of compossibles comes into being which is the best possible. He at once defines the will of God as this process of elimination and choice, which is rational because it implies a sufficient reason and therefore follows from the harmony of the ideas themselves. But the distinction introduces a factor of resistance or limitation into the nature of God himself, who can no longer be pure intellect, since the teleological nature of all of his ideas can no longer be realized. Since the best of all possible worlds is a fulfillment of only a part of the total of the ideas, this now involves contradiction. Hence the distinction between logical possibility and compossibility, however fruitful it may have been for later thought, destroys the consistency of the doctrine of ideas itself.

This distinction is, however, the first of the trends toward the individual and the empirical which appear in Leibniz's later thought, and which reflect an uneasiness at the imperfect pattern of analogies involved in his system of categories. To his early effort to sustain the theory that God does not fatalistically necessitate our acts, but infallibly inclines us to them, are now added

55. The first suggestions of this distinction occurred from 1675 to 1676 (Gerhardt, I:124, note 3). Later it is further explained by the theory, suggested by the solution of certain physical problems through maxima and minima, that every mechanical law is an optimal case of many possible laws. See the *Tentamen Anagogicum* (Gerhardt, VII:270–279; Loemker, pp. 477–484).

an increasing tendency toward temporalism[56] and the clarification of his apriorism by the admission that human knowledge is limited to phenomena and grounded in experience.[57] In the *De Rerum Originatione Radicali,* an analogy is used which suggests that matter or passive power is not derived from the ideas at all, but is somehow independent of them and imposes conditions to which creation has to adapt its ends. In opposition to Malebranche, Sturm, and others, there is increasing emphasis upon the activity of the monads themselves rather than upon God,[58] so that, whereas the *Discourse* began and ended its exposition with God, the *Principles of Nature and of Grace* and the *Monadology* build their outline on the nature of the individual and his powers. It is noteworthy, also, that the doctrine of ideas does not appear in these two papers of 1714.

IV

We may summarize by saying that Leibniz's doctrine of ideas is metaphysical and designed to combine and systematize his three basic interests: universal order, individual freedom (in the sense of the expression of order in an individual as completely as possible), and purposive force. Ideas, therefore, enter into our experience on three levels: as the harmonious and perfect logical ground for all existence; as the law of each individual series and of the phenomena resulting from the organized activities of related series; and as the structure of individual acts of knowledge and of will. The doctrine is not only the central unifying element in Leibniz's thought; it is also one of the most fruitful, for it relates a dynamic psychology and physics with a relational logic of possibility and with a teleological metaphysics supporting the whole variety of human experience, scientific and nonscientific.

In logic the ideas aid him in anticipating a modern approach

56. See A. O. Lovejoy, *The Great Chain of Being* (Cambridge: Harvard University Press, 1936), pp. 172 f., 255 f.

57. After 1702 the epistemological statements are in this vein. Cf. Gerhardt, VI:508, 533; Loemker, pp. 552, 556.

58. See *De Ipsa Natura,* 1698 (Gerhardt, IV:507, 509; Loemker, pp. 500–501, 502).

to logistic. Though he never completely breaks with the predicative viewpoint and has only occasional insights into an extensional logic, relational thinking is the foundation of all of his projects in the reform of logic and a universal characteristic. Yet logical relations are never free from their symbolic contents, as his use of the word *denominations* suggests, and the principle of sufficient reason serves to explain the analogical parallels between the various levels of symbolic knowledge. Though Leibniz continues to use Scholastic categories in arguing with Scholastics, he has almost completely rejected, by the period of the *Nouveaux Essais*, both the substance-property and the empirical qualitative view of reality; nominal essences are denied[59] while real essences, or the possibilities of things, are relations, which constitute, he says, "the largest field of our knowledge".[60] Nor can his often repeated remark that "there are no purely extrinsic denominations"[61] be interpreted as a theory of internal relations. This remark, indeed, is commonly made by him against those who, like Malebranche, tend to deny active substance to individual created beings. The organic structure of the ideas is relative to purposive function; a single perception is an organism; so also is a single many-valued monad, and so is the entire universe of compossible events.

As principles of force, the ideas permit Leibniz to correct the Cartesian geometrical physics and to provide a plausible synthesis of mathematical law, energy, and specific events. In psychology, they free him from both materialistic and soul-substance theories of mind[62] and support his theory of an unconscious and

59. *Nouveaux Essais*, bk. III, chap. 3, secs. 18, 19 (Gerhardt, V:273 f). Leibniz often calls ideas essences, but not in the sense of empirical or sensible qualities; these are phenomenal and without ultimate logical status, since they are confused. Real essences are metaphysical processes by which the pattern of ideas is actualized.

60. *Ibid.*, bk. IV, chap. 3, sec. 18 (Gerhardt, V:364).

61. Gerhardt, II:56 (1686); Loemker, p. 337. Cf. *Nouveaux Essais*, bk. II, chap. 25, sec. 1 (Gerhardt, V:211 [1704]).

62. Leibniz considered not only Hobbes but Descartes and Spinoza as materialistic. For Hobbes, see Gerhardt, I:85; Loemker, pp. 105–107, and later Gerhardt, IV:559; Loemker, p. 577. For Descartes, see Gerhardt, IV:299 f. (1679); Gerhardt, IV:283 (1680); Loemker, p. 272. Though some-

his teleological theory of memory, thought, and will. They also supply a more fruitful concept of individuality than either the materialistic one or one based merely on self-consciousness. What is perhaps most important of all, they supply a psychological support for his modified rationalism in epistemology and a metaphysical foundation for a realistic logic and theory of knowledge. Their original function of providing a norm for human values and a source of justice and harmony commensurate with power is thus enlarged by the most inclusive metaphysical burdens.

The ultimate question in interpreting Leibniz's doctrine of ideas seems to be this: can the failures of his doctrine be removed by a modification of his methods—without losing its values? The great failure was, as we have seen, their inadequacy to establish an individualism which squares with experience. Self-experience does in fact reveal ideas as active, purposive, and particularizing processes. And the analogical application of the results of this empirical fact to other areas of experience—mathematics and logic, physics, law and theology—may, if carefully done, be productive of new possibilities of understanding. But the *a priori* method, which seeks to establish a universe determined by ideas and then to prove the necessity, within that universe, of limitation, matter, error, and evil, is but the rationalization of a faith. Leibniz's *apriorism* is a product of his century. But his phenomenological perceptions into the interrelations of the mind with its world and the cautious effort to extend these perceptions by analogies, necessarily symbolic, to nature, life, and social relations, and perhaps even to an ontological reference, mark a permanent advance. To emphasize this method, of which Leibniz was a most skillful master, is to loosen the reins with which God holds existence, to see ideas as abstractions from the activity of spirits of which they are parts, to seek individual laws, not as creative of individual perspectives, but as relative to them, to abandon the Plato of dogma for an explicit temporalism.

---

times Leibniz uses a trace-theory of memory, he explains that traces are really acts of perception of past or future events (Gerhardt, IV:551 f.).

4

On Substance and Process in Leibniz

Leroy E. Loemker

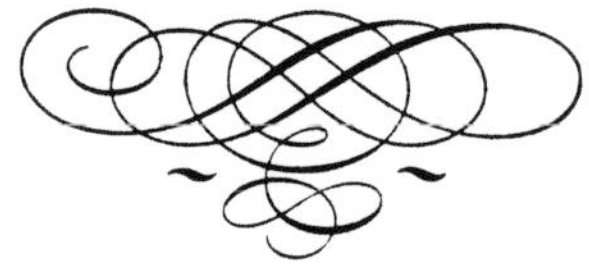

It is an irony of modern philosophy that Leibniz, who did more than any other thinker of his century to undermine the traditional doctrine of substance in the interest of a modern conception of change and dynamism,[1] should, in the last twenty years of his life, have applied most of the time and energy left him for philosophical thought to what may well be the longest and most persistent debate on the nature of substance which records have preserved.

Moreover, since this debate was carried out with correspondents schooled in either the Scholastic or the Cartesian tradition (or in that strange combination of the two which prevailed so widely in the late seventeenth century), it is a part of this irony that Leibniz's expositions of his doctrine, which was approaching a functional simplicity, had to be written in the terminological tradition which they used, with the result that they seem only rarely to grasp his meaning adequately. It is rather in those simpler interpretations of his thought written in the last years of his

This paper was first published in *Process and Divinity: The Hartshorne Festschrift,* edited by William L. Reese and Eugene Freeman (LaSalle, Illinois: Open Court Publishing Company, 1964), pp. 403–425.

1. Cf. the new concept of *force* which resulted from his studies in dynamics and was first given a metaphysical meaning in a published paper of 1694: *On the Correction of Metaphysics and the Concept of Substance* (Gerhardt, IV:468–470; Loemker, pp. 432–434).

life for the instruction of such interested laymen as Eugene of Savoy, Nicolas Remond, and Louis Bourguet that the clear, concrete, and empirically oriented accounts are to be found which still serve best as introductions (admittedly inadequate) to his thought.[2]

Leibniz's mature doctrine of substance stands at midpoint between the traditional theory of his predecessors—that which was criticized by George Berkeley and David Hume—and the process philosophy of our own century, from which the category is banished, at least in name, but in which its functions must still somehow be served. This discussion of the debate will be restricted to the intellectual exchanges with three men: Pierre Bayle, Burcher de Volder, and Bartholomew des Bosses. The first two were Cartesians of somewhat diverse interest, while the last named was a Jesuit Scholastic. Involved in this discussion will be, primarily, five perennial antinomies brought to the fore by Leibniz's new theory: the logical antinomy of universal and particular (and the ambiguity of their relation); the metaphysical antitheses of self-determinism versus external interaction and of order versus freedom; the psychological antithesis of disposition or habit versus particular act, and the ethical antithesis of power and justice (now tempered with love). These are all aspects of the same general issue; they are all Platonic in origin and inspiration; and the one great generalization of Leibniz's theory of substance proposes to resolve them all.

I

In a detailed reply to some of de Volder's criticisms, Leibniz offers a compact definition of substance. In essence, it is a permanent law determining a temporal sequence or series of events.

2. Particularly the *Principles of Nature and of Grace*, probably written for Eugene of Savoy but sent to Nicolas Remond de Montmort as well, and the so-called *Monadology*, which A. Robinet has recently suggested was sent to Remond to provide the basis for a new *De Rerum Natura* by the poet Fraguier. See G. W. Leibniz, *Principes de la nature et de la grace fondés en raison, Principes de la philosophie ou monadologie*, edited by A. Robinet (Paris: Presses universitaires, 1954). The letters to Louis Bourguet also contain clear expositions (Gerhardt, III:572–583; Loemker, pp. 661–665).

That there is a certain persisting law which involves the future states of that which we conceive as the same—this itself is what I say constitutes the same substance. If anyone concedes to me that there is an infinity of percipients, in each of whom there is a fixed law of the progression of phenomena; that the phenomena of these different percipients correspond with each other; and that there is a common reason for both their existence and their correspondence in the being we call God—this is all I claim in the matter and all I think can be claimed.[3]

A substance consists of two mutually dependent phases corresponding to the logical dimensions of intensionality and extensionality respectively—the "complete notion" or "the law of the individual," and the particular temporal series of "states" or perceptions which express this law. In traditional terms, the complete individual notion, concept, or law is the substance, which has two kinds of properties: the essences or enduring natures which are ingredient to it, and the particular events which change and which are particular actualizations of these essences. Logically speaking, a substance is a singular subject in which all of its abiding and changing predicates inhere, and it is identical to them; the subject is equal to the whole of its predicates. In mathematical terms, it is a functional law which determines all of the particular values which inhere in its complexly interrelated variables. It can equally well be regarded (as the second part of the quotation from the letter to de Volder shows) as a succession of events, understood as perceptive acts, continuously related to each other by an internal principle of order which determines them. Substance is, therefore, a uniformly ordered succession of such events.

For Leibniz, every individual thus consists of a combination of particular and universal in the new relationship of process and form (indeed, he revives the Scholastic designation of substantial form). These two inseparable aspects do justice, the one to his panpsychism, the other to his panlogism. When the new concept

3. Leibniz to de Volder, January 21, 1704, Gerhardt, II:264; cf. Loemker, p. 535.

of substance was first clearly explicated, in the *Discourse of Metaphysics* in 1686, Leibniz was engaged in logical studies involving the development, through the art of combinations, of *complete* or *integral* notions. This was to serve as the logical analog to the creation of individuals from the simple perfections of God.[4] Thus the *Discourse,* written for Antoine Arnauld, the first draft of which carries the title "A Treatise on the Perfections of God," emphasized the panalogistic aspect of substance—the logical constitution of the individual concept.[5]

At the time of the correspondence with Arnauld which followed, Leibniz had not yet worked out clearly such detailed problems as the nature of composite substances and the relationship between individuals, particularly the relations between mind and body, nor had he simplified his theory of the action and passion of the individual into a theory of perception and appetite. The concept of force was still lacking. During the Italian journey which followed, his interest was centered, aside from his historical task, upon problems of mathematics and dynamics, with the result that his new theory of individual substance was further developed to include the conception of primitive force; this must be understood as the metaphysical exigency or striving of the ideas comprising the individual notions to actualize themselves, or in other words, as the operative power of the very perfections of God as they are compounded and made complete in individual substances.[6] In *The New System on the Nature and Communication of Substances* (1695), Leibniz undertook the first published interpretation of his new doctrine, with particular emphasis upon the activism of the individual and the doctrine of harmony as an explanation of their relationships, but with a mere mention of "a kind of perception" as the act expressing this harmony. It was

4. For example, see the *Generales Inquisitiones de Analysi Notionum et Veritatum* (1686) (Couturat, pp. 356–399).

5. See particularly *Discourse,* secs. 8–13 (Gerhardt, IV:432–439; Loemker, pp. 306–311).

6. *On the Radical Origination of Things* (1697) (Gerhardt, VII:303; Loemker, p. 487); and Leibniz to des Bosses, February 5, 1712 (Gerhardt, II:435; Loemker, p. 600).

the *New System* which gave rise to the great controversy about substance; and it is worth noting that Leibniz's correspondents did not know the unpublished *Discourse* of 1686 in which the logical basis of his theory had been given. Thus his panpsychism, and its significance for dynamics, is clear in their minds, but his panlogism is obscured. Leibniz's last papers on logic were written in 1691 and 1692, and they mark no advance in his thinking about the metaphysical implications of logic.

But although Leibniz's analogies in these letters are drawn primarily from the functional concept of mathematics, the concept of force in dynamics, and the phenomena of life and consciousness, and although his thinking is increasingly occupied with time, process, and history, his concept of substance holds the panlogistic and panpsychistic aspects of his metaphysics together inseparably.[7]

II

From its earliest beginnings, Leibniz's thought had converged upon this unity of logic and process. His early philosophical speculations, before the years in Paris (1672–76), were eclectic, and his logical, juristic, and theological ideas were incompletely assimilated to each other. Yet there is underlying them all a metaphysical synthesis which assimilates Aristotle's doctrine of substance to Platonic souls and thus to the data of conscious life, without neglecting the mathematical Platonism of the new sciences of Kepler and Galileo. Certain phases of this combination may briefly be enumerated.

1. In the student work in which Leibniz's mathematical logic of combinations and commutations was first proposed, the *Dissertation on the Art of Combinations* (1666), there is a short metaphysical introduction which involves a metaphysics of ideas and their possible arrangements, in the course of which spatial, temporal, and dynamic orders are derived. This theme was not

7. See J. Jalabert, *La théorie Leibnizienne de la substance* (Paris: Presses Universitaires de France, 1947), especially the concluding chapter. Jalabert agrees that, though the panpsychistic aspects dominate the discussion after 1696, Leibniz never abandoned his panlogism.

developed, however, until ten years later, in the first logical papers of the early Hanover years, when Leibniz had acquired the mathematical tools needed for a clearer conception of logical addition—the ideas of variables and values in a functional relationship, of a mathematical determinant which is resolvable into successive lower and more abstract orders of determinants until the lowest order of simple elements is reached, and the physical device of a resolving of motion into momentary impetuses or conations.[8]

2. Leibniz's early papers on theological and juristic problems, written during his stay in Mainz, reflect a metaphysical theory of creation which anticipates some of his later principles. It views creation as a process of multiplication of the divine ideas, required by the infinite nature of God. Several quotations will show the Platonism involved.

> The substance of things is an idea. Idea is the union of God and creatures, as action is the union of agent and patient . . . N.B. Ideas are not in God except insofar as there are things outside of him. Thus a point is not a center without lines . . . The ideas of God and the substances of things are the same in fact, different in relation, as are action and passion. And since the substances of things are the action of God upon species, we must inquire how it is possible that his action upon one species is numerically the same as his action upon another.

Again, "In idea is contained ideally both passive and active power, both active and passive intellect. Insofar as passive intellect concurs, there is form."[9] This metaphysics of ideas provided the ground for Leibniz's early doctrine of harmony in theology, and of justice in jurisprudence.

3. If the first two examples show Leibniz's early tendency to

8. Gerhardt, VII:280–283. Cf. the marginal note to the Dialogue of 1677: "When God calculates and carries out his calculations, the world is made." See also the paper *On Universal Synthesis and Analysis, or the Art of Discovery and Judgment*, Gerhardt, VII:292–298; Loemker, pp. 229–233.

9. Academy Ed., VI, i:513. From a treatise on transubstantiation from 1668. See also Leibniz to Magnus Wedderkopf, May 1671 (Academy Ed., II, i:117; Loemker, p. 146); Leibniz's first letter to Antoine Arnauld (1671) (Gerhardt, I:72–73; Loemker, pp. 148–150); and *On the Elements of Jurisprudence* (Academy Ed., VI, i:437).

a panlogism, the next reflects his early panpsychism. In the *a priori* part of the *New Physical Hypothesis, The Theory of Abstract Motion,* published in 1761 and dedicated to the French Academy, Leibniz made an early attempt to find a common component of body and mind in motion. In this attempt he made use of Hobbes's concept of conatus as a simple momentary motion. Twenty years would pass before it became a momentary force.

> No conatus without motion lasts longer than a moment except in minds. For what is conatus in a moment is the motion of a body in time. This opens the door to the true distinction between body and mind, which no one has heretofore explained. Every body is a momentary mind, or one lacking recollection (*recordatio*), because it does not retain its own conatus and the contrary one together for more than a moment. For two things are necessary to sense pleasure and pain—action and reaction, opposition and then harmony—and there is no sensation without these. Hence body lacks memory; it lacks the perception of its own actions and passions; it lacks thought.[10]

Remarkable here is the theory that sensory feelings are momentary oppositions or resistances between opposed impulses and that memory, or the retention of a series' own past actions and passions, makes possible thought. There is no evidence that Leibniz at this time related this conception of a dynamic series as a succession of momentary motions to the role of the individual idea in creation, but when he succeeded in refining both notions, in the post-Paris period, the essentials of his theory of substance were outlined.

4. The psychological aspect of the notion of a serial order of events is brought out in a paper of 1679 published by Gaston Grua. Entitled *De Affectibus: Ubi de Potentia, Actioni, Determinatione,* it begins as a running commentary on Descartes's *On the Passions of the Soul,* but soon shifts to a description of the serial chains of thought (later, perceptions) which constitute the mind. Beginning with the basic proposition, *nos esse substantias,* Leibniz here resolves the mind into an interweaving of series of

10. Gerhardt, IV:230; cf. Loemker, p. 141. The theory of *conatus* or *impetus* is generally accepted in Scholastic works on physics at the beginning of the century.

cogitations, each of which is determined by an affect, and each of which aims at a perfection. Nowhere did he penetrate more deeply into a phenomenological study of consciousness or anticipate Whitehead more closely, and it is regrettable that he never resumed his thinking in this direction. A few quotations will show the nature of his analysis:

> An affect is a determination of the mind toward thinking of a certain thing in preference to other things.
>
> Attention is the determination toward thinking one thing above other things because these others are not remembered.
>
> A series is a multitude with a rule of order.
>
> The determination to a series of thinking is stronger to the degree that the rule of the series involves the more reality [or perfection].
>
> A series is thus ingredient in [ingredimur] thinking, so that we may discover in [the confused parts of thought] something which we seek. It can happen that diverse series become progressively ingredient so that we may choose what we find in each.[11]

Thus the mind, conscious and unconscious, is constituted not merely by one "series with a rule of order" but by many series which may determine each other, and sometimes envelop, one the other, or merge into each other. These subordinate series within the mind, or more generally, within the individual substance, provide a basis for the "subalternate maxims" (as Leibniz designates them in the *Discourse*[12]) or the laws of nature which are common to entire classes of individuals. It is to be regretted that Leibniz neither developed this idea nor built it into his mature system. But the paper on the affections does mark one point in the development of Leibniz's thought at which his panlogism and panpsychism are firmly bound together through the principle that generative individual concepts or laws and serial acts are united inseparably in each substance.

11. *De Affectibus, Ubi de Potentia, Actioni, Determinatione,* Grua, II: 512–537. The quotations are from pages 525–526 and 524.

12. Sections 7, 17; Gerhardt, IV:432, 442; Loemker, pp. 307, 314.

In its essentials, Leibniz's doctrine of substance was then complete, although it required his correction of Descartes's theory of motion and the conservation of momentum, and the development of the calculus, to provide him with his strongest analogical arguments from science and his clearest explanations of the relationship between a universal law and the particular instances or values of its variables.

III

It will be useful to enumerate some of the gains which Leibniz had achieved by this doctrine of substance.

1. *It eliminates the unempirical specter of a substance with spatial or temporal attributes but itself beyond definition.* This is the "substance" to which the Cartesians clung and which was found, by the time of Locke, to be without empirical support or rational necessity. Both souls and bodies are now reduced to continuous processes of active and passive states, the effects of forces originating in the ideas or laws which determined them. They are as habits which determine acts, as the fixed relations between variables which determine their values, as facts and the principles which describe their order. This is a concept of substance which lies well within the limits of scientific theory and verification (though complete verification would involve an infinite process of analysis).

2. *It claims to show the possibility that a perfect logical order may be coextensive with a spatio-temporal order of serial events.* There is necessary, of course, a narrowing of the logic of possibilities into a logic of the order of existence; this involves the principle of the best possible. However, by identifying Aristotle's dictum—that in an adequately analyzed proposition the subject must include its predicates—with the logical principle that the intensional meaning of a term must be equivalent to its extensional scope, Leibniz achieves a harmony of rational order with empirical totality.

Louis Couturat considered it a mistake of Leibniz to have developed a logic of intensionality rather than of extensionality. In fact, Leibniz's logical papers show the possibility of both types and the nature of their relation to each other. His metaphysics requires both. The modern trend toward nominalism, however, when it rejects intensionality, finds it impossible to explain order (save as a pragmatically justifiable verbal generalization by the observer). Metaphysically, the choice is one of explaining particulars in terms of an established order, as in Leibniz, or of explaining order as a function of the differing and chance particulars, as in Whitehead.

3. *Leibniz's doctrine of substance restores the old theological theory of the univocity of divine and creaturely attributes and develops it into an actual identity of the essences of created individuals with the perfections (finitely limited) of God himself.* This brings to the center of discussion again the traditional metaphysical and ethical categories as attributes both of God and of his creation and pushes aside such relational categories as extension and thought (which Leibniz could not regard as simple). But in place of the Aristotelian hierarchical structure of genera and species terminating in infima species, Leibniz adopts Spinoza's conception of substance as self-determining and applies it to each individual substance as a complete essence causing its existence. Thus, as Leibniz's discussion of Locke's distinction between real and nominal essences shows, Leibniz's theory of the essence or idea of the individual approximates the real essences which Locke considers unknowable, but which Leibniz regards as knowable imperfectly and in part.[13]

4. *Moreover, the shift which this theory of substance involves from a reference to things of ordinary perception to the microthings resulting from analysis, and from spatial to temporal and dynamic relations* (a shift which was not fully apparent to Leibniz's critics) *provided a more fruitful hypothesis for the explanation of physical as well as mental phenomena than did the alternative hypothesis of atoms.* The new atomism stopped with space and motion and failed to explain the qualities of composite bodies. Leibniz's theory supported the deepening of the physical

13. See *Nouveaux Essais*, bk. III, chap. 3, secs. 15–19 (Gerhardt, V:272–274; bk. III, chap. 10, secs. 19–21, Gerhardt, V:326–328). See also *New Essays on the Understanding*, translated by Alfred G. Langley (La Salle, Illinois: Open Court Publishing Co., 1949), pp. 315–318, 384–387.

sciences by the principle of force[14] and its conservation in closed systems of particles, and in the complex structures of life and mind as well.

5. *In particular, Leibniz's doctrine of substance provides his psychology with a firm basis for both acts and dispositions, making the latter the ground for the former.* It is true that the dispositional components of the mind (or of monads of a lower order) are conceived intellectually, as subalternate patterns of ideas ingredient in the complete notion of the individual. Yet they are not conscious ideas, though they may become known by inner perception or reflection. Indeed, this distinguishes self-knowledge from self-consciousness. To know oneself is by analysis and synthesis to penetrate as deeply as possible into the dispositional characters of which our complete law is the whole.[15] Acts proceed out of character, as particulars from universals, and their variety and order is determined by the order and arrangement (literally, the disposition) of the constants and variables in our nature. For the method of psychology, Leibniz's conception of analysis is significant—and perhaps comforting—at this point. He frequently shows, using algebraic and geometric problems, that though the selected terms and operations of an analysis may differ, and analyses of the same problem may therefore differ in apparent results, the terminal result, if it can be achieved, must always be the same. We may set out to achieve a psychic profile, or laws of motivation, or a typology of personalities, but regulative for all of these methods is an ultimate individual nature defined in simplest terms and relations, even though we can never achieve this definition because truths of fact involve an infinite process of analysis.

6. *In his new doctrine, moreover, Leibniz defined the nature*

14. Gerhardt, IV:468–470. Leibniz here makes explicit the distinction between his conception of force and the Scholastic notion of potentiality. The force operative in the monad (primary force) is a specific *impetus* or *conatus* implicit in the law of the individual, but actualizing itself, if not impeded, as successive appetites and perceptions.

15. See *Nouveaux Essais*, bk. II, chap. 27, secs. 6–23, in reply to Locke's theory of personal identity on this point (Gerhardt, V:215–227; Langley, pp. 241–256).

of the interrelationship between individual substances. One of his less fortunate metaphors, it is true, deprives the monads of windows—a figure singularly inconsistent with that other one describing them as living mirrors. Windowlessness, however, excludes only the possibility of an external causality or "influence" upon the individual; it does not exclude perceptions of the external from within. It emphasizes the completely self-determining nature of substances. Each, in every present state or act, "represents," "expresses," or "perceives" the entire world according to its point of view or the limitations imposed by its individual law. Every perception is the actualization of an idea, is internal to the perceiver but external to what is perceived (this is the realistic dimension of Leibniz's thought), and combines activity and passivity—the inert, material content of the perception which restricts it to "phenomena well founded." According to Leibniz, "Every mind is omniscient but confused."[16]

Such a harmony of interpenetrating perceptions, however, cannot assure the ontological harmony of the world, for, *however* complex the order of perceptions, they are all focused in the nature of the *percipient* and unattached, so to speak, to the *perceptum.* A world of such percipients would fall apart into a plurality of substances, as Bayle and others charged. The harmony of the existing world is assured, not by these perceptions, but by the common ideas or perfections of God ingredient in the complete concepts of the monads. The unity of the world is made possible only by the presence of God whose very attributes inhere, with finite differences, in our natures. Hence "God belongs to me more closely than my body," as Leibniz says in one of his most mystical formulations of his thought.[17]

7. *The conception of a harmonious order of distinct but (in spite of their differences) largely overlapping individual concepts thus supplies Leibniz with a new notion of levels of generality and abstractness in the scientific laws imbedded in both natural and spiritual or mental events.* The process of combinatorial syn-

16. From a fragment of the Paris period (Couturat, p. 10).

17. *On the True Theologia Mystica* (Guhrauer, I:411; cf. Loemker, p. 368).

thesis involved in the creation of this world may be grasped by the analogy to a matrix or determinant containing an infinite number of terms (the irreducible perfections of God) each of which will appear in this world in a particular range of finite values. The complete solution or resolution of this determinant will be an infinite number of complete notions, all containing each of the simple terms, but in a different order or disposition and with varying values. This complete resolution is reached, however, in an infinity of stages in which each term serves as a parameter related to a subordinate order of determinants, each stage involving reduction of the order of these determinants until they disappear. Thus, there appear, in the final complete concepts, various overlapping orders of identical configurations, each of which defines a class of events or abstract attributes and forms which constitute Leibniz's "subalternate regulations" or natural laws. No natural law, however, serves to define completely an individual monad. Each individual retains a uniqueness of nature.

8. *Leibniz's monadology thus involves a theory of causality approaching that of modern science and more adequate than current positivistic theories.* The individual monads and their concepts do not render mechanical laws unnecessary; mechanical laws are abstract aspects of God's creation of the monads. But they are descriptive and functional. All efficient causality resides in the individuals as *vis primitiva,* the actualization of the series; this is what Leibniz means in his frequently repeated remark that he had to return to the substantial forms of the Scholastics.[18] Scientific causality rests on the observation of *phenomena bene fundata* and consists of a description of the relationship between two regularly recurring types of observed events, one of which is relatively active, the other relatively passive, with respect to each other. These descriptive laws, however, are subject to such analysis as can be given to truths of fact; that is, when analyzed further, they may be seen to approach mathematical functions, and, ideally, the functional relations implicit in the monadic notions.[19] Science ideally involves, therefore, a bridging of the

18. *Discourse,* sec. 11 (Gerhardt, IV:435; Loemker, p. 309). Cf. Gerhardt, IV:345, 473, 478; Loemker, p. 454.

19. See Leibniz to Conring, March 1678 (Academy Ed., II, i:400); cf.

gulf separating macrocosmic from microscopic events and the reduction of causal connections to functional dependencies, though these are actually achieved only in dynamics, where the quantifiable elements are fairly exact analogues to the monadic acts and contents themselves. In less exact sciences the scientist must content himself with descriptive and externally related causes and effects. Leibniz anticipates Hume's analysis of causality, but completes it with a metaphysical theory derived from mathematics.

9. *Finally, Leibniz's doctrine of substance also provides him with his doctrine of freedom.* For the "spontaneity" of the monad, whether natural or spiritual, consists of its self-determination, that is, the determination of its actions and passions by the law of its nature which inheres in them. And this individual nature, being complete and concrete, lies beyond the determination of any of the subordinate regulations which are abstractions from it. Reflection and memory impart responsibility to spirit monads, but in no way supply their freedom; this resides in the exigencies of the law of each individual substance, and none of Leibniz's distinctions—between metaphysical and moral necessity, or between necessitating and inclining causes—can modify his determinism. The very important distinction between truths of reason and truths of fact, first introduced in Leibniz's essay *On Freedom* written in the early years in Hanover,[20] supports the contingency of this world as a whole and provides an explanation for man's empirical sense of freedom in his inability to reduce empirical knowledge to logical necessities, but it offers no help toward modifying his determinism. Thus divine creativity enters intimately into man and nature, but only in a way to deprive them of any internal indeterminism or genuine creativity.

IV

It is remarkable that this theory of freedom seems to have satisfied all of Leibniz's correspondents; not even Pierre Bayle,

Loemker, p. 189: "All things occur mechanically in nature; that is, by certain mathematical laws prescribed by God."

20. *Nouvelles lettres et opuscules inedits de Leibniz,* edited by Foucher de Careil (Paris: A. Durand, 1857), pp. 178–185; Loemker, pp. 263–266.

the alleged free thinker, nor Burcher de Volder, the Cartesian, questioned it. Yet they all raised the same question which is closely related to it: How can one explain the lack of "uniformity" in serial events which are determined by internal principles of order? How can sudden changes and abrupt variations occur in any substantial series of events?[21]

It is no doubt true, as Charles Sanders Peirce said of Leibniz, that "this great and singular genius was as remarkable for what he failed to see as for what he saw."[22] But clearly his correspondents shared with him this myopia which kept them from considering discontinuity, indeterminism, and other implications of science and moral experience. They were all distrustful of "libertinism"; they had a greater concern for order and law than for man's willfulness, and there was a commitment to glorify God, the great monarch and father, rather than to glorify the independence of his subjects.

The obvious shift in Leibniz's own thinking, after 1696, from an emphasis upon logic and panlogism to process, force, and panpsychism does not, however, bring him to regard his theory of substance with greater flexibility. He never relinquishes his theory of the completely determinant concept or law of the individual, though his physical studies of the total force of closed systems of bodies bring considerations of the nature of time, space, and composite bodies to the foreground of his thought, and his historical studies lead him to conjectures about the nature of progress.[23] One must regret the host of distractions, of uncertainties, and of diverse projects which prevented this great creative man, in the last two decades of his life, from further adapting his metaphysical views to these new concerns. It is in

21. Antoine Arnauld was uneasy about this deterministic doctrine, not because it denied a genuine freedom of choosing alternative actions, but because it implied traducianism—the law of Adam's nature must include not only his own acts, but also those of all his descendents (Arnauld to Leibniz, March 13 and May 13, 1686 [Gerhardt, II:15, 29]).

22. *Collected Papers of Charles Sanders Peirce,* edited by C. Hartshorn and P. Weiss (Cambridge, Mass.: Harvard University Press, 1934), p. 250.

23. See the concluding paragraphs of *On the Radical Origination of*

the letters written in answer to his critics that we must find the last refinements of his thought about substance and any tendencies to modify it.

The criticisms of his friends—in particular, of Bayle, de Volder, and des Bosses—may be treated under a few points:

1. The obscurity of the relationship between the law of the individual and the series of events involved in it. (This leads de Volder to suggest several radically different theories of substance —Spinoza's monism on the one hand, and a reification or substantialization of momentary events on the other.)
2. A difficulty in accepting the doctrine of pre-established harmony as a solution of the problem of the interrelationship between self-determining substances.
3. The problems of novelty and the need for God's creating new monads to explain it.
4. The nature of the spatial, inertial, and dynamic unity of composite bodies. (This involves the issue of whether composite bodies can be treated adequately as phenomena, or whether a metaphysical principle, more specific than that of harmony, is needed to explain corporeal unity.)

Among the first critics to examine the conclusions put forth by Leibniz in the *New System* was Pierre Bayle, who raised the first two of the above points. Bayle could not understand how a simple substance, determined by a law, could undergo so rapid and abrupt a variety of states, even of contradictory states. Nor could he understand how the self-determination of the monad could be compatible with its entering into relations with other monads. Indeed, since a monad's states are expressions solely of a nature created directly by God, how could a monad know (assuming it to be a spirit monad) that other monads exist? Rather, why should it not follow that either God and my monad alone exist, or that, in creating many monads, God has created not one universe but an

---

Things (Gerhardt, VII:307–308; Loemker, pp. 490–491); and Leibniz to Louis Bourguet, August 5, 1715 [Gerhardt, III:582–583; Loemker, p. 664].

infinity of them, each one private to an individual substance.[24]

Bayle himself preferred a direct interactionism on the ground that only direct causal intervention can explain the radical transitions which occur in successive states of consciousness.

I understand why a dog passes from pleasure to pain if we strike him with a stick just when he is very hungry and is eating some bread. But that his soul is constructed in such a way that he should feel pain at the moment he is struck even if no one were to strike him, and even if he were to continue to eat bread without difficulty or interruption—this I cannot understand.[25]

To this figure, Bayle adds, in the second edition of his *Dictionnaire historique et critique* (1702), a comparison of Leibniz's theory to a ship so constructed that it can arrive at a desired port by itself and without guidance.

In his replies, Leibniz once more outlines the theory of harmony implicit in the agreements, i.e., the actual identities, contained in the laws of the different series of actions involved in a system. But the criticisms lead him to a reaffirmation and amplification of his mechanism. The apparent lack of continuity in the actions of an individual results from our overlooking the complex multitude of unconscious perceptions which flow, at every moment, from the law of our nature. Just as a simple (i.e., an irreducible) mathematical function in which one variable contains, in each of its successive values, all of the corresponding values of other variables and yet, in spite of its simplicity, contains maxima, minima, and other variations in curvature, so the present state of every monad is continuous with those which precede and follow, and radical discontinuity seems to appear only because we con-

24. Bartholomew des Bosses raises an objection similar to this but the obverse of it. If Leibniz's theory were correct, he says, it would force God, in creating one monad, to produce all the rest, since the monad consists of a series of perceptions of all of them. But this would be a serious limitation to the freedom of God, who is not forced to do anything (Gerhardt, II:493; Loemker, p. 610).

25. Quoted by Leibniz in his *Clarification of the Difficulties which Mr. Bayle has found in the New System of the Union of Soul and Body* (Gerhardt, IV:518–519; Loemker, p. 493).

sider merely those perceptions to which we are attentive, or of which we are conscious.[26]

To make a ship which could arrive at a desired port without guidance (which Leibniz admits would be contrary to the nature of a ship), God would have to impose upon it a "particular faculty" extrinsic to its nature. He could do this, but it would have to be, not a Scholastic faculty, but a principle derivable from the laws of mechanics and applicable to the internal forces in the ship. Man himself, Leibniz adds, could make a robot capable of walking about the streets of a city, turning the proper corners, and arriving at a planned destination at the proper time.[27] Similarly, the inbuilt law of the individual series involves a purpose or final cause to which each internal event leads.

Thus there is implicit in Leibniz's reply to Bayle an amplification of his mechanism to include internal controls of the timing of events and "feedbacks" to assure the properly timed adjustments to the monadic environment. In our own century, we are fully conscious of the possibility and the utility of this expanded conception of mechanism, and it is remarkable that Leibniz should have conceived it within the limits of the mechanical techniques of his day.[28] Yet it is unfortunate that he never showed how such delayed and mutually adjusted actions could arise out of the compound law of the monad; it would involve a delayed order of successive temporarily operating principles, all of which must be defined in the complex total individual order. Since, as Leibniz frequently reasserts in correspondence, time is nothing but the succession of events, as space is their simultaneity, it is difficult to see how either could function as principles of determination within the eternal laws themselves.

De Volder's criticisms of the doctrine of substance, though

26. Gerhardt, IV:518–519. See also Leibniz to de Volder, January 21, 1704 (Gerhardt, II:264; Loemker, p. 534).

27. Gerhardt, IV:555; Loemker, p. 575.

28. Leibniz's invention of devices for producing a uniform movement of the pumps of the windmills used at the Harz silver mines, regardless of the speed of the wind, is an example of such a mechanism. Leibniz includes the greatest feats of outstanding arithmeticians in his mechanistic interpretation.

similar at points to Bayle's, involve certain misunderstandings of Leibniz's thought which grow out of de Volder's Cartesian convictions, and it is not surprising that the tone of Leibniz's replies to his unyielding repetitiousness sometimes changes from amicable deference to unconcealed irritation. Yet, he evoked from Leibniz his clearest, simplest definitions of both simple substances and composite, and his best accounts of their relationship.

It is on logical rather than metaphysical grounds that de Volder finds the doctrine unsupportable. Three points in his criticism are noteworthy:

1. If a substance is simple, as Leibniz claims, in the sense that it has no parts, then each substance must have a simple attribute and no two substances can have a common nature. Extension is such a simple attribute. It follows, then, that contrary to Leibniz's analysis, force must be a derivative mode of extension and therefore would apply only to composite bodies.

2. If substance is that which is self-contained and conceived in itself, then, as Bayle had maintained, it cannot give rise to such a variety of divergent successive modes. Perhaps, then, it would be better to regard each momentary state as possessing its own essence and nature, and therefore as being a momentary substance. Or, alternatively, it might be feasible to accept Spinoza's view that there is only one eternal substance.[29]

3. How can a persisting law be related to a succession of changing states or acts? Or how can an extended body be related to (or appear as the result of) disparate unities?[30]

Leibniz's clearest replies to de Volder's objections (the last two of which both Bayle and des Bosses also raise) are found in his letters of July 6, 1701, April, 1702, June 20, 1703, and January 19, 1706.[31] De Volder's proposals lead him not merely to reexamine the logical conception of substance and its implications for dynamic theory, but also to discuss such related problems as the spatial and temporal nature of intersubstantial relations.

29. De Volder to Leibniz, April 13, 1702, Gerhardt, II:235–238.

30. De Volder to Leibniz, January 5, 1706, Gerhardt, II:279.

31. Gerhardt, II:224–228, 239–241, 248–253, 280; Loemker, pp. 523–526, 526–527, 528–531, 538–539.

Many years earlier, Leibniz had criticized Spinoza's definition of substance as that which is in itself and is understood through itself; his comment was that, though substance may be regarded as in itself (this being true of his monads), it cannot be understood through itself.[32] He had also had misgivings about Spinoza's definition of attributes. To de Volder, he expressed his unhappiness with the innovation which attaches attributes to substance rather than to God and gave a conclusive proof that substances with differing but simple attributes cannot ever undergo a series of modifications or enter into relationship with each other. The variations within things and the interrelatedness among them require that substances have complex essences with some simple natures in common. It is this latter requirement which makes possible the "sympathy" which exists between monads.[33]

Extension, Leibniz asserted, is not a simple attribute, since it is compounded of number, continuity, and simultaneity; nor can it be a source of derivative force or power since the passive cannot give rise to the active. Extension is, in fact, an abstraction from the concrete temporal-spatial order of events given in our experience. In correcting Descartes's physics by accepting the primacy of force, de Volder must also make force prior to extension. Since "space is the order of possible coexistents and time is the order of possible inconsistents," both space and time "enter into all things," corporeal and incorporeal for "every change, spiritual as well as material, has its own place (*sedes*), so to speak, in the order of time as well as its own location (*situs*) in the order of coexistents, or in space."[34] Time is a dimension of the serial order of monadic events, space a dimension of simultaneous

32. In the *Notes on the Ethics of Spinoza* (1678), Gerhardt, I:139; Loemker, p. 196.

33. Gerhardt, II:240; Loemker, p. 527. Years later Leibniz accused Newton of having restored the old doctrine of the sympathists through his conception of gravity as a force acting at a distance. But this is in the realm of *phaenomena bene fundata* where abstract descriptive laws prevail; Newton's famous scholium in the second edition of the *Principia* shows the two men to be in agreement.

34. Gerhardt, II:253; Loemker, p. 531. See also Gerhardt, II:263; Loemker, p. 534. In another context, however, Leibniz writes to des Bosses, May 26,

events. Hence our experience of space rests upon the perceptual relations of the monads, and all perception has a spatial as well as a temporal dimension.

Leibniz's general answer to the question raised by all of his critics—what uniformity there can be in a series of acts and passions of such great apparent variation and continuity—is the answer given to de Volder: their only uniformity is that they follow from a uniform law.

To de Volder's suggestion that the problem of sudden and abrupt variations in serial events might better be solved by the Cartesian theory of the momentary creation by God of successive individual substances without duration, Leibniz makes no specific reply. Though he agrees that God's creativity is operative continuously in each monad, he cannot agree that the individual law or concept in which God's nature is effective can be eliminated from his creation, and the series reduced to momentary substantial complexes of perception, sensory feeling, and appetition. This would remove any permanent dispositional ground for the unity of the monadic series, and no source of its primary force or dynamism.

It has remained for thinkers of our own times, notably Alfred North Whitehead, to develop the theory suggested by de Volder which resolves each temporal continuity of being into momentary occasions, though this is done in the interest, not of the divine power, but of an intrinsic novelty and creativity. The modern view, in turn, has the problem of explaining the presence of enduring experiences and permanent dispositions in a continuous temporary succession of new events. The choice between Leibniz and Whitehead on this matter seems to be between deriving novelty and spontaneity from abiding order (which is impossible) or deriving order from spontaneity and novelty (which has its difficulties too).

The "perpetual progress" which Leibniz comes to see both in

1712 (Gerhardt, II:444; Loemker, p. 602): "In themselves monads have no situation with respect to each other, that is, no real order which reaches beyond the order of phenomena."

the life of the monad and in the world[35] would seem to involve novelty and creativity, but he prefers to consider it as growth determined by a predetermined law, after the analogy of the biological preformation theories of his day. Each present is always considered as "a natural consequence of its preceding state, in such a way that the present is great with the future."[36]

Only one concession does Leibniz make toward the recognition of true novelty, and this is made reluctantly in the midst of the long correspondence on substance with Bartholomew des Bosses. This discussion with a learned Jesuit mathematician and theologian turned upon theological issues. It is known chiefly for the discussion of the *vinculum substantiale,* a metaphysical solution which had been proposed by certain post-Tridentine theologians to explain the unitary properties of extension, mass, and motion, of composite bodies and to give them the metaphysical status needed, among other considerations, in the doctrine of transubstantiation.

The concession forced by des Bosses is related to this problem, but it is also related to that of the origin of the soul. Leibniz has argued that a spermatic animal can develop into a rational animal, and therefore an unthinking, unreflective substance can develop into a spirit monad. Des Bosses, who has earlier argued for a free interaction between monads as a source of the changes between them, maintains that this change from sperm to spirit would involve the creation, at a particular point of time, of a new monad, since the individual law of a dormant monad with only unconscious perceptions could hardly be the same as the law of a conscious, reflective monad. Leibniz, on the other hand, prefers to consider such a transformation a "transcreation" within the specifications of one single individual serial law. But he is willing

35. See note 22, above.

36. *Monadology,* sec. 22, Gerhardt, VI:610; Loemker, p. 645. Leibniz generally recognizes that monads grow in proportion to their activity and that the law of their nature is thus not only teleologically defined, but a law of growth. Cf. *Discourse,* sec. 15, Gerhardt, IV:440–441; Loemker, p. 313: "Whenever anything exercises its virtue or power, that is to say when it acts, it improves and enlarges itself in proportion to its action."

to admit that "it is possible for God to create new monads. Yet I do not assert definitely that new monads have been created by God."[37]

"Transcreation" within a determinate serial order can hardly be considered as more than equivocation. The possibility of God's creating new monads as filiations of old ones moves in the direction of Burcher de Volder's suggestion of the creation of a succession of temporally limited substances. But Leibniz could take no further step toward limited indeterminacy and creativity within creation. The demands of his own panlogism on the one hand, and the theological temper of the time on the other, which distrusted libertinism, prevented him from drawing the consequences of his own belief in progress, spontaneity, and moral responsibility. The choice of actions remained God's, the responsibility for them, man's.

The central issue underlying the discussion remains: Admitted that individual substance involves a series of actions or events determined by an immanent but perduring law, how is the unity of the two to be conceived and expressed? To this question Leibniz has no answer save the traditional one that law is to be its included events as subject which includes its predicates (whether permanent or changing), or as function to its variable values. This remains the mystery of the Platonic idea, active in bringing about imitation and participation, and Leibniz finally replies to de Volder as he had already done to Father René Tournemine when that Jesuit leader had pressed him on the nature of the union of soul and body: This union "is not a phenomenon and there is no concept and therefore no knowledge of it."[38] The only empirical clue, which does not reach the mystery, is the dynamic force of conscious perceptions arising out of habits or faculties.

V

The lasting force of Leibniz's doctrine of substance can be seen in our own time, in spite of our nominalistic aversion to persisting

37. Leibniz to des Bosses, April 30, 1709 (Gerhardt, II:371; Loemker, p. 598).

38. Leibniz to de Volder, January 19, 1706 (Gerhardt, II:281; Loemker, p. 539. See also Gerhardt, II:270; Loemker, p. 537).

laws and determinants. His achievement was the reduction of substance to ordered process; and the criticisms of the traditional empiricists, aimed at a substratum theory, did not really touch it, since the law of the individual, though not an object of experience, can be approached, both in science and in reflective self-awareness, through rational analysis.

It remains to ask, however, how his doctrine must be modified to do justice to freedom, genuine spontaneity and creativity, a real responsiveness to environmental changes, and moral decision and responsibility. All of these seem to demand a linear continuity of actions with momentary freedom from any total determinant —logical or mechanical.

In his letter of July 20, 1715, des Bosses argues that a system of interacting substances is "in greater conformity with the divine wisdom" than one in which individuals do not so influence each other.

> Which architect will deserve credit for greater wisdom in his art [he asks], one whose entire craftsmanship consists in his choosing stones that are not only already exactly square but also so fitted to each other by their nature that a most magnificent palace is put together out of them because of the mere fact that they have been brought together in one place . . . just as the poets narrate that as the Theban walls sprang up to the lyre of Amphion . . . Or is that architect rather to be preferred who constructs an equally beautiful palace from stones unfinished by nature and not corresponding to each other in such harmony, but which must be fitted by craftsmanship and adjusted in time and place?[39]

Leibniz replies with a third alternative.

> In reply to your analogy, I admit that the architect who rightly fits stones together acts with greater art than one who has found the stones already so prepared by someone else that they fall into order when merely brought together. But on the other hand I believe you will admit that the craftsmanship of the architect who can so prepare stones in advance will be infinitely greater still.[40]

39. Gerhardt, II:501; Loemker, p. 612.
40. Gerhardt, II:503; Loemker, p. 613.

Stones, it will be admitted, are poor analogies to monads. But their use does reveal an obliviousness, on the part of both Leibniz and his critic, to the significance of his panpsychism. To fit contemporary thought one would have to force the analogy further in one of two possible directions. Either the living "stones," the individual components of the cosmic structure, can freely develop their own forms, without preformation by a determining architect or law, so effectively that through their efforts a beautiful palace comes into shape of itself, without architect: this is the way of creative intelligence, and many find it difficult to hold in our century; or a builder—perhaps no longer an architect—is needed to assume a role, "consequent" to the individual's creative development of his own form, of redeeming the flaws and unfitnesses and building the best edifice possible under the circumstances. (Or there may be no building, and no possibility of one).

Whitehead is right, it seems, in showing that the choice is not between a panlogism and a panpsychism, or between spontaneity and order, but rather that the issue is about the proper relationship between the two. Life cannot be subjugated to logic, and the issue is how logic is properly subordinated to life. Recent metaphysics seems to be showing clearly that it is not necessary to reduce logic entirely to an instrument of creative purpose, but that a logically definable order may develop within a field of serial choices or self-determinations *and* interactions.

Such an order is needed as a regulative principle both for science and for human morals and values. Leibniz's theory provides the former, since his overlapping individual concepts or laws assure the validity of infinite empirical analysis, synthesis, and generalization. But he is deficient in the latter, for ethics requires that creativity burst through the determinism of law, and also that creativity operate with responsibility through the increasing regularity and persistence of disposition and purpose.

The traces of the development of a new notion of substance are to be found in recent discussions (though the new concept may be to the old very much as the lingering smile is to the vanished Cheshire cat). Bertrand Russell has set up as a fundamental postulate of science the relationships of "compresence" and "causal linearity" among a pluralism of space-time events to explain the continuity of structure in space and time respectively.[41] Frederic Fitch follows him in asserting the individual sufficiency of "causal chains of primary occasions" which he calls substances.[42] And Nathaniel Lawrence has defined the person as a causal chain of primary occasions of longer duration, of greater discontinuity, but characterized by "value, volition, attitude, disposition, etc."[43] Thus, substance as causal-formal "persistence" (Weiss) or "continuant" (Gotshalk) is reappearing in a reconsideration of the conservative aspect of fixation in creative serial orders. Yet the task of defining the proper relationship between the self-determination of an individual series and its interaction with other partly self-determined series is still incomplete. Leibniz was partly right; there is an individual nature which determines us, though not completely. He was wrong, however, in denying that our free choices can help determine our complete individual nature, and that the influence of other environing persons and things somehow also plays a role in this.

41. B. Russell, *Human Knowledge, its Scope and Limits* (New York: Simon and Schuster, 1948), pp. 196, 459, *et passim.*

42. F. B. Fitch, "Sketch of a Philosophy," in Ivor Leclerc, *The Relevance of Whitehead* (London: Allen and Unwin, 1961), pp. 95–97.

43. *Ibid.*, p. 163.

5

Leibniz on Matter and Memory

Milič Čapek

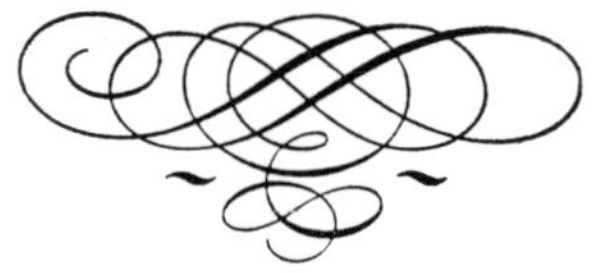

To AVOID possible misunderstandings and disappointments, I should clarify the title of this essay, for it may appear both inappropriate and too broad: inappropriate, since Leibniz had comparatively little to say about the problem of memory, at least about memory as we understand it today; too broad, because the problem of matter interested Leibniz throughout his life. Also the juxtaposition of the terms *matter* and *memory* seems rather odd: *matter* is of a very high generality, while *memory* denotes a particular group of psychological phenomena. The conjunction of these two terms may bring to mind Bergson's famous book, *Matière et mémoire.*[1] Although this association of ideas is not altogether irrelevant, it may nevertheless be quite misleading, for Bergson's book deals primarily with the problem of the relation of memory to the brain or, more specifically, with the relation of mental recollection to the corresponding cerebral trace. There was no such problem, so far as I know, in Leibniz's philosophy. This is probably because Leibniz's peculiar solution of the mind-body problem, a solution which may be characterized as a generalized form of occasionalism, prevented his formulating the

1. Henri Bergson, *Matière et mémoire*, fifth edition (Paris: Alcan, 1908); *Matter and Memory*, translated by Nancy M. Paul and W. Scott Palmer (New York: The Macmillan Co., 1911).

problem in the same terms as Bergson did and as we do today. Thus I still owe an answer to the question, Why did I choose this title?

The explanation is in a passage from Leibniz's early work dealing with the general principles of mechanics entitled *Theoria motus abstracti seu rationes motuum universales a sensu et phaenomenis independentes:*

> No conatus without motion lasts longer than a moment except in minds. For what is conatus in a moment is the motion of a body in time. This opens the door to the true distinction between body and mind, which no one has explained heretofore. For every body is a momentary mind, or one lacking recollection, because it does not retain its own conatus and the other contrary one together for longer than a moment. For two things are necessary for *sensing pleasure* or pain—action and reaction, opposition and then *harmony*—and there is no sensation without them. Hence body lacks memory; it lacks the perception of its own actions and passions; it lacks thought.[2]

The purpose of this paper is to analyze what was obviously Leibniz's view of matter and mind around 1670; to trace the development of his thought which led him to his particular view of that time; to indicate how certain elements of his view not only foreshadowed his mature thought, but how some of them persisted unchanged throughout his life; finally, to show how his view of the relation between the physical and mental, hinted at in the passage quoted above, exercised a decisive influence on some outstanding thinkers of the nineteenth and twentieth centuries. One of the most neglected aspects of Leibniz's influence was his formulation of the traditional problem of the mental and physical in terms of *time* rather than in terms of space. While Descartes—and after him a great majority of post-Cartesian theorists of knowledge until at least 1900—regarded the opposition of the mental and the physical as the opposition between the inextensive and the extensive, Leibniz was the first thinker, so far as I know, who hinted at the possibility of interpreting the difference between mind and matter in terms of *different temporal spans.*

2. Gerhardt, IV:230; Loemker, p. 141.

Leibniz's Thought Prior to 1670: From Atomism To a Geometrical Kinetism

According to Leibniz's own testimony, he emancipated himself from Aristotle before he was fifteen years of age. Leibniz recalled his solitary walks in the woods when he was confronting in his mind the thought of Aristotle and of Democritus. It was the influence of Democritus, mediated by Gassendi and Bacon, which prevailed.[3] Although he later departed from atomism, he remained loyal to mechanism in his philosophy of nature, even when he came to regard the mechanism of nature as a phenomenal manifestation of the spiritual and inextensive units. In his early treatise *De arte combinatoria* (1666), he enthusiastically espoused atomism as the only way to penetrate the secrets of nature ("*unica ista via est in arcana naturae penetrandi*"[4]). The more we perceive the positions and the shapes of the parts of which things consist, the better we know them, and it does not matter, says Leibniz, whether we call these parts atoms or molecules. Leibniz's atomism is, like the atomism of Gassendi, emended in a theistic sense, God being the ultimate cause of every motion. Leibniz attempted to give a proof of the existence of God as an infinitely powerful mover. What is interesting in this proof is that, already, at the time of his commitment to atomism, he claimed that each body consists of an infinite number of parts, and for this reason only an infinitely powerful mover is able to move them.[5] It would be unfair to regard this part of his treatise as incompatible with his own atomism, since he undoubtedly drew a distinction between infinite divisibility in a geometrical sense and in a physical sense; while he accepted the first, he rejected the latter. In other words, the atomic volumes are ideally divisible ad infinitum; physically, however, they remain indivisible. Leibniz obviously did not realize that his proof of the infinitely powerful mover was fallacious, since the mass of each body is finite in spite of the

3. Leibniz to Thomas Burnet (Gerhardt, III:205; Leibniz to Foucher, Gerhardt, I:371).

4. Gerhardt, IV:56.

5. Gerhardt, IV:32: "Demonstratio existentiae Dei."

infinite number of points which it contains; he overlooked the fact that the mass of each point is vanishingly small, and thus their infinite number can result in the total finite mass—whether we deal with the mass of the atom or of any macroscopic body. But we must not forget that Leibniz was then only nineteen and unacquainted with the principles of calculus.

Two other pieces from the same period reflect his commitment to atomism as well as his incipient doubts about the limits of the atomistic explanation. In 1666 he wrote a short treatise with a strange title, *A conjecture why Anaxagoras could have said that snow is black.*[6] Leibniz was wrong in regarding Anaxagoras—who was a qualitative pluralist—as an atomist in the Democritean sense; otherwise, his reasoning was sound. From the atomistic point of view, color is as subjective as any other secondary sensory quality; color is not inherent in things themselves. Since blackness is not a color, but the absence of color, any atomist (though not Anaxagoras) could claim that the constituent particles of snow are "black," i.e., without color. Thus this short treatise with a grotesque title turns out to be nothing but a defense of the subjectivity of colors, which was the basic tenet not only of atomism, but of any consistent mechanistic view of nature.

"The Confession of Nature against Atheists," which appeared in 1669, shows Leibniz's first doubts about the adequacy of the atomistic explanation—indeed, of any mechanistic explanation. Leibniz shows convincingly that, from the concept of a material body, neither its definite size nor its definite shape can be derived. Why, then, do the atoms have a particular shape or particular size?[7] The concept of abstract materiality filling space does not imply that the elementary particles should have this particular size and not another. Even Democritus was vaguely aware of this when he said that in principle the atom can be as big as the world;[8]

6. Gerhardt, I:8–9.

7. Gerhardt, IV:107: "Determinatam figuram et magnitudinem, motum vero omnino illum in corporibus sibi relictis esse non posse"; cf. Loemker, p. 111.

8. Aetios, I, 12.6, in H. Diels, *Fragmente der Vorsokratiker,* edited by

a worldlike atom would, in virtue of its fullness, be as indivisible as a tiny atom. Thus the smallness of the atoms always appeared as an empirically given datum, not derivable from the basic definition of matter. This, however, did not satisfy Leibniz's rationalistic mind; in his question, "Why this particular size or shape and not another?," we can discern the principle of sufficient reason which became later one of the central ideas of his philosophy. Even today Leibniz's curiosity appears far from being archaic; it characterizes every attempt at a complete rational explanation of reality. As Émile Meyerson pointed out,[9] in a completely rational world, empirical constants would disappear or, more accurately, they would cease to be bare data of experience, since they would be derivable from the more general laws. This program was to a considerable extent realized in physics and chemistry; thus the atomic weights and various chemical affinities of the elements ceased long ago to be bare empirical data, being now logically derivable from the electron theory. In this century, Einstein's wondering why the electrons have the same charge and mass, or Eddington's attempt to establish the relations between the most general physical constants, that is, to show that they are not logically independent, stems from the same principle of sufficient reason which inspired Leibniz to ask: "Why this particular shape or size and not any other?"

Leibniz showed the same inquisitive attitude toward the problem of motion and cohesion. While the concept of matter implies that of space, it does not necessarily imply its own motion, but only its own capacity of motion (*mobilitas*). Leibniz correctly recognized that the classical concept of motionless mass is free of contradiction. This is implied by the very law of inertia according to which a body with zero velocity will remain at rest as long as no external force acts on it. Leibniz, it is true, soon afterwards claimed that matter at rest is inconceivable since it would be indistinguishable from the portion of space it occupies; but this

---

Walther Kranz (Berlin: Weidmann, 1951–54), vol. II, 68A47; cf. Cyril Bailey, *The Greek Atomists and Epicurus* (Oxford: Clarendon Press, 1928), p. 126.

9. Émile Meyerson, *De l'explication dans les sciences* (Paris: Payot, 1921), II:211.

was at the time when he had given up atomism altogether. As long as he remained an atomist, he could not have held the view that the essence of matter consists in motion as he did later. Like Locke, and d'Alembert,[10] Leibniz insisted on the logical separability of matter and motion; and since he identified causal action with logical implication, as did the majority of classical thinkers, he concluded that motion which cannot be produced by matter itself, must have its separate, immaterial cause: God. It is also God who is responsible for creating the atoms with certain shapes and with certain sizes. We may suspect that Leibniz was guided in his reasoning by emotional factors, more specifically by a perhaps subconscious desire to save his religious belief; but this would not be entirely fair, for there cannot be any doubt that, from the strictly logical point of view, Leibniz was right. In classical physics the concepts of mass and motion were regarded both as logically independent and mutually inconvertible. Every change of velocity, whether in magnitude or direction, must come, not from mass itself, but from some external force. It is true that the atomists insisted on the co-eternity of matter and motion; but this co-eternity was a mere *empirical* correlation which has no bearing on the question of *logical* relation between these two concepts. Perhaps the atomists were more aware of this than we think; in one peculiar and puzzling passage of his commentary on Aristotle's *Physics*, Simplicius wrote that the atoms are *naturally* stationary.[11] Did he not want to say, in a rather clumsy way, that, according to the atomists, mass—including the mass of the atoms—does not imply motion, nor produces it?

Another reason for which Leibniz postulated God as a determining and efficient cause was cohesion. Here is his argument:

It is indeed truly and with good reason that Democritus, Leucippus, Epicurus, and Lucretius of old, and their modern followers, Peter

10. John Locke, *An Essay Concerning Human Understanding*, bk. IV, chap. X, sec. 10; J. d'Alembert, *Traité de dynamique*, Discours preliminaire, 1743; Gerhardt, IV:107.

11. Simplicius, *Physics*, 42.10, in Diels, *op. cit.*, vol. II, 68A47; cf. Bailey, *op. cit.*, p. 131.

Gassendi and John Chrysostum Magnenus, asserted that the whole cause of cohesion in bodies may be explained naturally through the interweaving of certain shapes such as hooks, crooks, rings, projections, and in short, all the curves and twists of hard bodies inserted into each other. But these interlocking instruments themselves must be hard and tenacious in order to do their work of holding together the parts of bodies. Whence this tenacity? Must we assume hooks on hooks to infinity? . . . There remains only one answer which these most subtle philosophers can make to such objections; they may assume certain indivisible corpuscles, which they call atoms, as the ultimate elements of bodies, which, by their varied shapes, variously combined, bring about the various qualities of sensible bodies. But no reason for cohesion and indivisibility appears within these ultimate corpuscles.[12]

Nevertheless, the atomists did have an explanation of cohesion; or, more accurately, they *did not need any,* since the cohesion of the atoms and of their parts—including the hooks, projections, etc.—followed from their definition: the atoms were assumed to be indivisible because their masses occupied the atomic volumes without leaving any interstices of void. It is such interstices which make possible the empirical divisibility of the macroscopic aggregates; nothing is divisible which is not already divided, that is, separated by the interstices of void—irrespective of how tiny such interstices may be. Any division of matter thus means nothing but an increase of such tiny interstices; and since the atom lacks these interstices, it is absolutely indivisible. Thus the absolute plenum guarantees its absolute indivisibility. For this reason Lactantius's objection that the hooks would eventually break away from the main body of the atom is silly, since it is due to a basic misunderstanding of the logic of atomism.[13] Leibniz was aware of this explanation; but he raised another objection, far more serious: if the cohesion of the atom is due to the gapless contact of its geometrical parts, should we not expect that, whenever the atoms come into contact, they will coalesce into a single body without the possibility of separation? This

12. Gerhardt, IV:108; Loemker, p. 112.

13. Kurd Lasswitz, *Geschichte der Atomistik vom Mittelalter bis Newton* (Hamburg & Leipzig: Leopold Voss, 1890; unchanged reprint, Hildesheim, Georg Olms, 1964), I:20.

should follow, if the contact is the only reason and cause of the cohesion; but this is contrary to experience. Leibniz could have added that this consequence would be fatal to the basic assumption of atomism—that the number of atoms is eternally constant. Leibniz was to raise the very same objection more than twenty years later, in his *Demonstratio contra atomos sumpta ex atomorum contactu* (1690).[14] In 1669 Leibniz merely concluded that cohesion can be explained only by the action of God and he regretted that "neither Gassendi nor any other of these most acute philosophers of our century" used such a wonderful opportunity to demonstrate the divine existence.[15]

The evidence of Leibniz's definite departure from atomism can be found in two of his letters to Thomasius, one of which was written in October 1668, and the second in April 1669. Although Leibniz in the latter letter insisted that he was "anything but a Cartesian",[16] it is obvious that Descartes's influence at that time was decisive. Leibniz, it is true, claimed that he owed more to Aristotle than to Descartes; but this claim was based on his unhistorical and arbitrary interpretation of Aristotle's ideas—as when, for instance, he interpreted the Aristotelian Form in the sense of geometrical shape. It is clear that Leibniz's own declaration "that only magnitude, figure, and motion are to be used in explaining corporeal properties" cannot in any way be reconciled with the basic tenets of Aristotle's physics and metaphysics. Arthur Hannequin was right when he wrote, in 1908, about the "Cartesianisation of Aristotle" by Leibniz.[17] Although Leibniz still tolerated the theory asserting the existence of the void,[18] he definitely preferred the Cartesian doctrine of a plenum; matter shares with space infinity as well as continuity; the individualization of matter into bodies is, according to him, caused not by

14. Gerhardt, VII:284–288; cf. Gerhardt, IV:108–109.

15. Gerhardt, IV:109; Loemker, p. 112.

16. Gerhardt, I:16: "Tantum abest ut Cartesianus sim."

17. A. Hannequin, *Études d'histoire des sciences et d'histoire de la philosophie* (Paris: F. Alcan, 1908), II:46; Joseph Moreau, *L'univers leibnizien* (Paris: E. Vitte, 1956), pp. 27–28.

18. Gerhardt, I:16: "Mihi enim neque vacuum neque plenum necessarium esse, utroque modo rerum natura explicari posse videtur"; cf. Loemker, p. 94.

the interstices of empty space as the atomists believed, but by *motion.* This is especially obvious from the following passage:

> But discontinuity can be introduced into the formerly continuous mass in two ways—first, in such a way that contiguity is at the same time destroyed, when the parts are so pulled apart from each other that a vacuum is left; or in such a way that contiguity remains. This happens when the parts are left together but moved in different directions. For example, two spheres, one included in the other, can be moved in different directions and yet remain contiguous, though they cease to be continuous. This makes it clear that, if mass were created discontinuous or separated by emptiness in the beginning, there would at once be certain concrete forms of matter. But, if it is continuous in the beginning, forms must necessarily arise through motion . . . For division comes from motion, the bounding of parts comes from division, their figures come from this bounding, and forms from figures; therefore, forms come from motion.[19]

This is nothing but an orthodox Cartesian view, formulated by Descartes in his *Principles of Philosophy.* Leibniz was certainly acquainted with it, even though he then knew Descartes's ideas only from secondary sources.[20] There was, however, one difference; unlike Descartes, Leibniz insisted even then—more than twenty years before his famous letter, "Whether the Essence Of a Body Consists In Extension" (1691)[21]—that matter is irreducible to extension and, consequently, that physics is not altogether reducible to geometry. Although matter requires space for its existence, it is something different from space which it fills; its essence consists in impenetrability, *antitypia, "impletio spatii,"* as Leibniz will still say much later in 1689.[22] But was this really a difference which separated him from Descartes? Did not Descartes say the same thing in different words when he denied the existence of the void? The main ambiguity of Descartes's philosophy consists in the uncertainty whether he tried to reduce matter to space or space to matter. It is true that he held matter to be

19. Gerhardt, I:18; Loemker, p. 96.
20. Hannequin, *op. cit.*, II:27.
21. Gerhardt, IV:464–467.
22. "Phoranomus seu de Potentia et Legibus Naturae," edited by C. I. Gerhardt in *Archiv für die Geschichte der Philosophie*, I (1888): 576–581.

equivalent to space; but his space was a gapless, continuous plenum, it was full—but full of what? Impenetrability of matter is implied in Descartes's philosophy as much as it is explicitly asserted by Leibniz. Leibniz's Cartesian orientation at that time is also visible from his refusal to admit the existence of anything other than extension and thought. Thus when he restated in the first letter to Thomasius his argument for the necessity of the nonphysical cause of motion on the grounds that the concept of matter does not imply the concept of motion, he concluded that this cause must be spiritual since, besides bodies, no other entities are conceivable except minds.[23]

It may sound paradoxical, but it can be said that, with Leibniz's departure from atomism in 1668–69, the main trends of the future development of his thought had begun to take shape—or at least they are discernible in retrospect. His transition from atomism to Cartesian mechanism did not basically affect his life-long commitment to mechanism in natural philosophy. At the same time his insistence that motion is underivable from geometry and from mass, and that its existence points to its spiritual cause foreshadowed his development toward what is usually designated as *metaphysical dynamism*. The tension between these two trends, which was never successfully removed, became much more acute when a year later—in 1670—the first signs of his panpsychic view of reality appeared in his *Theoria motus abstracti*.

Leibniz's Doctrine Around 1670: Matter as "Instantaneous Mind"

This treatise, *Theoria motus abstracti*, contains the general principles of mechanics established in an *a priori*, rationalistic fashion or, as the subtitle of the treatise explicitly says, "independently of sensory appearances."[24] In the same year another treatise appeared, *Hypothesis physica nova* or *Theoria motus concreti*, in which it was shown how general principles are

23. Gerhardt, I:11: "Cumque extra corpus nihil sit cogitabile praeter ens cogitans seu mentem, erit mens causa motus."

24. Gerhardt, IV:220–240.

modified when they are applied to concrete physical phenomena.[25] Near the beginning of this article, I quoted a passage from the former treatise. In order to understand the first crucial sentence of that passage, "No conatus without motion lasts longer than a moment except in minds," we must first explain the meaning of the term *conatus* used by Leibniz. The term itself is clearly borrowed from Hobbes, whose influence on Leibniz at that time was even stronger than that of Descartes. Leibniz's enthusiastic letter to Hobbes written in July 1670 shows this clearly.[26] Both Descartes and Hobbes accepted the mathematical continuity, that is, the infinite divisibility, of space and time, and Leibniz followed in their tracks. But since the concept of motion implies both space and time, it must share the characteristics of both; it must share their mathematical continuity. In other words, motion must be divisible ad infinitum as much as space and time are; it must be continuous even in its smallest spatio-temporal intervals. For this reason Leibniz rejected the view of Gassendi, who assumed one single constant velocity of all motions in nature; the observed differences in velocity were due, according to Gassendi, to the fact that each of the slower motions consisted of the motion of the same constant velocity interrupted by small intervals of rest ("*quietulis interruptus*").[27] This implied that motion is discontinuous. But as Leibniz correctly saw, such a view is incompatible with the law of inertia, which requires that whatever is in a uniform rectilinear motion must persist in such motion, and whatever is at rest must continue to be at rest unless some external force intervenes. Thus the law of inertia would be violated twice at each elementary pause: first, when a body stops without being arrested by any external force, and then when it resumes its motion again without any action from without. It is strange that Gassendi did not see his own inconsistency; strange, since he himself contributed to a correct understanding of the principle of inertia and experimentally verified one of its consequences—to

25. Gerhardt, IV:177–219.

26. Gerhardt, I:82–85; Gerhardt, VII:572–574; Loemker, pp. 105–107.

27. Gerhardt, IV:229. Leibniz himself in 1689 conceded that it was also his original view. Cf. "Phoranomus seu de potentia et legibus naturae," *loc. cit.*

wit, that a body dropped from the mast of a moving ship does not fall behind, since while falling it retains the velocity of the ship.[28] (Incidentally, there was one surprisingly modern feature in Gassendi's apparently strange view: that there is a certain *maximum velocity* which no body in nature can exceed; we know today that this is one of the central ideas of relativity theory.)

In accepting the mathematical continuity of space, time, and motion, Leibniz—again like Hobbes—began to grapple with the basic problem of the infinitesimal calculus—that is, with the nature of the infinitely small elements of space, time, and motion. Leibniz definitely accepted actual infinity; in the first two paragraphs of the former treatise, he explicitly stated that there are actual parts in a continuum and that they are actually infinite in number.[29] This followed, for him, from the infinite divisibility of space, time, and motion. But these parts or elements must be differentiated from the *minima* which do not exist; for there is no such thing as a minimum of space and time. Such minima would themselves consist of parts; in other words, being themselves still divisible, they would not be minima at all. Leibniz here tried to say in a rather clumsy way that Kant later stated much more clearly in his *Critique of Pure Reason*: "Space and time are *quanta continua*, because no part of them can be given save as enclosed between limits (points or instants), and therefore only on such fashion that this part is itself again a space or a time. Space therefore consists solely of spaces, time solely of times."[30] Points and moments are *inextensive*. Leibniz corrects Euclid's definition of a point in the following way: "A point is not that which has no part, or whose part need not to be considered, but *that which has no extension*, or whose parts *lack distance* . . ."[31]

Two observations should be made here. First, in claiming that

28. Cf. A. Koyré, "Gassendi: le savant," in *Pierre Gassendi: Sa vie et son oeuvre* (Paris: Albin Michel, 1955), pp. 64–65 (on Gassendi's experiment at Marseille in 1641).

29. Gerhardt, IV:228: "Dantur actu partes in continuo . . . eaeque infinitae actu."

30. I. Kant, "Anticipations of Perception," *Critique of Pure Reason*, translated by N. Kemp Smith (London: Macmillan & Co., 1958), sec. B 211.

31. Gerhardt, IV:229, sec. 5; italics added [my translation].

the elements of extension are themselves without extension, Leibniz began to move in the direction of his later view that both extension and matter are mere phenomena, even though "well-founded phenomena," based on units which themselves are neither extensive nor material. Second, by speaking of the parts of a point which do not have any distance ("*partes indistantes*"), Leibniz apparently held the strange view that the points themselves have an intrinsic complexity. While this view remained absurd as long as the points were understood in an exclusively geometrical sense, it became meaningful when they become qualitative units having psychological or quasi-psychological character. The monads of Leibniz's later philosophy are precisely such units—indivisible, without parts, yet still intrinsically complex (though not composite)—containing qualitative diversity within their indivisible unity. Thus we may say that the inextensive elements of *Theoria motus abstracti* are in this sense the ancestors of Leibniz's monads. Incidentally, Leibniz's view that space and time consist of inextensive and durationless elements was explicitly upheld by George Cantor and Bertrand Russell;[32] this view pervaded classical physics and to a considerable extent is present even in contemporary physics.

Leibniz held a similar, though not an identical, view on the nature of an instant. Like geometrical points, instants are inextensive, yet still complex; their parts, which Leibniz designated by the scholastic term "signs" (*signa*), are *indistantes*, that is, without distance or extension ("*citra distantiam et extensionem*"), though they are still *one after another*. Leibniz's thought on this point clearly shows the signs of uncertainty and even of inconsistency; how can there be any succession within the indivisible inextensive (i.e., *temporally* unextended) instant? His argument was that, in any accelerated motion, there is an increase of velocity at any instant, "but to increase presupposes an earlier and a later. So one sign is necessarily earlier than another at the same given

32. G. Cantor, "Über verschiedene Theoreme aus der Theorie der Punktmengen," *Acta Mathematica* VII (1885): 105–124; Bertrand Russell, *Principles of Mathematics*, second edition (London: Allen and Unwin, 1937), p. 468.

instant, even though without distance or extension."[33] It is evident that Leibniz was led to this view by kinematic consideration. It was precisely the problem of *velocity* which led him to the formulation of the concept of conatus.

In the same way that points are the elements of space and instants the elements of time, *conatus is the element of motion;* it is an infinitesimal motion, in a modern notation *ds/dt,* if *ds* is a differential of space and *dt* a differential of time. But since Leibniz insists on the point-like character of the elements of space and time, and since he apparently did not know that the ratio of both differentials can have a finite value—he was then not yet in possession of the infinitesimal calculus without which the concept of instantaneous velocity cannot be properly understood—he believed that the only way to account for observably different velocities was to assume different magnitudes of either *ds* or *dt.* He decided to keep the equality of instants ("*instans instanti equale*"), since he believed that such equality was required by the uniform flow of time which makes it possible to represent time symbolically by uniform, rectilinear motion. (It is clear how close Leibniz was then to Newton's absolutist view of time.) But this meant for Leibniz that the space differentials are *unequal,* or, in his language, that the points are not equal: "*punctum puncto . . . maior est*"![34] The differences of magnitude between spatial points account for the differences between the elements of motion which are different for different velocities while they are all greater than the conatus of a body which is at rest. Leibniz tried to convey the meaning of his thought by an arithmetical analogy: while the ratio of rest to motion is comparable to the ratio of zero to unity, the ratio of conatus (i.e., of the element of motion) to motion itself (i.e., to a motion through a certain distance in a finite interval of time) is comparable to the ratio of unity to infinity. Needless to say how far from satisfactory Leibniz's solution was; it is true that he was groping toward the notion of different orders of infinitesimal quantities, but his insistence on the point-like character of conatus was, to say the least, grossly

33. Gerhardt, IV:230, sec. 18 [my translation].
34. *Ibid.*

misleading. How self-contradictory his language is, is shown by the following quotation:

> *One point of a moving body at the time of conatus,* or in a time less than any assignable time, *is in many places or points of space,* i.e., the body will fill a part of space greater than itself, or greater than it would fill at rest or if moving more slowly, or if striving in one direction only. Yet this space is still inassignable or *consists in a point.*[35]

How can one extensionless point be larger than another? How can one point be in several points? This is a contradictory statement similar to that quoted above, which asserted that the parts of the durationless instant can be one after another. Leibniz obviously wanted to avoid the Eleatic conclusion about the impossibility of motion; this is why he claimed that a moving body occupies a larger space than the same body at rest—the very opposite of Zeno's claim in his paradox of the flying arrow. But we should not be unduly severe of Leibniz. To what extent did the differential calculus which Leibniz helped to create settle the difficult problem of motion within a durationless instant? Is such motion possible at all? What about Bertrand Russell, who at the beginning of this century claimed that "Weierstrass, by strictly banishing all infinitesimals, has at last shown that we live in an unchanging world, and that the arrow, at every moment of its flight, *is truly at rest*"?[36] Zeno then would be right. But is it not preferable to agree rather with Whitehead that "a state of change at a durationless instant is a very difficult conception," or, more definitely, that "nature at an instant" is nothing but a fiction, since it fails to include change as the ultimate fact?[37] Were not William James—and long before him, Pierre Gassendi—right when they insisted that the mathematical durationless present is a mere conceptual fiction?[38] Was not Bergson basically right

35. Gerhardt, IV:229–230, sec. 5; Loemker, p. 140 [last italics mine].

36. Russell, *Principles of Mathematics*, p. 347.

37. A. N. Whitehead, *An Enquiry Concerning the Principles of Natural Knowledge* (Cambridge: Cambridge University Press, 1919), p. 2.

38. W. James, *The Principles of Psychology* (New York: Henry Holt & Co., 1890), I:608; P. Gassendi, *Syntagma philosophicum, Opera Omnia* (Florence, 1727), p. 197.

when he pointed out that the true nature of motion cannot be properly understood when we consider it only under its geometrical aspect, that is, when we confuse motion with the motionless trace it leaves behind in space? By confusing motion with its trajectory, we naturally tend to believe that "to an extremity of the line corresponds an extremity of duration"—that is the instant. But, as Henri Bergson observed, "the instant is what would terminate a duration if the latter came to a halt. But it does not halt."[39]

We know that Leibniz was then gradually groping toward the realization that motion as well as the whole physical world cannot be exhaustively described in terms of geometry and mechanics. Although in 1670 he was still far away from this insight, there are symptoms in his thought which pointed in this direction. His physical world was then still nearly completely geometrized. Although he insisted then, as much as in his previous treatises, on the irreducibility of *materia prima* and motion to space, his matter was geometrized even more than matter in Cartesianism. This is obvious in his treatise *Theoria motus abstracti*, especially in his laws of impact. If Descartes arrived at the incorrect laws of impact because he failed to take into account the vectorial character of velocity, Leibniz committed an even worse mistake —in failing to consider the *masses* of clashing bodies. Thus David Selver was correct when he claimed that, in his abstract mechanistic-mathematical conception of matter, Leibniz even went beyond Descartes;[40] and Leibniz himself was right when he characterized his mechanics as "*phoronomia elementalis.*" It is true that, like Descartes, he tried to account for the individuality of physical bodies by motion; it is motion of various kinds which diversifies the homogeneous ether into what appears to us as physical bodies. But we should not be deceived by the spuriously dynamic character of the claim which he made two years later,

39. Henri Bergson, *Duration and Simultaneity*, translated by Leon Jacobson (New York: Bobbs Merrill Co., 1965), p. 53.

40. David Selver, "Die Entwickelung der Leibnizischen Monadenlehre bis 1695," *Philosophische Studien* III (1952): 258.

in 1672, when, in his letter to Antoine Arnauld, he wrote that the essence of a body consists in motion.[41] For his approach to motion was almost exclusively geometrical. I say "almost," since Leibniz was aware that motion is irreducible to matter or space; but this correct insight was obscured by the fact that his attention was captured mainly by the *geometrical* aspects of motion. He defined motion as *"mutatio spatii,"* change in space—there is hardly any doubt that his emphasis was on *spatii* rather than on *mutatio*. And since he believed that time is adequately symbolized by a uniform rectilinear motion,[42] he applied the same spatializing approach to time as well. Time must share with its spatial symbol—a geometrical line—mathematical continuity; that is, it must be divisible in infinitum; and in the same way as any geometrical line is a dense continuum of dimensionless points, time must consist of an equally dense continuum of instants which are themselves devoid of temporal thickness. Classical physics shared this conviction with Leibniz; in truth, the unanimity on this point was only in this century challenged by those few physicists who timidly and hesitantly considered the possibility of the "atomic" or "chronon" theory of time.

This is the reason for Leibniz's famous definition of matter as *"mens momentanea"*—"instantaneous mind," devoid of any recollection of the immediately previous moment. In the physical world there is complete externality of the successive moments; there is no prolongation of the past into the present, since the present is a continuously shifting knife-edge boundary separating the past from the future and is thus also *external* both to the past and to the future. But by calling matter an "instantaneous mind", Leibniz consciously contrasted it with the mind whose present is *not* instantaneous, since it has a certain temporal span by which it merges with immediate memory or recollection. This temporal span is necessary for the diversity of the mental content; or, as Leibniz elaborates, "two things are necessary for *sensing plea-*

41. Gerhardt, I:72: "Essentiam corporis potius consistere in motu, cum spatii notio magnitudine et figura, id est extensione, absolvatur"; cf. Loemker, p. 148.

42. Gerhardt, IV:230: "Tempus exponitur motu uniformi in linea eadem."

sure or pain—action and reaction, opposition and then *harmony* —and there is no sensation without them."[43] In other words, the awareness of time is impossible without the perception of difference, without a rudiment of comparison, and such comparison *takes time*—no matter how short—and as such implies an immediate, elementary memory. In this respect Leibniz was probably influenced by his master Hobbes, who claimed that consciousness is possible only as the *consciousness of difference*: "To perceive one and the same thing is equivalent to not to perceive at all."[44] The terms *opposition* and *harmony* recall Heraclitus's view of becoming as a synthesis of opposites. In more modern terms, the true psychological duration—Bergson's *durée réelle*—is heterogeneous; the awareness of change is always the awareness of the present within the context of the immediately antecedent past; the consciousness of the present, merged with immediate memory, constitutes a diversified, yet indivisible, dynamic whole.

But by contrasting matter as "momentary mind," devoid of immediate memory, with mind as a temporally extended, past-embracing process, Leibniz hinted at the possibility of approaching the problem of the mental and physical from a completely new angle, considerably different from that adopted by Descartes and all those who were, often without realizing it, influenced by him. "This opens the door to the true distinction between body and mind, which no one has explained heretofore."[45] For more than two centuries nobody entered the door which Leibniz opened—indeed, not even Leibniz himself. He never departed from the view of mind described above; even in the mature stage of his thought, he insisted on the identity of mind and memory. Thus in the letter to Princess Sophie of Hanover in 1706, he wrote that the presence of minds is necessary for the conservation of the past; and as late as 1710, consciousness was defined as memory: "*Conscientia est reflexio in actionem, seu*

43. Gerhardt, IV:230; Loemker, p. 141.

44. *De corpore*, part IV, chap. XXV, sec. 5: "Adeo sentire semper idem, et non sentire, ad idem recidunt."

45. Gerhardt, IV:230; Loemker, p. 141.

memoria actionis nostrae ita ut cogitemus nostram esse."[46] In other words, in order to recognize a certain previous action *as our own,* we must remember it; if consciousness could not transcend the mathematical present, the very meaning of the possessive pronoun "mine" would be unintelligible. Indeed, the meaning of "I," of our own self, would not be possible either; Leibniz explicitly says this in his *Discours de Metaphysique,* XXXV: "*Nostre personne, c'est à dire le souvenir et la connoissance de ce que nous sommes.*"

From Leibniz to Bergson and Whitehead: The Lasting Ambiguity of Leibniz's View

Why did Leibniz never explore the possibility of a new approach to the mind-body problem at which he himself hinted? This will become clear by contrasting his philosophy with those who *did* explore this possibility. Only two thinkers, so far as I know, tried to reformulate the relation of the mental and the physical in terms similar to those of the young Leibniz. The first was Bergson who, in *Matter and Memory* (1896), defined the difference between the mental and the physical in terms of different temporal or mnemic spans. Later, in his Huxley lecture at the University of Birmingham in 1911, Bergson explicitly recalled Leibniz's view of matter as "momentary mind" (*un esprit instantané*).[47] It is impossible to consider here even superficially all the aspects of Bergson's theory of the mind-body relation and in particular his view of matter, as it is expounded in the last chapter of *Matter and Memory.* Let us only say that this is the most important, though the most frequently overlooked, part of Bergson's philosophy—indeed, so important that without it a major part of his philosophy remains either unintelligible or appears as a mere semi-literary essay of about the same character as the romantic *Naturphilosophie* of the German post-Kantian idealists. What is important in this context is that, in spite of the

46. Quoted also in Émilenne Naert, *Mémoire et conscience de soi selon Leibniz* (Paris: J. Vrin, 1961), p. 19; cf. also p. 17.

47. Henri Bergson, *L'Energie spirituelle,* second edition (Paris: Alcan, 1919), p. 5.

affinity of Bergson's view with that of the young Leibniz, there was one important, fundamental, difference. For Leibniz, physical events were strictly instantaneous, that is, without any duration whatever. A present moment in the physical world was an infinitely thin, "knife-edge" present devoid of any temporal thickness. From this view, which he shared with the whole world of classical physics and a large part of contemporary physics, Leibniz never departed. On the other hand, to Bergson, who in this respect was followed by Alfred North Whitehead, this was only approximately true. For him, physical events still *endure*, even though their duration is vanishingly short and thus they are never equivalent to mathematical, durationless instants.[48] It is true that their "life-time"—to use the term now used in microphysics—is so negligibly short in comparison to our psychological present, that they may *for practical purposes* be regarded as instantaneous. This modified Leibnizian view was stated with great clarity by Whitehead in one of his last essays:

When memory and anticipation are completely absent, theire is complete conformity to the average influence of the immediate past. There is no conscious confrontation of memory with possibility. Such a situation produces the activity of mere matter. When there is memory, however feeble and short-lived, the average influence of the immediate past, or future, ceases to dominate exclusively. There is then reaction against mere average material domination. *Thus the universe is material in proportion to the restriction of memory and anticipation.* According to this account of the World of Activity there is no need to postulate two essentially different types of Active Entities, namely, the purely material entities and the entities alive with various modes of experiencing. The latter type is sufficient to account for the characteristics of the World, when we allow for variety of recessiveness and dominance among the basic factors of experience, namely consciousness, memory and anticipation.[49]

The quoted passage suggests that there is a definite correlation

48. Henri Bergson, *Matière et mémoire*, fifth edition, pp. 230–231; Henri Bergson, *Creative Evolution* (New York: The Modern Library, 1944), p. 220.

49. Cf. the essay "Immortality" in *The Philosophy of Alfred North Whitehead*, edited by Paul A. Schlipp (Evanston & Chicago: Northwestern University, 1941), p. 695 [italics added].

between the mnemic span and the *degree of indeterminancy;* with a reduced temporal span, "the average influence of the immediate past" dominates, and the element of novelty which constitutes the specificity of each event becomes negligible on the macroscopic level; or, as Bergson wrote in the concluding pages of *Matter and Memory:*

> Absolute necessity would be represented by a perfect equivalence of the successive moments of duration, each to each. Is it so with the duration of the material universe? Can each moment be mathematically deduced from the preceding moment? We have throughout this work, and *for the convenience of study,* supposed that it was really so; and such is, in fact, the distance between the rhythm of our duration and that of the flow of things, that the contingency of the course of nature, so profoundly studied in recent philosophy, must, for us, be practically equivalent to necessity.[50]

Thus, as early as 1896, three decades prior to the formulation of the indeterminacy principle, Bergson had the courage to challenge the accepted dogma of physical determinism in claiming that underlying the apparently strict causality of daily experience is the contingency of microphysical events; or, more accurately, that the appearance of macroscopic determinism is due to our macroscopic—or, rather, *macrochronic*—perspective. Bergson even then was not completely alone; although he does not refer in the passage quoted above to Émile Boutroux by name, it is clearly the author of *De la contingence des lois de la nature*[51] to whom he refers, perhaps also to Charles Renouvier. I doubt that Bergson was then aware of the penetrating article of C. S. Peirce, "The Doctrine of Necessity Examined,"[52] which appeared several years before *Matter and Memory,* and boldly challenged classical determinism. The correlation between the concept of a mathematical instant and rigorous classical determinism—although it is fairly obvious in the second form of the uncertainty principle ($\triangle E \cdot \triangle t \geqq h$)—would require a more extensive explanation.

50. Henri Bergson, *Matter and Memory,* pp. 330–331 [italics added].

51. Second edition (Paris: F. Alcan, 1895).

52. Originally published in *The Monist* II (1891–92): 321–337 and reprinted in the *Collected Papers of C. S. Peirce,* edited by C. Hartshorne and P. Weiss (Cambridge: Harvard University Press, 1960), VI, 28 ff.

I have previously discussed it in different places, where I tried to show how much the trends in twentieth-century physics are consonant with the anticipatory insights of the Boutroux-Peirce-Bergson contigentism.[53]

It is on this point that the chasm between the panpsychism of Leibniz and what may be called "Neo-Leibnizian panpsychism" is most conspicuous. Leibniz's panpsychism is rigorously deterministic; on this point there can be hardly any disagreement. In his view of the physical world Leibniz never departed from the basic premise of his mechanism. It is true that in his mature thought the physical world lost its original naively realistic character and became a phenomenon—"a well-founded phenomenon," "*phaenomenum bene fundatum*"— whose underlying metaphysical ground consists of inextensive qualitative monads related in a rigorously deterministic fashion by the system of the pre-established harmony. The nature of his phenomenal world was described by Leibniz in his mature thought by basically the same mechanistic models as in his *Theoria motus concreti.* In his essay *Antibarbarus physicus,* written—according to Professor Leroy Loemker's kind information—probably around 1702, he insisted as strongly as he had in 1670 that everything in nature must be explained *per figuras et motus*—by shapes and motions; that every action must be explained in the form of direct contact: *nullum corpus moveretur nisi impulsu corporis tangentis;* consequently, that to admit any kind of action at a distance, such as gravity, is nothing but a thinly disguised return to the occult qualities of the Scholastics. Although Newton is not directly named, it is only too clear that it is he whom Leibniz regarded then as *Barbarus physicus*—a barbarian in physics. This became quite obvious in Leibniz's later unfinished correspondence with Newton's disciple, Samuel Clarke. Leibniz apparently never departed from the mechanistic, Hobbes-Cartesian view of matter

53. Cf. Milič Čapek, *The Philosophical Impact of Contemporary Physics* (Princeton: D. Van Nostrand Co., 1961), especially chap. 16, "The End of the Laplacian Illusion"; Čapek, "The Doctrine of Necessity Re-examined," *The Review of Metaphysics* V (1951): 11–54; and Čapek, "La théorie bergsonienne de la matière et la physique moderne," *Revue philosophique* 143 (1953): 28–59.

in which the atoms of Gassendi were replaced by the aetherial plenum whose local complications are individual bodies. It is then hardly surprising that, in *Antibarbarus physicus*,[54] he explicitly referred to Descartes and Hobbes in support of his own view. Thus despite very important modifications of his thought after his sojourn in Paris, some basic features of Leibniz's thought are clearly discernible in his early phase, including the dualism of the inextensive realm of mental qualities underlying the apparent extensive and instantaneous world of matter. By hinting that the physical world is a limit-case of the world of mind, Leibniz indicated the way in which this dualism could be overcome; what prevented him from doing so was that, in his metaphysics, he always remained rigorously deterministic, and as a physicist he always remained resolutely mechanistic, though in a Cartesian rather than in an atomistic fashion. Neither his deterministic metaphysics nor his mechanistic physics is compatible with what I termed the "neo-Leibnizian panpsychism" of the Bergson-Whitehead variety.

But even Leibniz's identification of consciousness with memory, undoubtedly the most important point common to him and the two process philosophers mentioned above, was far more ambiguous than it appeared in the form which Leibniz gave it in *Theoria motus abstracti*. While in both Bergson and Whitehead such identification is equivalent to the denial of what William James called the "knife-edge" mathematical present, it is highly doubtful that Leibniz intended it in this sense. Introspective evidence against the durationless pointlike present is quite obvious: there is no such thing except in the geometrizing imagination of some philosophers. The psychological present has a certain duration and as such it merges with the immediate past. This is why the retention of the past is temporally coextensive with the duration of the present; in other words, why consciousness is *mnemic* by its own nature. Even Bertrand Russell, who certainly cannot be suspected of any hostility to the concept of mathematical continuity, did not dare to deny this. Without realizing how much

54. Gerhardt, VII:337–344.

he agreed in the following passage with the hated Bergson's view of time, Russell wrote:

> In that case [i.e., if we deny that two successive sounds can form one temporally extended experience], the perception of change will become inexplicable, and we shall be driven to greater and greater subdivision, owing to the fact that changes are constantly occurring. We shall thus be forced to conclude that one experience cannot last for more than one mathematical instant, which is absurd.[55]

It is true that some, not many, philosophers claimed that the concept of the infinitely short-lived experience (that is, experience which would last *no* time) is meaningful. In 1896, C. A. Strong defended this concept against William James; and before him, Alexius Meinong complained about "*horror puncti*" ("the dislike of the concept of a point") and insisted that the very fact of the specious present requires the existence of one *single instant of time* in which the temporally extended manifold of the specious present is unified. This distinction between *the temporally extensive field* of the psychological present and *the rigorously instantaneous* act which unifies this field is also implied in C. D. Broad's diagram symbolizing the psychological experience of "the sensible present."[56] This was also Leibniz's view.

Underlying this distinction between the temporally extensive content and the instantaneous act is the gratuitous assumption that the unity of any experience, including temporal experience, must reside in the indivisible unity of the mathematical point or mathematical instant. In such a view time is considered only from a "separative" and not a "prehensive" perspective; temporal diversity is regarded as a multiplicity of *mutually external* units. No wonder that under such assumptions unity can be found only in the indivisibility of a single point-instant. But there is no such

55. B. Russell, "On the Experience of Time," *Monist* XXV (1915): 217.

56. C. A. Strong, "Consciousness and Time," *The Psychological Review* III (1896): 156; Alexius Meinong, "Das zeitliche Extensionsprinzip und die successive Analyse," *Zeitschrift für die Psychologie und Physiologie der Sinnesorgane* VI (1894): 434 f.; C. D. Broad, *Scientific Thought* (London: Kegan Paul, 1923), p. 349.

separation between the unifying, instantaneous act and the temporal diversity of the content. The whole distinction is artificial and stems historically from the equally artificial distinction between the "form" and "content" of knowledge. The so-called unifying act is not located at a certain instant *within* the specious present nor on its frontward edge, but it is *coextensive* with it, being as temporal, as enduring, as its "content" itself. The mythological character of "instantaneous psychological acts" was clearly shown by William Stern in his rebuttal of Strong's polemic against James.[57]

Yet, this also seemed to be Leibniz's view, not only at the period of his *Hypothesis physica nova*, but apparently throughout his life. In 1671, in order to safeguard the unity and incorruptibility of the soul, Leibniz identified it with a mathematical point: "*mentem consistere in puncto seu centro*," since only points are truly indivisible. Leibniz was well aware that this approach to psychological reality is geometrical, and he conceded it explicitly. From the indivisibility of the point follows its indestructibility, and the *impossibility of forgetting*.[58] It is true that later Leibniz recognized that this early identification of souls with points was made when his philosophy was not yet mature;[59] the monads, metaphysical units, replaced the pointlike souls which supposedly exist in space, since space itself became for Leibniz "the order of coexistence." Even in 1671 his pointlike souls were not mere geometrical points, since they had an *inner complexity* and *qualitative diversity*, each of them being "a small world contained

57. W. Stern, "Die Psychische Präsenzzeit," *Zeitschrift für die Psychologie und Physiologie der Sinnesorgane* IX (1897): 326—349; cf. also Čapek, "Memine Ergo Fui?," International Congress of Philosophy, Thirteenth, Mexico, 1963, *Memorias* (Mexico: Universidad Nacional Autónoma de Mexico, 1963), pp. 415–426.

58. Gerhardt, I:61 (Leibniz to Duke John Frederick); cf. Gerhardt, I:72 (Leibniz to Antoine Arnauld): "Cum enim sit a me demonstratum, locum verum mentis nostrae esse punctum quoddam seu centrum, ex eo deduxi consequentias quasdam mirabiles de mentis incorruptibilitate, de impossibilitate quiescendi a cogitando, *de impossibilitate obliviscendi*" [italics added].

59. Gerhardt, II:372, Leibniz to des Bosses, April 24, 1709.

in a point" (*"eine kleine in einem Punkte begriffene Welt"*).[60] The affinity with the later intrinsically diversified monad as *"mirror de l'univers"* is unmistakable; indeed, one may ask whether the monads of Leibniz's later thought do not differ from his pointlike souls only in one respect, that they are no longer located in a containerlike space.

But if Leibniz modified his view about the assimilation of the mind to a geometrical point, it seems rather doubtful that he ever gave up his view of the psychological present as a strictly durationless instant. As late as in his *Monadologie* (sec. 47), he explicitly claimed that the monads "are born, so to speak, by continual fulgurations of the divinity from moment to moment." Is the term "moment" understood here in a strictly mathematical sense? A number of other passages in Leibniz indicate that it was so. In spite of occasional hesitations,[61] Leibniz persistently held the view that the continuity of motion and time is only apparent and that, underlying its spurious and purely phenomenal continuity, there is a dense *discretum* of durationless instants. His view that motion and time consist in what he called *trans-creatio*, that is, in the acts of annihilation and subsequent re-creation, had not changed from 1676 to 1705 when he wrote to Burcher de Volder: *"Nam de tempore non nisi instantia existunt"*—"of time nothing exists but the instants."[62] In his view of reality as being annihilated and re-created by God at each instant, Leibniz was very close to Descartes and the Arabian atomists, and the discovery of the infinitesimal calculus only strengthened his proclivity toward "arithmetization of the continua." There is hardly any question that in this respect there was lasting influence of Leibniz on Bertrand Russell. It is only natural that in accepting the infinite divisibility of time and change—both being inseparable in his relational theory of time—Leibniz regarded psychological time as a dense mathematical continuum of perpetually perishing, discrete, durationless instants. The observation of

60. Gerhardt, I:61.

61. These hesitations were pointed out by W. Gent, *Die Philosophie des Raumes und der Zeit* (Hildesheim: Georg Olms, 1962), I, 189–194.

62. Gerhardt, II:279.

Poincaré, Bergson, and Weyl that the modern concept of mathematical continuity is really a "discontinuity infinitely repeated"[63] applies to Leibniz as well, and it would be unfair to judge him too severely for the mistake which is so common today.

But if Leibniz's psychological instants are devoid of duration, what can possibly be the meaning of memory—even of immediate memory—in the passage quoted at the beginning of this essay? The only possible answer would be that given by C. A. Strong in his defense of the mathematical instant: "Our consciousness of even the nearest past must be ideal, not actual; representative, not intuitive." In other words: "The lapse of time is not directly experienced, *but constructed after the event*."[64] Even Russell found this view absurd; the perception of duration or of change must itself be temporally extended or it will not be possible at all. How can the past, which is *completely external* to one "really present" knife-edge instant, be "re-presented" (in an etymological sense) in this instant? Meinong himself admitted eventually that, within the framework of his own view, the consciousness of succession is inexplicable.[65] Both Descartes and Leibniz took refuge in the omnipotence of God. Such difficulties are inevitable if reality is reduced to a durationless instant floating between two ontological noughts—the nonexisting future and the nonexisting past—and if the genuine continuity of the process is broken into a spurious continuum, in truth the *discretum*, of mutually external and fictitious instants.

From Leibniz to the Mind-Dust Theory: The Fiction of "Imperceptible Sensations"

Related to, though not entirely identical with Leibniz's view of infinitely divisible, in truth, infinitely *divided*, time is his view

63. Cf. the references in Čapek, *Philosophical Impact of Contemporary Physics*, pp. 316, 331.

64. C. A. Strong, *op. cit.*, pp. 156, 155 [italics added].

65. Meinong, *loc. cit.*, p. 446: "Nobody doubts that we really have the representations of motions, of the succession of the tones, etc., but nobody knows what these representations are (niemand weiss so recht, wie diese Vorstellungen aussehen)."

which had a definite influence in both the nineteenth and the twentieth centuries: his theory of *petites perceptions*. His illustration of this theory from *Nouveaux Essais sur l'Entendement Humain* is fairly well known: in order to hear the roaring of the sea, we must perceive the sound of each individual wavelet; and since the sound of a single wavelet is too faint to be perceived consciously, it must be registered unconsciously; if it were not, then we would not be able to perceive even ten thousand wavelets together, since ten thousand psychological zeros cannot result in any conscious sensation. This idea of Leibniz to resolve conscious sensations into unconscious subsensations was probably the first theory of the psychological unconscious; it gave rise to the famous "mind-dust theory" which was effectively criticized by William James in his *Principles of Psychology*.[66] James pointed out that the basic fallacy underlying this atomistic theory of mind is what is today known as "the fallacy of composition"; from the unquestionably composite character of the stimulus—in this case a large number of the individual wavelets—it is wrongly inferred that the resulting perception itself must exhibit the same composite structure. In James's concise and trenchant language, the idea of a pack of cards is not a pack of the ideas of each single card; nor is the perception of table with four legs made of five subperceptions, four of them each corresponding to one single leg and the fifth one to the top; the perception of *table* is experienced as a genuine unity, *Gestalt*, and therefore *is* a genuine unity; for, "the essence of feeling is to be felt, and as a psychic existent *feels*, so it must *be*."[67] James concedes that an individual wavelet affects our physical organism, including our nervous system; but to claim that to such subliminal *physiological* modification corresponds a subconscious subsensation is a sheer mythology. It is only too obvious

66. James, *Principles of Psychology*, vol. I, chap. vi, "The Mind Stuff Theory."

67. *Ibid.*, I:163. Twenty years later James upheld the Berkeleyan principle *esse est percipi* in psychology as resolutely as he had in 1890: "A material fact may indeed be different from what we feel it to be, but what sense is there in saying that a feeling, which has no other nature than to be felt, is not as it *is* felt?" (*Some Problems of Philosophy* [London: Longmans, Green, & Co., 1911], p. 151.)

that Leibniz created his concept of *petite perception* in analogy to the concept of differential in the calculus; "subsensation" is nothing but a differential in psychology. But, unlike in mathematics, the "integrative" or "associative" method cannot be fruitful in psychology since it leads to the artificial atomization of our introspective experience.

How far this atomization was pushed can be shown graphically in one thinker who was not only influenced by Leibniz, but who elaborated Leibniz's idea of "psychological differential" in a systematic, original, and far more concrete way. In 1870, Hippolyte Taine wrote the book *De l'Intelligence,* in which he applied the associationistic method of Hume, Condillac, and James and John Stuart Mill, not only to the introspectively discernible diversity of our mental life, but even to what British empiricism regarded as *minima sensibilia,* that is, the irreducible atoms of experience. According to Taine, even the simplicity of sensory qualities is only *apparent,* each quality being only *apparently* indivisible; further analysis discloses that these spuriously indivisible sensations are made of the succession of subsensations of a lesser intensity and of a far shorter duration. Taine illustrates it by describing the experiments made by Hermann von Helmholtz and others which showed how the succession of separate sounds produced by the teeth of the rotating Savart wheel is fused into the musical quality of the lowest pitch when the rate of the rotation is increased, and how a further increase of the rotation speed results in the sensations of the higher and higher pitch. From this and from other facts—for instance, from Helmholtz's explanation of the difference of musical timbre by means of the upper harmonics—Taine concluded that the sensation of tones is only *apparently* simple, being "in reality" composed of the more elementary homogeneous subsensations of which we are not aware. In this way, he tried to reduce the differences of quality to the differences of quantity, more specifically, to the differences of intensity, of duration, and of the rate of succession of these homogeneous, though subconscious elements. In a footnote he then explicitly related these elements to Leibniz's *perceptions insensibles.*[68] The passage itself is worth quoting *in*

68. H. Taine, *De l'intelligence,* fifth edition (Paris: Hachette, 1923), I:187.

extenso, since it characterizes *the atomistic approach* of the nineteenth-century associationism which, via Ernst Mach, Bertrand Russell, and early Ludwig Wittgenstein, passed into the logical atomism of this century:

We get a glance here at the obscure and infinite world extending beneath our distinct sensations. These are compounds and wholes. For their elements to be perceptible to consciousness, it is necessary for them to be added together, and so to acquire a certain bulk, and to occupy a certain time; if their group does not attain this bulk and thus not last this time, we observe no change in our state. Nevertheless, though it escapes us, there is one; our internal sight has limits; outside these limits, internal events, though real, are for us as though they did not exist. They gain accessions, they undergo diminutions, they combine, they are the composed, without our being conscious of it.

They may even, as we have just seen in the case of sensations of sound, have different degrees of composition . . . beyond the grasp of consciousness. The elementary sensations directly making up our ordinary sensations are themselves compounded of sensations of less intensity and duration, and so on. Thus, there is going on within us a subterranean process of infinite extent, its products alone are known to us and are only known to us in the mass. As to elements and their elements, consciousness does not attend to them, reasoning concludes that they exist; they are to sensations what secondary molecules and primitive atoms are to bodies; we have but an abstract conception of them, and what represents them to us is not an image, but notation.

Taine then applied this reductive method to other sensory qualities, and he envisioned the hopeful eventual result of his "mental chemistry" in the following way:

We conceive . . . that the elementary sensations of the five senses may themselves be aggregates, composed of the same elements, and therefore, like the distinct sensation of hearing and sight, they may be reduced to a single type. If so, there would be but one elementary sensation capable of various rhythms, as there is but one nervous texture capable of various types.[69]

And further:

69. *Ibid.*, pp. 187–188; the preceding quotation is from the English translation by T. D. Haye (New York: H. Holt and Co., 1889), pp. 116–117.

> At the foundation of all bodily events we find an infinitesimal event, imperceptible to the senses, movement, whose degrees and complications constitute the rest, whether the phenomena be physical, chemical, or psychological. At the foundation of all moral events, we guess the presence of an infinitesimal event, imperceptible to consciousness, whose degrees and complications make up all the rest, sensations, images, and ideas.

Taine then concluded that the physical and mental (or, as he said, "moral") events are two parallel aspects of one and the same event, "two translations of one and the same text" in the sense of the theory initiated by Spinoza and adapted by the majority of psychologists and epistemologically more sophisticated biologists of the last century.[70]

This is true not only of the last century, however. The reason I dealt with Taine so extensively was not only because of the affinity of his thought with that of Leibniz, but also because the main features of his double-aspect theory can be found, in a contemporary version, in Pepper and Feigl. Furthermore, the genetic connection of the contemporary version with Taine's—and thus ultimately with Leibniz's—view can be traced quite clearly through the thought of Herbert Spencer. Although Spencer seemed to suggest, in the preface to the second edition of *The Principles of Psychology*, that it was Taine who made his ideas known in France, all the circumstantial evidence suggests that it was the other way around:[71] the atomistic analysis of the sensations; the examples by which this analysis was illustrated; the belief in a "single primordial element of consciousness" which, in combining itself with other elements of the same kind, produces all the apparently tremendous diversity of our introspective experience; finally the belief that this primordial element is a mere subjective aspect of the nervous impulse—all this is absent in the first edition of *The Principles* and appears in

70. *Ibid.*, p. 235.

71. Taine, who was an exceedingly modest and unaggressive person, called attention to this fact only in his private letter to Théodule Ribot, January 11, 1873 (*H. Taine: Sa vie et sa correspondance*, III:215–217.)

the second edition, after the publication of *De l'Intelligence.* But there is hardly any question that it was thanks to the greater popularity of Herbert Spencer's massive philosophical and psychological work that this Neo-Spinozistic—or should we say Neo-Leibnizian?—version of the psychological parallelism influenced late nineteenth- and twentieth-century thought. For our purpose, suffice it to say that the Taine-Spencer reduction of the sensory qualities to the succession of subsensory micro-events correlated with the elementary nervous processes was revived by E. B. Holt in his contribution to the co-operative volume, *The New Realism,* in 1912, while the almost identical view was expounded by Stephen Pepper in "A Neural Identity Theory of Mind," published in Sidney Hook's *Dimensions of Mind.*[72]

The characteristic feature of this view is its physicalistic orientation which is clearly in line with the present popularity of the behavioristic approach in psychology and related sciences. Although the mental and physical "aspects" are placed *verbally* on the same footing, there is a definite tendency in all the thinkers referred to above toward a materialistic, at least to an *epiphenomenalistic,* view according to which the mental qualities are not genuine wholes, but *aggregates* of the more elementary events related in one-to-one relation to the physical events of the brain. This is particularly obvious in the treatment of the psychological present. The very term "specious" by which it is characterized suggests that it is not a genuinely indivisible quality, but that it is "in reality" composed of the exceedingly shorter subevents, which are then "fused" into a spurious simplicity of color, sound, and other qualities, whether sensory or emotional. The main, though often unacknowledged, source of this view was the conviction that *the only genuine present is the point-like mathematical present of the physical world* (we should say now more accurately "the mathematical present of the textbooks

72. E. B. Holt, "The Place of Illusory Experience in a Realistic World," in *The New Realism,* by E. B. Holt et al. (New York: The Macmillan Co., 1912), pp. 303–373; S. Pepper, "A Neural Identity Theory of Mind," in *Dimensions of Mind,* edited by S. Hook (New York: New York University Press, 1960), pp. 37–56.

of classical mechanics") and that the psychological present must consequently be spurious, "specious," since it is *not* durationless. This is obviously the same fallacious assumption which has pervaded Western thought since the time of Zeno, and which apparently was shared by Leibniz. It is needless to repeat James's criticism of the "mind-dust theory," Ehrenfels's analysis of "temporal *Gestalten*," and a nearly unanimous rejection of the knife-edge present in psychology, in order to conclude that the so-called "specious" present is *the only authentic present in psychology*, while the so-called "true mathematical present" is specious, unauthentic, spurious. In other words, the psychological present is a *datum* which, being experienced as an enduring indivisible event, *is* an enduring indivisible event, and to speak of any "illusion of consciousness" or—what is the same—to invent the fictitious *perceptions insensibles* or Meinong's "instantaneous acts" is sheer mythology.

What, however, is the status of the *physical present*? There is in our time strong circumstantial evidence that even physical time is *not* divisible ad infinitum; the quantum phenomena suggest that there is a definite limit to the divisibility of time which *excludes* the physical reality of instants. It is true that "*amor puncti*" is still too strong among the physicists to make universal their doubts about the legitimacy of the concept of the instant. But even if we concede that physical instants are unreal, the difference between the rhythm of psychological duration and physical time is still enormous; the span of the psychological present is fantastically wider than the span of the concomitant physical events. This is, in my view, the main stumbling block to the double aspect or identity theory which is based on the assumed one-to-one correlation between the physical and mental events. But there is clearly no such correlation in the case of the psychological present. A single flash of color, the shortest perception of sound, a pang of pain, a pulse of thought—all such events, no matter how evanescent for us—still correspond to an enormously long succession of elementary physical events; from the point of view of the physicist they are *enormously long histories*.[73] The

73. William James became aware of this difficulty in 1895, i.e., five years

situation is certainly paradoxical: both types of present are genuine, physical as well as mental; nevertheless, there is no one-to-one correlation between them. The correlation between the mental and the physical in the light of the genuine reality of the psychological present is clearly "one-to-many" or, rather, "one-to-very-many"; and irrespective of how uncomfortable this is to our symmetry-loving minds, it is a *fact imposed by experience*. For this reason the mental and the physical *cannot* be identical.

Conclusion

Thus Leibniz's view of the mind as far as its relation to time is concerned was strangely ambiguous. In one sense, mind for him was timeless; in another sense, it was instantaneous. It was *timeless* in the sense that the future states of the mind are the attributes of the individual monad which inheres as timelessly in the individual spiritual substance as the predicates inhere in the subject. From this point of view, as Bergson observed, "the history of an isolated monad seems to be hardly anything else than the manifold views that it can take of its own substance: so that time would consist in all the points of view that each monad can assume toward itself, as space consists in all the points of view that all monads can assume toward God."[74] In another sense, the mind for Leibniz was *instantaneous* as his Cartesian theory of perpetual trans-creation suggests; for of time nothing is real except its instants, more accurately, only *one* of its instants. But this paradox is only apparent: the concept of timeless eter-

after the publication of his *Principles.* Why has the psychological present a certain minimum durational span, contrasting with the instantaneous character of the physical events? "*Why just this amount of time, neither more nor less?*" (*Collected Essays and Reviews* [New York: Longmans, Green and Co., 1920], p. 398). It is utterly superficial to answer this objection by claiming that the corresponding neural impulse has the same duration. For the "unity" of such an impulse is merely functional; in it millions of elementary physical elements and millions of successive physical events are involved. The contrast to the absolute indivisibility of any sensory or introspective quality cannot be greater.

74. Bergson, *Creative Evolution,* p. 384.

nity eliminates succession as effectively as does the concept of a single durationless instant; for this reason it is hardly surprising that these two notions were often treated interchangeably—timeless eternity and Eternal Now (*Nunc stans, Totum simul*) were regarded as synonymous terms.

More ambiguous and paradoxical in the light of what we have just said is Leibniz's opposition of matter, as an instantaneous entity—"instantaneous mind" devoid of memory—to mind possessing its own past. If *all* the monads without exception are born by continual fulguration of the divinity from moment to moment; or, in other words, if all of them are perpetually perishing and perpetually being re-created in continual "transcreation," then it is obvious *that the spiritual monad is as much confined within a single instant as the so-called "material monads."* In what sense then can mind—in opposition to matter *retain* its own past? The only plausible answer to such a question is that the term "retention," for Leibniz, was either understood metaphorically or that he was groping toward its correct meaning, without, however, fully attaining it. The logic of his system did not allow any place for genuine retention of the past; what it *did require* was that, after the immediate preceding state of each monad perished forever, it was immediately replaced by a new instantaneous state in which all previously destroyed states of this particular monad were *instantaneously* reflected. For Leibniz, the idea of the instantaneous mirroring of the past did not represent any difficulty. We have seen that the monad, though point-like, reflects the whole contemporary universe, being a "small world concentrated within a point"; we can then understand that, at each moment, the monad was "its whole history concentrated in a single instant." But it is clear that in such a view there was no place for immediate memory nor for any dynamic continuity of which immediate memory is merely one aspect. What Leibniz called *"recordatio"* should be understood in a strictly etymological sense: the awareness of a present *record* of the past, not the immediate grasp of the past. In this respect there is only a difference of degree between Leibniz's *recordatio* and the "faint images" of Hume or the "temporal signs" of Rudolf Lotze or engrams of R. Semon; they are all *within the present* and *external* to the past. Instead of regarding the perishing of the past and the emergence of novelty as two complementary aspects of the dynamic continuity of any process, Leibniz artificially disjoined these two aspects in regarding temporal process as a series of successive destructions and re-creations in the same way as did Descartes and much more recently, as did Charles Renouvier, who in this respect influenced even the first phase of James's philosophy. In this way the immanence of the past within the present became impossible and memory could at best be nothing but "veridical illusion."

Thus, contrary to Leibniz's own words, his view implied that mind is as much devoid of genuine memory—*carens recordatione*—as is matter in his own philosophy. His own fascination by the concept of mathematical instant—the fascination undoubtedly strengthened by the whole trend of classical physics and by his own discovery of the infinitesimal calculus—prevented his exploring the possibility of a new formulation of the mind-body problem, the formulation at which he himself hinted. The door which he, in his own words, opened to a new solution, he never entered. And nothing indicates more the ambiguity of Leibniz's thought on this point than the fact that two divergent—indeed, antagonistic—solutions of the mind-body problem can be traced to his influence: Bergson's solution in *Matter and Memory* and the mechanistically oriented identity or double-aspect theory.

6

Leibniz and the Analysis of Matter and Motion

Ivor Leclerc

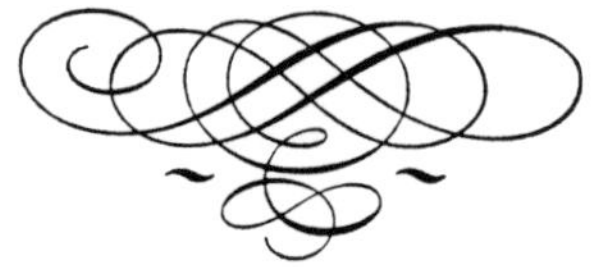

THE ADVANCES in physical science in the twentieth century have necessitated some important changes in concepts which were fundamental to the post-Newtonian cosmology, concepts such as space, time, and matter. Because these concepts were fundamental, they were accepted as ultimate, not only by scientists, but also by a great many philosophers. It is not surprising, therefore, that the changes in these concepts introduced in this century have been felt to be revolutionary and that their acceptance has not been entirely thoroughgoing—in fact, the changes necessitated are even more far-reaching than is realized by all but a few.

There is another concept—motion—which is equally fundamental to the post-Newtonian cosmology; but this concept, it is almost universally supposed, has not been affected by the recent advances. The meaning of *motion,* it is assumed, is clear and evident; motion is something ultimate, and there is just no way to conceive of it other than as it has been thought of during the past few centuries. This assumption, I shall argue, is an error; twentieth-century developments have affected the concept of motion no less than they have affected the others. The reason, in part, is that the concept of motion is intimately bound up with the modern concept of matter; consequently, the change in the latter inevitably involves the former also.

The thought of Leibniz on the topic of motion is of special relevance to us today. That motion is not an ultimate, irreducible notion was clear to Leibniz in the seventeenth century, but his insight was virtually ignored in his day, and it has continued to be so down to the present. There is particular value in the fact that Leibniz's analysis and criticism came at a time when the modern concept of motion had come into dominant acceptance after a long period of development. Leibniz's awareness of that development was a significant factor in his recognition of what the concept entailed. Indeed, there is no better way to come to this recognition than to see the concept in its development.

This development of the modern concept of motion is so much a concomitant of the development of the modern concept of matter that it cannot be understood in its full implications without a consideration of the development of the concept of matter: this is where we must start. It is a long and complicated account;[1] here we cannot do more than indicate some of the salient points.

A main feature of this development was a gradual transformation of the Aristotelian concept of *hylē*, a process which began in the late middle ages and reached its crucial stage in the seventeenth century. For Aristotle, *hylē* (which had been rendered as *materia* in Latin) is the principle which is correlative to *eidos*, form; *hylē* is that which receives form or definiteness, that which is formed. It is not to be understood as a "stuff"—there is, for example, an intellectual *hylē*, as well as the sensible *hylē* found in body. Also, *hylē*, per se, is not to be thought of as a self-subsistent entity, one which is capable of a separate existence, distinct from form. It cannot so exist since, in itself, it is devoid of all the determinations necessary to being; in Aristotle's words, "By *hylē* I mean that which in itself is neither a particular thing nor of a certain quantity nor assigned to any other of the categories by which being is determined."[2] Thus, for Aristotle, *hylē* was a relative and analogical concept; it is relative to the par-

1. I have gone into this at some length in a forthcoming book, *The Nature of Physical Existence*, Muirhead Library of Philosophy (London: Allen & Unwin; New York: Humanities Press, 1972), chapters 8–11.

2. *Metaphysics* 1029^{a}19–21 (Ross translation, with substitution of *hylē* for *matter*).

ticular *ousia* or existent in question and its form, and it is arrived at by analogy and always understood analogically: as the wood out of which the bed is made stands to the fully formed bed, so generally stands *hylē*, that which is formed, to the entity, whatever it is, which exists as formed.

This Aristotelian conception of *hylē*, or matter, as a principle correlative to form was maintained all the way down to the sixteenth century, but in the Scholastic period some important changes occurred which tended to weaken the essentially analogical nature which the concept had for Aristotle. Averroes, in the twelfth century, accepting Aristotle's designation of *prōtē hylē* (prime matter) as pure potentiality, interpreted this doctrine as entailing that the forms must be contained in matter, to be educed therefrom by God. But this tended to imply that there is matter with a distinct status of its own, which is a departure from the Aristotelian analogical conception. This tendency to conceive of matter as an entity per se went much further in the next century. Richard of Middleton conceived of matter as having a minimum of actuality, since it is in the power of God to create matter without form, had he willed to do so. Henry of Ghent and John Duns Scotus both maintained that there is an "essence" of matter not derivable from form, e.g., the form of corporeity as held by Avicenna. Before them, Roger Bacon too had conceived of matter with its own essence different from form. The potentiality of matter, he maintained, is not a mere passive capacity to receive form; the potentiality of matter is constituted by a positive craving in matter for its perfection. This he explained in terms of the Augustinian doctrine of "seminal reasons"; a seminal reason, according to Bacon, "is the very essence of matter which, being incomplete, can be brought to completion, as a seed can become a tree."[3]

Thomas Aquinas continued this tendency away from the Aristotelian conception, his divergence indeed being of a kind which was to have very considerable consequences for the future. In

3. *Opera hactenus inedita fratris Rogeri Baconis* (Oxford: Oxford University Press, 1905), II, 84; cf. E. Gilson, *History of Christian Philosophy in the Middle Ages* (New York: Random House, 1955), p. 298.

his scheme, matter ceased being a general correlative to form, but was confined to the realm of sensible existence. Further, in this realm Aquinas conceived of matter as the principle of extensive quantity. For Aristotle, the categories of quantity and quality were analyzed in terms of form, and subsequent thinkers followed him in this. Aquinas now took the category of quantity out of form and ascribed it to matter as such. Thereby, matter became extensive stuff. It remained for him, however, a correlative of form; matter was not conceived of by Thomas as an independent existent, as substance.

Aquinas had continued the Neoplatonic emphasis on the ontological primacy of form over matter. But the tendencies we have pointed to resulted in a sixteenth-century reversal of emphasis: it was matter which came to be thought of as primary, though still remaining the correlative of form. Form came to be conceived of in its relation to matter as the soul of matter, and soul was the principle of activity of matter. Thus physical substance was conceived of as material substance, but it was ensouled matter. The next and crucial stage in the development of the modern conception of matter came in the next century, initially in response to scientific rather than to explicitly philosophical inquiries.

A number of medical men, among whom were Paracelsus, Fracastoro, Cardano, Scaliger, and William Gilbert, were concerned with the problem of chemical change. They came to the conclusion that the elements do not alter as maintained in the Aristotelian analysis, but remain constant in chemical change, and that accordingly this change must be constituted by a proportional variation of quantity of the elements. This position was plainly akin to that of the Greek atomists, the explanatory possibilities of whose doctrine was seized upon. This position was also consonant with the tendencies to conceive of matter as substance. The elements of physics and chemistry thus came to be identified with the philosopher's matter, and therewith another change was introduced in the concept of matter. The medical thinkers conceived of the elements as in themselves unalterable *ongkoi*, bulks —this Greek word being rendered *corpuscula* by Daniel Sennert. Thus the term *matter* acquired the connotation of bulky stuff.

In the early seventeenth century, Daniel Sennert, David Gorlaeus, and Sebastian Basso in particular began to see some of the philosophical implications of the new theory. If the corpuscles are in themselves unchanging, then in chemical combination the only change which can occur is the change of these corpuscles from one place or locus to another, e.g., when numbers of them are brought together, or when they group together, in different patterns. According to this theory, the only motion allowable is locomotion.

In addition to the concept of motion, however, this theory affects the basic understanding of being or actuality. Since Greek times, the close correlation between motion and being or actuality had been recognized, and the Greek insight was epitomized by Aristotle's doctrine of motion (*kinēsis*) as fundamental to nature (*physis*), the concept of *physis* being closely related to *ousia,* being. As Aristotle put it, in his famous definition: "Nature (*physis*) in the primary and proper sense is the being (*ousia*) of things which have in themselves as such a source of motion (*kinēsis*)."[4] This Greek conception was determinative through the middle ages into the renaissance; and from the twelfth century on, it was specifically the doctrine of Aristotle which was influential. In the Aristotelian analysis, the *kinēsis* of natural things (i.e., those things whose nature intrinsically involves *genesis,* becoming) is fundamentally constituted by each thing's achieving its actuality (*energeia*). That is to say, every natural existent or *ousia,* since it is in becoming (*genesis*), involves a transition from its potentiality (*dynamis*) to its actuality (*energeia*). It is this transition from *dynamis* to its achieved *energeia,* actuality, which is its *kinēsis,* motion.[5] This *kinēsis* may involve *phora, translatio,* i.e., a going from here to there, locomotion, but this locomotion does not constitute the fundamental sense of *kinēsis.* Thus, for Aristotle, *kinēsis* is far from being reducible to change of place; basically, *kinēsis,* motion, is the transition from potentiality to actuality.

This Aristotelian doctrine was seen by Gorlaeus to be in-

4. *Metaphysics* 1015^{a}14–16 [my translation].

5. Cf. *Physics* III. 201^{a}27–29: *ἡ δὲ τοῦ δυνάμει ὄντος* [*ἐντελέχεια*], *ὅταν ἐντελεχείᾳ ὂν ἐνεργῇ οὐχ ᾗ αὐτὸ ἀλλ' ᾗ κινητόν, κίνησίς ἐστιν.*

consistent with the new theory of the elements as changeless corpuscles, and he attacked the Aristotelian contrast of *dynamis-energeia,* potentiality-actuality, maintaining that actuality is not to be educed from potentiality. Actuality is the sheer *existence* of the thing, distinguishing that thing from nothing, nonexistence. The corpuscles or atoms of the new theory simply *are*: they do not *become,* that is, they have no internal process of change, that which Aristotle had conceived as *kinēsis.* It was Sebastian Basso—who undoubtedly had an influence on later thinkers like Pierre Gassendi—who specifically tackled the problem of motion. Prior to Basso, the concept of motion was still very largely under the influence of mediaeval Aristotelianism. For example, Basso's contemporary, Francis Bacon—whose contribution to the development of the corpuscular or atomistic theory was by no means negligible—enumerated nineteen different kinds or species of motion.[6] Basso maintained that all kinds of motion are ultimately reducible to change of place, that is, of locomotion. This came increasingly to be the accepted idea—indeed, it was not long before the essential meaning of the term *motion* came to be "change of place," a meaning which has been retained to the present day as the fundamental meaning; this is why we today have such difficulty in grasping the earlier meaning of the term.

This new concept of motion, therefore, is the outcome of a new idea of actuality, one which does not involve becoming. In this connection, Bernardino Telesio in the sixteenth century had already gone back to Parmenides. Gorlaeus and Basso appealed to Plato and Democritus. These two thinkers also, like their predecessors Telesio and others (who had thought in terms of matter as ensouled), insisted that the corpuscles or atoms have an inherent power or force. But this force has nothing to do with becoming; the atom *is,* fully, with its power. That is, this power or force is not one of internal change; rather it is that whereby there is external change, namely change of place. It is the force

6. Cf. *Novum Organum,* edited by T. Fowler, second edition (Oxford: Oxford University Press, 1889), II, 48.

whereby there is locomotion. Thus in the new theory the only *kinēsis,* motion in the original sense, which is possible is locomotion.

In the new doctrine, therefore, motion is as fundamental to the concept of "nature" as it is in the doctrine of Aristotle. Indeed, the Aristotelian definition of "nature" is simply carried over—but with a very different concept of "motion." Physics, the science of nature, now becomes the science of locomotion. The subjects of motion are pieces of matter which themselves fully *are,* involving in themselves no internal process of becoming but only change of places. This is the essential mechanical conception of nature upon which was based the epoch-making advance from J. Kepler and Galileo through Descartes to Christiaan Huygens and Newton. On this basis, physics could be conceived as a kinetics or kinematics, or, indeed, as phoronomy, as it was by Descartes. The most concerted attempt to achieve a pure kinetics—that is, to understand all nature in terms solely of material particles and their locomotion—was made by Huygens.

During this period of scientific advance there occurred a parallel philosophical advance involving clarification of the concept of "matter." This philosophical development was largely a carrying through to conclusion of implications which had begun to reveal themselves even in the preceding renaissance thought. Descartes and Gassendi represented two divergent outcomes of this development.

Ever since the rise of the concept of matter as an independent existent or substance—in contrast with the previously held Aristotelian concept of matter as a principle correlative to form—it was seen that the pertinence of some of Aristotle's arguments could nevertheless not be ignored. One relevant consideration which came to the fore in renaissance thought was that, if matter constitutes body, then matter is per se bulky and extended. This means that whatever exists as a physical existent is bulky, "full." Now this entailed, as Aristotle had pointed out, that, since all that which exists is "full," there could accordingly be no void; i.e., a nonfull means nonexistence, and since what does not exist cannot be extended, a "void" would mean an extended nonexistent, which is exactly "nothing." Thus thinkers had previously accepted Aristotle's view that "void" strictly could only mean a place where a macroscopic body is not but might be. This unoccupied extent must in actuality be occupied by a fine, subtle matter—usually called "aether"—which is not evident to the senses. By some, the aether was thought of as a continuous fluid; by more strict adherents of the corpuscular theory, however, such as Giordano Bruno and, later, Huygens, the aether was conceived of as itself corpuscular.

Descartes's conception of matter was the outcome of this entire line of consideration. The fundamental feature of matter is that it extensively fills every place: matter is the "full," and there cannot be anything else physically existing. Thus the defining characteristic or essence of this existent is "extension": it is a *res extensa.* It is not that matter "has" extension, among other attributes; extension, for Descartes, is the sole attribute necessary to *constitute* matter. Extension is as such geometrical, and therewith we have the fundamental basis of the new quantitative physics, according to Descartes.

But this physics involves not only the quantitative, measurability; it also involves motion, i.e., locomotion. Here Descartes ran into difficulty, for if matter be constituted solely by extension, this excludes "power" or "force"—which the renaissance thinkers had conceived of as an inherent feature of matter. But there can be no locomotion—change of place—unless there be some kind of force or power. Since for Descartes this could in no way be inherent in matter—"extension" in no respect entails "force" —he had no alternative but to bring "force" or "power" in from outside the physical: God's is the force or power which brings motion into a wholly inert matter.

Starting with the renaissance thinkers, another line of consideration led to Gassendi. This consideration was involved in the increasingly accepted corpuscular theory. This theory had to face the Aristotelian arguments concerning the divisibility of the continuum. Aristotle had maintained that, since continuity necessarily implies infinite divisibility, it follows that the atomic theory is false. The concept of an "atom" is that of a not-further-divisible particle (it is *a-tomos,* uncuttable), but since this supposed atom is extended, it is continuous, and thereby divisible, ad infinitum.

Bruno, Lubin, and Basso had struggled hard to find a way round the Aristotelian objection to atomism, but they did not validly manage to extricate themselves from what Leibniz was fond of referring to as the "labyrinth of the composition of the continuum"; they had sought to reduce the mathematical point to a physical entity, insisting on its necessary extensiveness. Gassendi considered himself to have found a way out of the difficulty by insisting on the fundamental difference between the mathematical and the physical. The mathematical continuum is certainly infinitely divisible, but it does not follow that therefore the physical existent is also infinitely divisible. Physical or material atoms are those bodies which are ultimately simple, i.e., noncomposite. They are, it is true, mathematically divisible, but that pertains to thought; in physical actuality, they are not divided nor divisible.

Gassendi, like Descartes, accepted, with his predecessors, that the fundamental characteristic of matter or physical existence is that it is "full." But adhering to a strict atomistic theory, he could not, like Descartes, conceive of the primary feature or meaning of "fullness" to be extensiveness; a strict atomism must admit an extensive nonfull, i.e., a void. Gassendi maintained that the "full" means the "solid"—sheer dense "stuff." So the ultimate character of matter for Gassendi is "solidity," and by virtue of this, he held, the atoms of matter have size (*magnitudo*) and shape (*figura*). This theory is certainly open to the Cartesian objection that extensiveness is not entailed in solidity, conceived as the ultimate feature of physical *existence*, as indeed the theory tacitly admits, since according to it, *non*existence, i.e., the void, also is extensive. Further, on the idea of solidity as ultimate, the relation of the mathematical to the physical or matter is left completely inexplicable. However, despite the weight of these arguments, the Gassendist conception of matter as solidity finally gained the majority adherence, many Cartesians also deserting their master in this respect. Many thinkers, like John Locke, sought a compromise, conceiving of "solidity *and* extension" as the ultimate character of matter.[7]

7. Cf. John Locke, *An Essay Concerning Human Understanding*, bk. II, chap. VIII.

But Gassendi's idea of matter—and certainly also no less the compromise one—runs into difficulty regarding motion analogous to that involved in the Cartesian conception: for "locomotion" is no less entailed in "solidity" than it is in "extensiveness." Gassendi was indeed quite clear about this, and, like Descartes, he had to resort to God for the "force" to put the atoms into motion.

What occurred in this entire development through Descartes and Gassendi and beyond them is that, with the clarification of the concept of "matter," there was lost to matter that feature of "power" or "activity" whereby it moved. It was far from being the case that this feature of "power" was regarded as undesirable, unwanted, or unnecessary; it is that "power," "activity," was seen to be inconsistent with what had come to be analyzed as constituting the essence of matter—extension or solid stuff, or solidity and extension. Extension just simply is *not* "active," nor does it in any respect entail "activity"; and the same holds for solidity; rather, both extension and solidity are the very converse: passive and inertial.

Now this theory makes acute a fundamental philosophical problem, that of the explanation of motion. Two thinkers in particular came to see clearly that this problem had to be faced, and that this was necessary indeed for the sake of physical science—which consideration made the recourse to a *deus ex machina* additionally unacceptable. These thinkers were Newton and Leibniz.

Newton adhered to the conception of matter as it was then most widely accepted. He expressed this view clearly in his *Opticks*:

> It seems probable to me, that God in the Beginning form'd Matter in solid, massy, hard, impenetrable, movable Particles, of such Sizes and Figures, and with such other Properties, and in such Proportion to Space, as most conduced to the End for which he form'd them; and that these primitive Particles being Solids, are incomparably harder than any porous Bodies compounded of them; even so very hard, as never to wear or break to pieces; no ordinary Power being able to divide what God himself made one in the first Creation.[8]

Matter is purely passive—as Newton says, "mov*able*," i.e., capa-

8. *Opticks* (New York: Dover, 1952), p. 400.

ble of being put into motion. In itself, matter possesses only a *vis inertiae*. But, Newton insists:

> The *Vis inertiae* is a passive Principle by which Bodies persist in their Motion or Rest, receive Motion in proportion to the Force impressing it, and resist as much as they are resisted. *By this Principle alone there never could have been any Motion in the World. Some other Principle was necessary for putting Bodies into Motion*; and now they are in Motion, some other Principle is necessary for conserving the Motion.[9]

The concept of matter does not permit the required "active principle" being found in matter as such, as an inherent attribute or feature of matter, and Newton, like Descartes and Gassendi, maintained that it must therefore come from outside matter. Newton, following Henry More, held the "active principle" to be God. But in his conception, unlike those of Descartes and Gassendi, this was not an appeal beyond the scheme of the world. For Newton, God is "a powerful ever-living Agent, who being in all Places, is more able by his Will to move the Bodies within his boundless uniform Sensorium, and thereby to form and reform the Parts of the Universe, than we are by our Will to move the Parts of our own Bodies."[10]

Leibniz was not at all impressed with this doctrine; he saw it as involving the fallacy of a *deus ex machina* no less than did the doctrines of Descartes and Gassendi. Nor indeed did this particular doctrine of Newton's have any wide appeal to his contemporaries and successors. Leibniz was in accord with Newton in insisting on the insufficiency for physics of a purely passive matter, that some "active force" had to be acknowledged as necessary. But, he insisted, this "active force" must be found "within" matter and not be something brought in from the outside. He adduced a variety of physical considerations to "prove that the body contains something dynamic by virtue of which the laws of power are observed. It therefore contains something besides extension and antitypy, for no such thing can be proved from these two alone."[11]

9. *Ibid.*, p. 397 [italics added].
10. *Ibid.*, p. 403.
11. Leibniz to de Volder, Gerhardt, II:184; Loemker, p. 520.

The insistence by Newton and Leibniz on an "active force" became widely accepted in the eighteenth century, and physics developed into a "dynamics" instead of the pure kinetics of Huygens, the term "dynamics" having been accepted from Leibniz. Little more was accepted from Leibniz, however, than that the active force must be something "in" matter. But what this amounted to was a recurrence during the eighteenth century to one aspect of the renaissance conception of matter. This is, of course, not quite true of the later Kantian development, but this had relatively little effect on scientific thought. What I want mainly to point out is, first, that this eighteenth-century recurrence to the renaissance concept of matter involved an ignoring of the philosophical issues; and second, that this eighteenth-century concept, after the important seventeenth-century philosophical developments, was thoroughly unsatisfactory. This condition continued through the nineteenth century, and twentieth-century physical theory is paying the price in a great deal of confusion.

It was the singular genius of Leibniz to have seen with remarkable clarity where the trouble really lies, and his analysis is still of the greatest significance—indeed, it is highly pertinent to the twentieth-century situation. The difficulty, Leibniz saw, lies in the concept of matter and the correlative concept of motion as these had developed and unquestioningly had been accepted by his time, as they have been since. What was then—and still is—requisite is to subject these two concepts to the closest scrutiny and analysis, and this is what Leibniz did.

Two of the most fundamental features of matter in the seventeenth-century development of the concept, as we have seen, were extension and solidity. This implies that these features are ultimate and primitive, that the concept of them is not capable of being analyzed. Leibniz challenged that implication. As he put it in a letter to de Volder:

> The Cartesians think that some substance can be constituted by extension alone because they conceive of extension as something primitive. But if they undertook to analyze the concept, they would see

that extension alone cannot suffice for an extended being, any more than number suffices for the things that are enumerated.[12]

His own analysis is summarily expressed in this passage, also in a letter to de Volder:

> I do not think that substance is constituted by extension alone, since the concept of extension is incomplete. Nor do I think that extension can be conceived in itself, but I consider it an analysable and relative concept, for it can be resolved into plurality, continuity, and coexistence or the existence of parts at one and the same time. Plurality is also contained in number, and continuity also in time and motion; coexistence really applies to extension only. But it would appear from this that something must always be assumed which is continuous or diffused, such as the white in milk, the color, ductility, and weight in gold, and resistance in matter. For by itself, continuity (for extension is nothing but simultaneous continuity) no more constitutes substance than does multitude or number, where something is necessary to be numbered, repeated, and continued.[13]

Extension was being accepted—as indeed it still is by most—as a quality inherent in a thing. Leibniz's basic argument is that extension is erroneously conceived of as a quality or as inhering analogously to a quality: *extension is a relation.* I would mention here that in this century the analysis made by Alfred North Whitehead, quite independently of Leibniz, comes to the same conclusion, namely, that extension is a relation.

Now if extension be a relation, it cannot pertain to just one single entity, as can a quality. This means that extension, as a relation, is a feature of a plurality, and not of a single entity. Thus, when there is extension, there must be a plurality of entities in relation. Further, the relation between the plurality which constitutes extension is a relation between a contemporary plurality only, in which the relation features, as Leibniz put it in the above passage, as something "continuous and diffused" between the contemporary plurality.

It will not be necessary for our present purposes to pursue this analysis further; suffice it to say that extension is not an ultimate

12. Gerhardt, II:240–241; Loemker, p. 527.
13. Gerhardt, II:169–170; Loemker, p. 516.

primitive quality, but a relation, and it is accordingly a feature pertaining to a plurality. What is the significance for the concept of matter?

Leibniz does not conclude that therefore matter is not extensive. Matter *is* extensive, and indeed as a fundamental feature, as the entire seventeenth-century development had made abundantly clear. Moreover, it is these extensive material bodies and their locomotion which constitute the subject-matter of the science of physics.[14] Leibniz agrees that this must be accepted. The error of the prevalent doctrine, he maintained, lies in the ontological analysis of matter, the analysis of the kind of being which is to be accorded to matter. Starting with the late mediaeval departure from Aristotle and continuing through the renaissance to Leibniz's own day, matter had come to be accepted as an ultimate existent, as a substance. The corpuscular and atomistic doctrine produced a refinement: not a macroscopic body, but each corpuscle or atom constituting a macroscopic body is a substance, and each is an instance of "matter," which is to say, each has the ultimate features of extension and solidity.

But if Leibniz's analysis of extension as a relation be correct, then the final constituents of bodies, i.e., the substantial existents, cannot be extensive, for, if they were, they would themselves be composite, and thus could not be substances or ultimate physical existents at all. In other words, it is impossible that the ultimate existents be "material." Leibniz maintained accordingly that it is necessary to distinguish two kinds of entity, which are distinct and different in ontological status. There are, on the one hand, the ontologically ultimate or primitive existents—which he termed "monads," and which in themselves are nonextensive; and, on the other hand, there are the material bodies, which are extensive. The latter, the material bodies, have monads as their constituents. But "matter" is not merely a collective name for a group of monads. Matter is the name of a distinct kind of entity, having features different from those of the constituents. The distinctive

14. Cf., e.g., "Specimen Dynamicum," Gerhardt Math, VI:234–254; Loemker, pp. 435–452; "On Nature Itself," Gerhardt, IV:504–516; Loemker, pp. 498–508.

features of matter—extension, solidity, inertia, etc.—are constituted by relations between the constituent monads. I have given Leibniz's analysis of extension as a relational feature; in this paper I cannot undertake an exposition of Leibniz's analogous analyses of solidity—which he shows to be reducible to antitypy or impenetrability—and inertia; nor can I go into much detail here as to how these relational features are derivative from the ontologically different features of the individual monads. It is sufficient for the moment to have brought out, first, that matter is an entity with a nature distinct and different from that of the ontologically primary existents; and second, that matter is a derivative entity, the distinguishing features of this entity, matter, being constituted by the *relations* between the primary existents.

We must now consider the concept of motion, which will be seriously affected by Leibniz's analysis of matter. In the concept of matter which Leibniz rejected, matter was taken to be ontologically ultimate, and along with this went a particular conception of motion: motion means change of place, i.e., motion is locomotion, and this was thought of as something ontologically primitive. Leibniz insisted, however, that this concept of motion (locomotion) is far from being ultimate and primitive: analogously to extension, locomotion can be analyzed into constituents, and what is more, it too is relational.

When we subject the concept of locomotion—change of place—to analysis, it is evident that there is, first, the factor of "change," and second, there is "place"—not only one place, but at least two; for the concept involves a change from one place to another place. So, manifestly the concept of locomotion is complex, and clearly it involves a plurality. Moreover, the concept of locomotion must pertain to a plurality, since the concept of locomotion, change of place, can have no significance for an entity considered purely in itself, without respect to anything else. For this concept to have any meaning, there is necessitated a complex of relations: first, between the entity in question and "its place"; second, between that place and another place where the entity is not but will be as a result of the change which constitutes locomotion. This situation is far from being metaphysically simple. Motion is not to be conceived analogously to an inhering quality.

Also, there is involved the very important problem of the meaning and ontological status of "place." But I shall leave aside this problem and deal with the other factor relevant here: that of the "change" involved in locomotion.

First, we have to note that this factor of change too is relational, for it means the "*transition* between one place and another." The factor of "change" refers to the "transition" in distinction from the "places," but it is a transition *between* the places. Thus this transition has no meaning except in relation to a plurality—of places, at least. That is to say, this transition can have no significance in respect of an entity considered purely in itself; the concept of "transition" pertains not to a single entity in itself, but to a relationship between a plurality. The concept of locomotion, therefore, is definitely a relational concept.

The analysis has to be pushed further, however. As with "place," so with the "transition" involved in locomotion: there is the problem of its ontological status and meaning. Leibniz was clear that it is philosophically superficial to take it to be some ultimate kind of occurrence or datum about which nothing further can be said. It was evident to Newton and Leibniz—as indeed it was to Descartes and Gassendi and other philosophically acute thinkers—that the transition of locomotion is impossible without some "act" or "active force."

Implicit in this is that there is a very important distinction between the "act," on the one hand, and the "transition," on the other, and this was recognized by those theories which ascribed the act to God and the transition to matter. But after Newton, this distinction came to be blurred or indeed not to be recognized; the act and the transition were implicitly identified—so that, today, when "activity" is spoken of, it usually means quantity of locomotion. It was the great merit of Leibniz clearly to have seen that the distinction between what I have called the "act" and the "transition" is one of first importance, and further so fully to have appreciated the implications of this distinction. One of the most important implications is that the transition of locomotion is the outcome of, and is thus derivative from, the quite different "transition" involved in the act. In other words, Leibniz saw that there is a transition involved in act, but that this is ontologically a different and distinct transition from that involved in locomotion. The former is ontologically primary, while the latter is derivative. Moreover, this ontological difference means that the transition of act is not, and does not involve, locomotion or change of place; it is a transition quite different from that of locomotion, and must necessarily be so. Leibniz was very clear about this, and he was also clear that in maintaining this he was returning to Aristotle. As he put it:

> It was thus necessary to restore and as it were, to rehabilitate the *substantial forms* which are in such disrepute today, but in a way which makes them intelligible and separates their proper use from their previous abuse. I found then that their nature consists of force and that there follows from this something analogous to sense and appetite. . . . Aristotle calls them *first entelechies.* I call them, more intelligibly perhaps, *primitive forces,* which contain not only the *actuality* or the *completion* of possibility but an original *activity* as well.[15]

In my previous brief analysis of the Aristotelian doctrine, I showed that the fundamental *kinēsis* for Aristotle is the transition from potentiality to actuality, this being basic to the very *einai,* "to be," of an *ousia* or individual existent. That is to say, *kinēsis* is the ultimate transition involved in the act of becoming. This is the more readily appreciated when we remember that the prototype of an Aristotelian *ousia* is a living being; the "act," *energeia,* of a living being is the actualization of its potentiality (the acorn becomes an oak, the boy becomes a man), and *kinēsis* is the transition involved in that act of becoming. Leibniz's position is fundamentally in accord with this. His ultimate existents, the monads, are *active* beings; their "act" is that of *perceptio.* As Leibniz put it in the *Monadology,* "This is the only thing—namely, perceptions and their changes—that can be found in simple substance. It is in this alone that the *internal actions* of simple substances can consist."[16]

The important advance which Leibniz made on Aristotle was to distinguish this internal *kinēsis* very clearly from the transition

15. "A New System of the Nature and Communication of Substances," Gerhardt, IV:478–479; Loemker, p. 454.

16. Gerhardt, VI, sec. 17, 609; Loemker, p. 644.

of locomotion. In Aristotle, the latter is subordinate, but he seems often to conceive of it as nevertheless sometimes *involved in* the fundamental *kinēsis*. Leibniz has shown that this cannot be the case. Locomotion is wholly derivative, and only confusion can result from conceiving the fundamental act as itself locomotive. Locomotion is not only not fundamental, but it is of a different order and kind from the transition involved in the ultimate act of the existent. In Leibniz's doctrine, the monads act—they perceive; and this act is intelligible in the case of each monad considered purely by itself, without regard to any other—insofar as perception involves a relation, it is for Leibniz "phenomenal." The concept of locomotion, on the other hand, necessarily involves relations; it is derivative and does not pertain to the monads as such. Locomotion pertains exclusively to a plurality; it is a feature of a plurality, the plurality which constitutes "matter" or "body."

This analysis by Leibniz makes clear the nature and status of locomotion and its essential connection with the modern concept of matter. Leibniz displays too how the "active force" upon which locomotion is dependent can be "in" matter, without that "active force" itself being a feature of matter per se. For Leibniz, locomotion is derivative from this "active force" of the monads, locomotion being the resultant change of locus of monads relatively to each other. I refrain here from discussing the details of Leibniz's analysis so as not to obscure the basic position—this obscuring, it seems to me, has all too frequently occurred, the wood not being seen for the trees.

Further, it is important not to be sidetracked and prevented from recognizing the fundamental distinctions which Leibniz made on account of finding his doctrine of the phenomenality of relations unacceptable, as has frequently happened from his own time onward; for the validity of these distinctions is not dependent upon that doctrine of the nature of relations.

Leibniz's distinction between the monads or fundamental existents and their acting, on the one hand, and the derivative matter or bodies and their locomotion, on the other, is one of the greatest significance at the present time. Research in physical science in this century has entered a new stage with the discovery of "micro-entities." But they continue to be called and treated as "particles." That is, thought about them proceeds on the presupposition that they are not different in kind but only smaller than the particles of matter, the atoms, which were the subject matter of the physics of the previous centuries. But these entities are different in basic respects: the laws of motion of the so-called classical physics do not hold for them; they exhibit "quantum" characteristics, and a new mechanics has had to be developed. However, they continue to be thought of as "material bodies" in motion. But might it not be that these categories are inappropriate in this realm? Might it not be that in this realm we are concerned with a different order of entities, a primary order, and their "acts," and not with a derivative order of entities and their locomotion? A significantly different interpretation of data becomes possible if the presupposition be abandoned that the only "activity" of elementary entities is "locomotion."

It may well be crucial for the future to recover an understanding of the fundamental distinctions which it was the tremendous achievement of Leibniz to have made, distinctions which were blurred again by Kant—or at least by the way in which Kant was understood—and which subsequently were lost sight of almost completely. Now that the inadequacy of the foundations of the physics of the last few centuries to the twentieth-century developments is more fully coming to be appreciated,[17] there is a great deal to be learned from Leibniz in our effort to reconstruct our foundations.

17. This point has been very well brought out by Milič Čapek in his *The Philosophical Impact of Contemporary Physics* (Princeton: D. Van Nostrand Co., 1961).

II

Assessments

7

Leibniz's Conception of Philosophical Method

Leroy E. Loemker

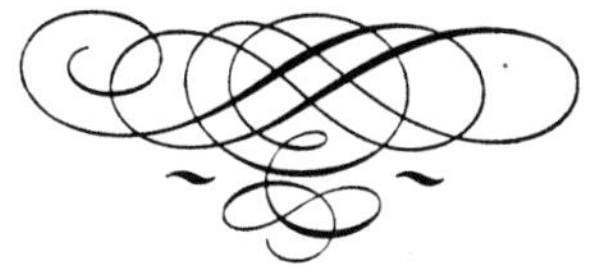

SINCE FORMULATIONS of method are impossible without a definition of the ends which the method is to achieve, and, furthermore, can usually be stated adequately only after the efforts to attain that end are examined, we shall undertake a brief description of the method of Leibniz's philosophizing before examining his own descriptions of the philosophical method.

More than two hundred and fifty years after his death, ac-

This paper was first published by Verlag Anton Hain K.G., in *Zeitschrift für Philosophische Forschung* XX (1966): 507–524, the issue commemorating the two hundred and fiftieth anniversary of the death of Leibniz.

The discussion here is based largely on the following works: *Dissertatio de Arte Combinatoria* (1666), Gerhardt, IV:27–104; selections in Loemker, pp. 73–84; *Nova Methodus discendae docendaeque jurisprudentiae* (1667), Academy Ed., IV, i:261–364; selections in Loemker, pp. 85–90; *De Modo perveniendi ad veram corporum analysin et rerum naturalium causas* (1677), Gerhardt, VII:265–269; Loemker, pp. 173–176; Leibniz to Herman Conring (1678), Gerhardt, I:193–199; Loemker, pp. 186–191; *De synthesi et analysi universali seu arte inveniendi et judicandi*, Gerhardt, VII:292–298; Loemker, pp. 229–233; *De modo distinguendi phaenomena realia ab imaginariis*, Gerhardt, VII:319–322; Loemker, pp. 363–366; *Nouveaux Essais sur l'entendement humain*, IV.

counts of the method of Leibniz vary with the interpretations and adaptions of his thought itself. At the beginning of our century Bertrand Russell gave a brilliant exposition of the analytic nature of Leibniz's thought, assuming his purpose to be the analysis of propositions into their ingredient concepts and reasons and rejecting as contradictory the more speculative aspects of his work. Ernst Cassirer, on the other hand, though also interested in the analytic nature of the thought, discovered in it a neo-Kantian pattern. Several decades later, Dietrich Mahnke found the clue to his method in a combination of symbolic representation with eidetic *Wesensschau* and found this combination necessary for his purpose of reconciling a metaphysics of individuality with a universalizing mathematics. More recently, Leibniz's method has been diversely interpreted as the formulation of "Leibniz-languages" or axiomatic systems capable of being unified by one inclusive "Leibniz-language" (by Heinrich Scholz), or as a dialetic process (by H. H. Holz and others), or (by the recent analysts) as the giving of sound reasons for one's beliefs.

Leibniz's method did in fact involve the giving of clear, distinct, and adequate formulations of old beliefs and the giving of reasons to support or to refute them. Since distinctness and adequacy involve analysis, it was therefore analytic in this sense.[1] But it was more. Since it aimed at a comprehensive grasp, as distinct and adequate as possible, of the universe, and also at a formulation of this inclusive perception in a *philosophia perennis* which rejected the false but preserved the true in all preceding intellectual traditions, it was also synthetic. And it was synthetic in no merely additive sense, but in a way which involved the analytic discovery of first principles and conceptions which should support unity, not merely in philosophy, but in theology, law, and the sciences as well.

1. Thus Leibniz writes to de Volder, March 24/April 3, 1699: "The more we analyze things, the more they satisfy our intellect," and later he reveals the motive for his voluminous philosophical correspondence: "Objections which have any weight always serve to clarify the nature of any issue" (Gerhardt, II:168 ff.; Loemker, pp. 515–518).

I

A comprehensive view of Leibniz's method of philosophizing is possible in the context of the broad development of his thought from his first academic dissertations to the formation of his mature system and its refinement in the controversial correspondence which filled the last two decades of his life.

His philosophical ideas begin in a boldly announced and fragmentary eclecticism, loosely held together by several traditional syntheses, but gradually developed by the opening out of new problems and perspectives and by refined analysis into a harmonious and thoughtfully explicated system.

The eclecticism of his thought is an inevitable result of his effort to achieve a perennial philosophy and of the varied practical projects for which this philosophy was to provide the unifying and motivating basis. The wonder is that he succeeded so well in bringing the separate intellectual preoccupations of his early work into so strong an interrelationship as is shown in the mature thought. Among the variety of relatively independent points of view in his early writings, the following more conspicuous ones may be singled out:

1. A theoretical development of the art of combinations, inspired by the revival of Raymundus Lullus's *Ars Magna*, and regarded as a ground for calculating all possible combinations of primary terms or truths in every field of learning, from which the true and useful combinations may then be selected by empirical tests or other teleological considerations (the first intimation of the principle of the best-possible)
2. A metaphysical interpretation of mathematical terms and relations, intended to support the combinatorial art and probably suggested by Erhard Weigel's attempt to conciliate Aristotle and Euclid
3. A commitment to nominalism and mechanism probably inspired by Thomas Hobbes (though the preface to Marius Nizolius's work *On the True Principles of Philosophy* [1670] already suggests his freeing himself from this commitment)
4. A conception of the order of knowledge, derived from ency-

clopedists such as John Alsted, John Amos Comenius, and John Bisterfeld, and perhaps through them from Francis Bacon, according to which the central disciplines of metaphysics and logic (conceived as sun and moon) provide the first principles of being and of truth, respectively, by which the great circle of the sciences and arts is illuminated

5. An adaptation of the metaphysics of Nicholas of Cusa and of Giordano Bruno, which explicates the microcosm-macrocosm relationship by means of a doctrine of ideas which are identical in God's unity and in the reflecting or echoing plurality of created beings—such a metaphysics served as a support in the early period for both the theological and the juristic studies
6. A concern about humanizing education and giving it a rational structure
7. A practical philosophy of law, justice, and moral obedience built upon the notions of power (from Hobbes), wisdom (from Plato), and love (from St. Augustine)
8. The beginnings of a conception of continuity and functional relationship suggested in his studies of doubtful cases and other casuistic problems in law
9. Studies of the nature of bodies and motion with the earliest suggestion that the concept of momentary motion could serve to resolve the distinction between mind and body
10. An effort to supplement Hobbes with an *Elementa Mentis* which should provide the concepts needed for answering not only epistemological, but also metaphysical and theological questions
11. A growing attachment to the method of Euclid as the ideal of logical order and certainty in knowledge

These various beginnings Leibniz never abandoned, but rather refined through analysis and amplified through further experience, until a coherent and fully explicated system resulted. That he soon began to recognize the impossibility for finite minds to achieve a completely demonstrated order of being can be seen clearly in the papers and letters of successive periods, and by 1695 he had begun to refer to his philosophy as a hypothesis, though one "which is consistent within itself and with phenomena" and therefore "more than an hypothesis."[2] Moreover, he found the ideal method of demonstration, however impossible for the philosophy as a whole, relatively successful in certain particular sciences, and he often urged that the primacy of concepts and of principles must be regarded as relative to their utility in providing *a priori* grounds for the disciplines to which they are applied.

II

When Leibniz's descriptions of the method of philosophy are examined, it must be admitted that he never succeeded in presenting a distinct, unambiguous, and adequate account. He did, however, discuss the problem of method in all stages of his thought beginning with his university years, and however different the contexts in which these discussions occur, they are formulated in terms of the traditional treatment of method which he had learned from others, and never escape entirely the ambiguities and difficulties which this tradition involved. That method consists of analysis and synthesis, or of resolving and compounding, was agreed upon by all, whether logicians, medics, or founders of the new sciences, such as Galileo. There was general agreement that this tradition had its origin in Galen's treatise on method and that it was based originally on Aristotle. All agreed, also, that method presupposes order,[3] and since order had been recognized as one of the transcendentals which characterize all being, method is thus assured of a foundation in reality.

2. See, for example, the *Système Nouveau de la nature et de la communication des substances* (1695), Gerhardt, IV, sec. 17:486; Loemker, p. 459; the *Eclairicissement des difficultés qui Monsieur Bayle a trouvées dans le système nouveau* (1698), Gerhardt, IV:518; Loemker, p. 492; and letters from Leibniz to de Volder, March 24/April 3, 1699; April 1702, Gerhardt, II:168, 239; Loemker, pp. 515, 526.

3. Cf. Jacobi Zabarella, *de Methodis* (Cologne: Lazari Zetzneri, 1957) and Zabarella, *de doctrinae ordine apologia*, edited by W. Risse (Hildesheim: Georg Olms, 1966). Zabarella refutes those who try to subsume both method and order under the common genus of doctrine, yet holds that order can have meaning only within particular disciplines and has no interdisciplinary relevance.

Order provides the assurance that an *adaequatio intellectus ad rem* is possible, and this assurance appears in the seventeenth century in the principle that, as ideas become clear, distinct, and adequate (i. e., "equated to" order), they are true.

Within this area of agreement, however, there is room for much ambiguity and disagreement in interpretation, and these confusions are still traceable in the discussions of method in Leibniz. Four of them deserve particular notice.

There is disagreement and ambiguity about the end of philosophical method. Does method aim merely to impose upon what is already known a desired or better order, or does it aim to discover (in the language of the century, to "invent" or come upon) new truth? For convenience, we shall call the former view the narrow conception, the latter the inclusive conception of method. The narrow conception fits the old tradition of erudition dominant in the Renaissance; the latter reflects the new spirit of science.

Whether Aristotelian or anti-Aristotelian in plan, the logic books of the sixteenth and seventeenth centuries agree in taking the former, narrow position. They follow a common plan of three or four parts, of which the last part is devoted to method. In his early writings, Leibniz, too, conforms to this plan.[4] The common division assigns the first two parts to invention (or Topics) and judgment (or Analytics) respectively, and the section on method is limited to the proper disposition or arrangement of what is known. In Petrus Ramus's *Dialectica*, part III, devoted to *Canonics* or *Didactics*, method has to do with the proper ordering of what is known for the purpose of teaching or of aiding the learner. In the *Logica Hamburgensis* of Jung, whom Leibniz regarded highly as a logician, the first two parts offer a fresh treatment of the principles governing both necessary and probable reasoning, and those governing necessary and probable reasoning separately, but the third part is restricted to the *ordo didascalia* or the *via doctrinae*.[5] In Bacon's *Advancement of Learning*, in which the spirit of erudition still dominates over that of discovery,

4. See the *Nova Methodus*, part I, secs. 24–26; Loemker, p. 88.

5. Joachim Jung, *Logica Hamburgensis* (Hamburg: B. Offerman, 1638; unchanged reprint, Hamburg: J. J. Augustin, 1957).

method is subordinate to the survey of the fields of knowledge and the gaps between them, though Bacon does look forward to the *Novum Organum* in his proposal that "knowledge that is delivered as a thread to be spun on, ought to be delivered and intimated, if it were possible, in the same method wherein it was invented."[6] Even the Port Royal Logic, which reflects Descartes's new conception of method, discusses it in Part IV, after the treatment of ideas, judgments, and reasoning, and retains the old narrow conception, combining it with the new:

On peut appeller generalment methode, l'art de bien disposer une suite de plusieurs pensées, ou pour decouvrir la vérité quand nous l'ignorons, ou pour la prouver aux autres quand nous la connoissons deja.[7]

The more inclusive interpretation of analysis and synthesis, on the other hand, had already been advocated by the forerunners and founders of modern science. The physician Jean Fernel discussed both methods in connection with the treatment of illnesses and wounds, as did Paracelsus, his enemy. These and other Aristotelians applied them, as did Zabarella later, to the discovery of unknown causes from observed phenomena, and the application of known causes to desired effects (i.e., healing or cure), respectively. But it was Galileo who provided the new method for science by putting the analysis of causes or determining circumstances within the context of the original perception or intuition of a hypothesis and then proceeding to support this hypothesis, first by a synthesis in experimental design, and then by deduction (also synthetic) from primary concepts and principles.[8]

6. See Francis Bacon, *The Advancement of Learning*, edited by W. A. Wright, fifth edition (Oxford: Clarendon Press, 1920), part II, sec. XVII, nos. 4, 11. Bacon himself does not discuss analysis and synthesis, but recognizes it as "a vulgar and received" "diversity" of method (no. 11).

7. "In general one can call method the art of arranging well the sequence of many thoughts either to discover the truth when we are ignorant of it, or to prove it to others when we already know it" (Antoine Arnauld and Pierre Nicole, *La logique ou l'art de penser*, fifth edition [Paris: Guillaume Despres, 1683], IV partie, chap. II, p. 396 [my translation]).

8. "The Third Day's Dialogue," in *Two New Sciences*, translated by H. Crew and A. de Salvio ([New York: Macmillan Co., 1914], pp. 153 ff.), is

Thus analysis and synthesis were adapted to the discovery of truth by relating them to observation and experiment, on the one hand, and by their deduction in Euclidean order from first principles, on the other.

It was the Euclidean conception of order, and the double method of analysis and synthesis which it supports, that provided Leibniz with the enveloping unity of his thought and also with the regulative ideal for his method in particular disciplines.[9] In contrast to the procedures of Descartes and Spinoza, whom he criticized for identifying possibility with necessity, Leibniz's attempt to apply this ideal served to increase the distinctness and certainty of knowledge, but it could not, alone, serve the end of discovery. To combine the goal of the best possible arrangement of known truth with that of discovery, he found it necessary to combine the method of analysis and synthesis based on Euclidean order with that based on the analytic-synthetic ordering of observation and experimental verification. Even in the deductive synthetic proce-

---

perhaps the clearest and best-known instance of this method which moves from an analysis of the problem on the common-sense level, proceeds to an elaborately designed experimental procedure for verification by observation, and finally sets up a demonstration from definitions and first principles. See also the brief discussion in the *Dialogue on the Great World Systems*, edited by Gide Santillana (Chicago: University of Chicago Press, 1953), pp. 59–60.

9. In the three formulations of geometry which Leibniz recognized, there is an interesting interplay of intuitive and analytic procedures:

i. In Euclidean demonstration, the argument moves sometimes by a direct implicative procedure which conforms to Zabarella's definition of synthesis: given *a, b, c, d,* etc., the truth of the theorem *A* follows; *a, b, c, d,* etc., are necessary and sufficient reasons for *A*. But sometimes the less comprehensive and stringent indirect proof by a *reductio ad absurdum* occurs: If the theorem *A* were false, it would follow that the necessary (but not necessarily sufficient) reason *c* which it entails would be false, but *c* is true; therefore *A* must be true. This method is used by Leibniz in the paper "Primae Veritates."

ii. Descartes's geometry uses algebraic analysis but also synthesis by fixing and quantifying spatial relations, deriving and applying the essential theorems from Euclid. This method Leibniz extends to apply to transcendental curves and pushes into the realm of new variables in dynamics.

iii. Leibniz's own geometry of relations (*analysis situs*) abstracts from quantity and operates upon equations of similarity or congruence, using an analytic procedure based on an intuition of relations.

dure of the "Primae Veritates,"[10] in which he derived the basic principles of his philosophy (including those which concerned individual substance and the physical order) from the principle of identity, he did this through the introduction of definitions which allowed a particularization of the principles to fit the empirical context.

A second ambiguity in the method of analysis and synthesis involves, not the aim of the method, but the subject matter to which it is applied. In his examination of the true nature of bodies and causes, Leibniz himself distinguished two kinds of analysis: "One of bodies into various qualities, through phenomena or experiments; the other of sensible qualities into their causes or reasons through reflection."[11] More generally, there is a distinction between material and conceptual analysis, or between analysis *a parte rei* and *a parte rationis.* This was an issue even within the Aristotelian tradition, for Zabarella held that method must be applied only within disciplines, while Bartholomew Keckermann of Danzig, who was his student in logic, regarded method as applying to things.[12] In other traditions, the atomists analyzed *de rebus,* even though their analysis and synthesis were themselves largely conceptual, while Ramus applied method to discourse; analysis and synthesis are involved in the proper didactic arrangement for the learning of subject matter.

Leibniz's theory of *perception* enabled him to resolve this difficulty, for perception is the direct prehension of objective reality but in various degrees of indistinctness and inadequacy. As such, perception comprises two dimensions, sometimes called representation (or expression) and ratiocination. Method applies to the latter, discursive dimension of perception, which is thus guaranteed objective relevance even though it operates primarily with passive content, or the *materia prima* of perceptions. Thus, in general, analysis and synthesis are *a parte mentis,* but as reflection becomes increasingly distinct and adequate, it "ade-

10. Couturat, pp. 518–523; Loemker, pp. 267–271. See also note 9 above.

11. *De modo perveniendi ad veram corporum analysin,* Gerhardt, VII:268; cf. Loemker, p. 175.

12. Zabarella, *de Methodis* and *de doctrinae ordine;* B. Keckerman, *Systema Logica* (Frankfurt: J. Stöckle, 1628).

quates" more and more nearly to the simple qualities and the ordered structure of reality.

It is important to recognize, too, that perception is of two kinds: external, in which the *materia prima* is sense-data; and internal, in which the reflective structure of perception and appetite and the concepts of order involved in them are themselves given. Thus analysis and synthesis applied to external perceptions provide with increasing adequacy the knowledge of an objective order which remains phenomenal but is increasingly "well-founded" in the logical order of existence, while analysis and synthesis applied to internal perceptions provide an empirical approach to the nature of individual substance itself. A combination of both is required as the basis for a metaphysics of monads.

A third ambiguity, already alluded to above, concerns the scope of synthesis and the possibility of arriving at unity. Werner Jaeger has described the fundamental difference between Aristotle and Plato in terms of this issue, pointing out that, in rejecting Plato's dialectic, Aristotle opened the way for the independent movement of separate disciplines united only through the fundamental concepts and principles which he had himself first brought to light.[13] In this restriction of system to the separate disciplines, Leibniz does not, like Zabarella, follow Aristotle, and yet, in spite of his professed Platonism, his use of analysis and synthesis is more like Aristotle's than like Plato's, for he is inclined to qualify the convertibility of the transcendental *unum* with the whole. The whole to which it might be applied is but a realm of the undefined simple perfections—a "region of ideas" which comprise all possibilities, and God himself achieves a concrete unity only in the selective act of creative providence in which finite substances come into being, the unity of this pluralistic order of existence consisting of its growing harmony ("unity in diversity") as the individuals achieve greater perfection. Thus the realm of all possible worlds is capable of analysis into the abstract

13. W. Jaeger, *Aristotle: Fundamentals of the History of his Development*, translated by R. Robinson, second edition (Oxford: Clarendon Press, 1948), pp. 369–372.

first principles and, in a formal way, the simple attributes, but not of synthesis, while the synthesis achieved in the created order takes a form, not of any concrete unity such as Kant's antinomies would shatter, but of a plurality of individuals of which each, from its limited point of view, reflects an always imperfectly conceived "whole" without spatial, temporal, causal, or telic boundaries.

Thus, Leibniz directed the method of analysis and synthesis *ad rem* in his chemical studies and pre-eminently in his dynamic studies, but in a more concrete way *ad mentem* in his metaphysics, for the method rested on the presupposition that, in the end, not merely all relations, but all primary attributes, qualities, and accidents in the world are logical in character and dependent upon mind.

There is a fourth distinction in the application of the method of analysis and synthesis which leads to a difficulty, if not an ambiguity, with respect to the role of relations in the doctrine of method. This is the distinction between the analysis of concepts and of propositions. The latter establishes the attribute of truth or falsehood, the former merely that of meaningfulness or meaninglessness.

Leibniz's earlier writings show that he was aware of this distinction, but even in his later studies he failed to relate the two adequately. In the *Nova Methodus* (1667), he undertook a simplification of Descartes's four rules of method (mistakenly assigned to the *Meditations*) in two formulae: "No word is to be accepted without being explained, and no proposition is to be accepted without being proved."[14] Descartes's criteria of clearness and distinctness he found "deceptive in endless ways." But he himself gave no further indication of what he considered the proof of a proposition to be.

On the other hand, in the academic *Dissertation on the Art of Combinations* (1666), Leibniz explored a method of exhausting the possibilities of knowledge and of utility through a calculation of the possible ways of combining the concepts which are pri-

14. *Op. cit.*, part I, sec. 25. A revision note from the 1690s qualifies this in many ways, limiting the rules to derivative notions and propositions and distinguishing between a logic of probability and one of necessity, corresponding in part with the distinction between truths of fact and of reason.

mary for a particular discipline, often including in these primary concepts such complex relational structures as mandates in law, stops in organ construction, and syllogistic figures and modes in logic.

Thus he held to two distinct methods of synthesis and analysis: the combinatorial which operates with logical entities treated as terms, and the Euclidean, which deals with propositions in the form of theorems and their analytic components—axioms, definitions, and simpler theorems. And he never gave a careful account of the relation between these two models of method. In two later studies of method, the *De synthesi et analysi universali* and the *Generales Inquisitiones,* he began with the discussion of incomplex and complex terms and the relations of combination and later leaped to the method of verification through analysis and synthesis by the Euclidean model.

It seems clear that Leibniz must have intended these two methods to be used successively; first, the test of the meaningfulness of terms by the combinatorial method of consistency and resolvability into primitive, empirically supported concepts, and then the application of Euclidean methods of proof to the propositions which contain these tested terms. It also seems clear that although he always recognized a problem in the complexity of the relations involved in judgment, the models which he set up for demonstration and verification were limited to the copula in the propositional form "S is P," in which the "is" must be read "contains." Leibniz is therefore regarded by most students of his logic as undertaking to reduce all relations, for purposes of logical demonstration, to the relation of intensional containment or inclusion, an undertaking which he must have seen could not be carried out and could not, even if successful, serve in the demonstration of most truths, but only for such implications as are involved in the Aristotelian syllogism.

III

It is true that, although Leibniz made little effort to develop a relational logic on broader grounds, he did recognize, not merely a host of relations between terms taken *in recto*, but also some taken *in obliquo*, though he made a weak attempt to reduce some of these to a direct connection. Thus he gave the following list of "transcendent" terms involved in internal or external perception, most of which are relational and verifiable:

> From imaginability or activity of thought there arise certain affections of being . . . similarity, difference, dissimilarity, contrariety, genus, species, universal, particular . . . But from consensibility and coexistence there arise the following forms of connection: whole, part, order, one, many, necessary, contingent, togetherness, cause, etc.[15]

Sensible qualities, on the other hand, are of two kinds, those "sensed (i.e., later, perceived) in the mind itself" and those perceived "by means of mediating bodily organs." Perceivable in the mind itself are only two qualities, thought and causality.[16] Leibniz's logical studies, therefore, must be regarded as aiming at an ideal of necessary implication which undertook to combine the combinatorial relationship by which terms are validated, and which he variously symbolized as addition or multiplication, with a propositional calculus by which the propositions of the form "S includes P" in which these terms occur are verified. To this logical viewpoint he was attracted by the consideration that it should be possible in many contexts to develop further the form "S includes P" into its more adequate species "S=P" by completing the subject or predicate or both. Such a completion would have supplied the formal logical basis not only for the equations of dynamics which have to do with the motion and living force of bodies or systems of bodies before and after impact, and for causal relations in which the total cause must at least equal its effect, but also for the basic metaphysical relation of equality between the complete notion of a substance and the totality of its attributes and properties, whether essential or accidental. Moreover, such complex equated propositions could be verified, after the analogy of algebraic and geometric solutions, by a process of analysis which should reduce them, if true, to identities, or at

15. See the "Generales Inquisitiones" in Couturat, p. 357.

16. *Nova Methodus*, I, secs. 33, 34. The term "affections of being" indicates that Leibniz thought of these relations as transcendentals.

least to a point "at which the difference from identity is less than any assignable amount."[17]

This last distinction, however, which already introduces the difference between truths of reason and truths of fact, is most difficult to interpret, and in fact Leibniz never discusses the criteria by which a process of reduction which is infinite but approaches a point in which "its difference from identity is less than any given amount" can be recognized. He seems here to be misled by a very weak analogy to convergent infinite series in mathematics. Thus we must conclude that, although Leibniz's method of verification by reduction to identity may be successful in empirically empty truths of reason which are tautological in this sense and have to do entirely with logical and mathematical possibility[18] or with "necessary truths," it cannot be applied to judgments of fact, since these cannot be reduced to the *a priori* components which are contained in them.

It must be concluded that Leibniz's studies in logic neither provide a basis for the successful clarification and adequation of propositions involving relations other than that of subject-predicate inclusion, nor do they provide a logical criterion for the truth of judgments of fact as opposed to those of reason. Leibniz's logical studies do not adequately support a general methodology, and it is not surprising that he dropped them in the last decade of the century, and turned increasingly to matters of fact.

IV

In our discussion of Leibniz's resolution of the ambiguities involved in the traditional method of analysis and synthesis and of the failure of his logical studies to provide an adequate basis for his method, the goal of his method has assumed a new form. It still includes the discovery of new truth when it is derivable from old truth or from new experiences molded into acceptable

17. See, for example, the "Generales Inquisitiones," secs. 66, 73, 74, in Couturat, pp. 374–377.

18. Leibniz himself seems to recognize this in sec. 61 of the "Generales Inquisitiones," where he asserts that contingent truths require resolution into infinity.

form through the use of *a priori* principles. It still includes also the aim of arranging known truth in the best order, since a definite Euclidean order is presupposed by his method. But it can be best formulated as the attainment of certainty in our knowledge through its adequation to things, by the twofold process of the analytic reduction of beliefs to first principles and primary concepts, and the ensuing synthesis, in demonstrative order, of the particular laws or rules, and the completely defined concepts applicable to the various fields of investigation.

Of course Leibniz recognized that a unitary, inclusive "system as a whole" is possible only to God, and that even for God, a deductive system beginning with the simplest notions (undefinable and therefore literally infinite) and the most abstract logical principles would lead only to theorems expressing logical necessity, and therefore only possibilities, without a distinctive, selective mode of reasoning which can determine particular substances and the theorems describing their natures and relations. God must have a method of analysis and synthesis, but it remains unknown to us save in the formal principles, abstracted from all qualitative content, which we can derive in logic and mathematics, and more particularly in our ability to demonstrate by means of the calculus of maxima and minima that the laws or "subordinate rules" by which phenomena are ordered are the best of all possible laws which might have been applied to them.

Thus we may hold that the principles of analytic and synthetic method discussed here apply to man's effort to achieve certainty under the circumstances of his finite nature. From that point of view, the "system as a whole" (whose first principles themselves —particularly the principle of the best possible—must be particularized to apply to existence, space, time, causality, and finite realms of order) is divided into two diverse areas of truth, corresponding to logical possibility and existence. As we have already seen, truths of reason and truths of fact, even though their realms of reference interpenetrate, are verified according to two different criteria—the former, by reduction, in a finite number of analyses, to identity; the latter, by some kind of serial approximation to an identity whose criteria Leibniz is unable to set up. Indeed, he seems to confuse the endless process of adequation of truths of fact to reality through analysis and synthesis, with an endless approximation to a simple identity by analytic reduction. Only in his later years, notably in the examination of John Locke's *Essay*, does he set up a more adequate account of the verification, or better, the justification, of truths of fact.[19]

It remains to examine briefly the restrictions under which the method of analysis and synthesis operates as a process of verification on the different levels of truth in Leibniz's philosophy. These levels, which are determined by the degrees of concreteness and of complexity of meaning which both the principles and notions assume, may be presented in simplified form as a revision of Plato's divided line. We list in order the disciplines involved in each level of thought, the type of analytic content and form (or concepts and principles), and the type of truth.

A. 1. (*Rational theology* centered in the ontological argument) *Metaphysics* (I.), *Logic*, and *Pure Mathematics* as formal sciences of the necessities applying to all possible being and thought, i. e., reproducing in symbols the structure of God's thought
   2. The perfections of God individuated into complete concepts, and the first principles of all thought[20]
   3. Truths of Reason

B. 1. *The Anagogic Science*
   2. God's teleological determination of the best possible world of individual substances and laws
   3. Metaphysical determinations of the anagogical process in natural laws and order

C. 1. *Metaphysics* (II) as theory of existence
   2. A spatio-temporal plurality of individual substances, with a growing harmony of their activities (perceptions)
   3. Truths of fact (metaphysical), supported by internal experience

19. See especially *Nouveaux Essais*, bk. IV, chap. 11, secs. 8, 14.

20. In the review of Locke's *Essay*, written in French in 1695–1696 (*Nouveaux Essais*, Academy Ed., VI:5), Leibniz writes: "Mais les idées primitives sont celles dont la possibilité ne sçauroit être demonstrée par d'autres plus simples, et ces idées, à le bién prendre, ne sont autre chose que les attributes de Dieu."

D. 1. *Natural Sciences*
  a) Functionally ordered
  b) Causally ordered
2. Phenomena *bene fundata* and the laws or forms of their ordering
3. Truths of fact (scientific)—statements of observation, particular and generalized

E. 1. a) Sense perceptions—real or illusory
  b) Internal perceptions
2. a) Judgments of objective perception
  b) Judgments of mental activity and passivity

The higher orders are ingredient in and entailed or presupposed by the lower, but they can be known by us only through abstractive analysis from them. As one moves down the line, the *a priori* principles involved in knowledge become more concrete through contextual definition, but they also become both insufficient (though necessary) to determine truths of fact and more relative and subject to failure and change in the face of more refined instruments of observation and new problems. Metaphysics (I) is, for humans, void of empirical content; even the ontological argument which provides what unity it may have is a formal argument. At the lower end, judgments of perception receive meaning only from similarity to remembered previous perceptions, and this similarity is the lowest minimal application of the principle of unity.

The application of the method of analysis and synthesis to the process of adequation in the various levels of truth may now be briefly characterized.

A. It must be remembered that "the labyrinth of the continuum and the infinite" separates God's thoughts from ours, and therefore limits human knowledge of the truths of fact and their analysis. The process of analysis by which God imposes definitions, and therefore finiteness, upon the continuous possibilities constituted by his own perfections, and the process of synthesis by which he combines the finite essences into complete notions and various possibilities of the combination of these complete notions into possible worlds, and by which he is able to "calculate" the superiority of one of these worlds as simpler in its fundamentals and fuller in its attainments—all this lies beyond the finite limits of our experience and rational powers.

We can, however, by analysis of the *a priori* principles necessary to support our knowledge of facts, arrive at primary principles, and by analysis of the empirical content of our judgments, we can arrive at some intuitive grasp of primitive ideas, "which are in truth, nothing else but the attributes of God." Moreover, by abstraction from the principles which we use in our analysis of truths of fact, we can reproduce, in symbols and abstracted from all empirical reference, the laws of rational order and of necessary implication which divine thought itself obeys and which are the primitive principles necessary to all *a priori* principles of our sciences. This abstractive symbolic analysis and synthesis comprises the systems of pure logic and mathematics.

B. The anagogical use of reason, like the necessary forms of reason, belongs to God, not men. Yet here, again, man can provide some examples of teleological reasoning in the determination of specific scientific laws, such as the principles of catoptrics and dioptrics, through a calculation of the maximal or minimal instances of an infinite number of possible laws explaining the phenomenon. This process is thus an extension of the analytic discoveries of mathematics, and mediates between the realm of mathematical necessities and the facts of this existing world—even as God's application of the principle does.

C and D. It is in the realm of created order, and on the two levels of the metaphysics of existence and of well-founded or "real" phenomena, that truths of fact have their place, and it is with the verification of these truths that method is most concerned. This is the region to which "mixed truths" (as Leibniz calls them) apply—truths which are compounded of prior truths of reason and simpler truths of fact, of which Leibniz says that "they have only that certainty and generality which belong to the observations" from which they are generalized.[21] "*All truths,*" he had written Conring much earlier, "*can be resolved into definitions, identical propositions, and observations*—though purely intelligible truths (i. e., what he later calls truths of reason) do not

21. *Nouveaux Essais,* bk. IV, chap. 11, sec. 14.

need observations."[22] The truths of reason which are necessary but not sufficient for the truths of fact which are built upon them take the form of necessary conditionals, that is, hypothetical propositions, the connections of whose parts does not rest upon observation but on logical necessity. It is about these that Leibniz wrote Conring:

> When we arrive eventually at already known truths by starting from assumptions of whose truth we are uncertain, we cannot conclude from this that the assumption is true, as you rightly warn, unless we make use in our reasoning of pure equations or propositions that are convertible or whose subject and predicate are equally inclusive.[23]

Thus some reference to fact, introduced through definitions arising out of the particular context, is already required for the derivation of *a priori* principles valid for individual sciences, so that there is some degree of mutual influence of principles on facts, and facts on principles. A shift in the analysis of concepts in a problem (for instance, a shift from events to processes) may involve a shift in the principles applicable *a priori* in the generalized solution of the problem (for instance, a shift from a principle of sufficient causality to a principle of functional dependence between variables).

The same interplay of fact and principle may be discerned in Leibniz's study of the opposite process, which begins with the perception of particulars and then proceeds to the analysis and generalization of concepts and laws by an increasingly but never completely determinant application of *a priori* principles.

E. The lowest level of the scale of knowledge and of being is concerned with distinguishing "real" from imaginary phenomena. The paper with this title deals with the identification of perceived objects as real, even though they are admittedly phenomenal because their perceived qualities are dependent upon the process of perception and need further adequation.[24] The

22. Gerhardt, I:194, 195; Loemker, pp. 187, 188. Leibniz to Conring, March 19, 1678.

23. *Ibid.*

24. *De modo distinguendi phaenomena realia ab imaginariis* (Gerhardt, VII:319–322; Loemker, pp. 363–366).

process of justifying the existence of a phenomenon is one of finding reasons of a perceptual and conceptual kind which support it. These reasons, Leibniz argues, are internal or external to the phenomenon. The internal reasons are abstractions from the perceived phenomenon itself—its vividness, complexity, and internal congruence. External reasons for its existence are its congruence with preceding phenomena; the rational support which the hypothesis of its reality receives from these remembered phenomena (here the principle of causality is suggested on the lowest phenomenal level); the discovery of common reasons for it, which are assumed to hold for the future as well as the past; its consensus with "the whole sequence of life"; its consensus with the witness of others like myself, and "the most powerful criterion of the reality of phenomena, sufficient even by itself . . . success in predicting future phenomena from past and present ones."[25] The reality of phenomena, supported by these reasons, does not permit absolute demonstration, since the internal reasons are merely analytic abstractions of qualities from the phenomenon itself, and the external reasons are either other phenomena, past, present, and future, with which it is related, or, in addition, certain metaphysical presuppositions, supported by experience, which are entailed by it or by the reasons given to support its reality—myself and other selves capable of memory, of communication, and of inference from present to future experiences. Thus metaphysical convictions serve in the affirmation of the reality of phenomena, not as *a priori* principles, but as presuppositions.

A second level of knowledge of fact which Leibniz discusses, but which he drops in his later thought, is the knowledge of substances from their perceived qualities.[26] This too proceeds by abstractive analysis and synthesis, that is, by offering correlative abstractions from the phenomena as reasons for the substance—notably, figure, number, and motion, which the mechanistic philosophies of his day regarded as basic categories. But fol-

25. Gerhardt, VII:320; Loemker, p. 364.

26. In his plan for an *Elementa Physicae*, from the early Hanover years, Leibniz proposes to deal with the analysis of qualities in the first part, and with the subjects of qualities, or existent bodies, in the second. See Loemker, pp. 277–289.

lowing his criticism of Descartes's theory of extension and his laws of motion, this argument ends with the establishment of the reality of force. Later, therefore, in opposition to Locke, who held that directly perceived qualities must be referred to the substances upon whose nature they depend, but whose real nature cannot be known, Leibniz holds that the causes and other relations between phenomena must remain phenomenal, but that the force required in higher phenomenal laws itself requires a metaphysical explanation.

A third level of truth about well-founded phenomena is the empirical discovery of causal connections between unanalyzed phenomena and an empirical induction from these to generalized causal statements. Such causal induction involves little analysis and is close to John Stuart Mill's induction by simple enumeration. As Leibniz shows in the *Discourse on Method,* sections 14–16, this involves the observation of two complex phenomena (one of which may be mental in the special case of the mind-body problem), which occur together and which differ in their apparent degree of activity or passivity. To distinguish the more active from the less active, and thus the cause from the effect, the categories of active and passive force are involved, but do not imply a concept of efficient causality. Empirical generalization is still relatively self-sufficient, without a strong formative role of *a priori* principles.

In those sciences which are built on analysis and mathematical generalization, on the other hand, the formal principles of mathematics impart a strong element of necessity when applied to inductive generalizations made from experience, though these *a priori* principles involved are still subject to revision when new techniques and fields of observation compel it. It is on this level that Galileo's application of the method of analysis and synthesis becomes most fully applicable, and the ordering of knowledge in the form of an axiomatic system becomes possible. Yet the life and real relevance of a science depend on the primacy of experience, which can compel a readjustment of the *a priori* forms when necessary.

Truths of fact in the natural sciences thus involve a double movement of *a priori* principles downward with a gradually decreasing determinative role in the organization of perceptual data, while the inductive generalization of experience acquires a gradually increasing quality of necessity, as more exact and analytic formulations of primary principles are used in their ordering, yet without losing their contingent character. As a result, the verification or justification of any judgment of fact in the field of the natural sciences may require both analysis of the *a priori* principles and the previously verified judgments which are entailed by it in the sense of being false if it were false, but it involves also a further synthesis, particularly of the problematic kind which leads to an experiment designed to reveal its falsehood, or, if possible, its truth, in a more empirical context.

C. In the case of the metaphysics of existence, the same process of verification and adequation is pertinent, but the primary empirical perceptions are internal, providing support for judgments about our own nature, and, by analysis, for the categories of being which our natures entail. With further support from external perceptions, they also make possible inferences to the existence of other monadic substances. Here the essences of individuals are capable of being analyzed, not in such abstract forms as figure, number, and motion, but, very imperfectly, into finite and limited selections of the simple perfections of God. Moreover, the first principles are applicable more directly than they are in the sciences—the principle of sufficient reason in its teleological form of best-possible being applicable to the universe as a whole and to each part of it, and the principle of identity being actualized as the equivalence of each substance with its essences and the series of actions which ensue from them. Thus the justification of our judgments of existence is possible through an analysis of the first principles which they entail and which partly determine them, and in addition through empirical verification by internal perception and its generalization to apply to other individuals and through the further concepts and principles which they make available for the interpretation of our experiences in the empirical sciences.

As a result, the criterion for the justification of truths of fact, metaphysical as well as scientific, comes to appear very much like a coherence or consensus criterion, but with its three components—the determinant formative role of *a priori* principles, the test of fitness (*convenientia*), and the confirming function of derivative principles and empirical verification in the sciences—separated, each given its appropriate place. The metaphysics of existence thus serves a regulative role and supplies significant categories for the sciences, as the metaphysics of possibility serves a regulative but not a determinative ideal for their mathematical formulations. And however inadequately finite thought grasps it, the whole system—considered as a rational axiomatic order in which a harmony of disciplines and the knowledge of a harmony of existents and their actions come to be from primitive concepts and first principles—remains a regulative ideal of order within which all method can operate.

8

Leibniz and the Limits of Empiricism

Leroy E. Loemker

Leibniz's philosophy has been interpreted from a great variety of differing perspectives, none of which has been adequate to bring total order to his insights. No philosophy has suffered more from the one-sidedness of its interpreters than has the thought of this many-sided genius. The reason for this is less in the comprehensiveness of his thought than in the enormous scope of his practical vision and projects. He was the firm opponent of all philosophical sectarianism; the goal for which he strove throughout his intellectual endeavors was the *philosophia perennis* which should conserve and systematize all that was true and valuable in the many sects, rejecting all that was false. It should provide the first principles for an *encyclopedia,* an encirclement of scientific doctrine. To be encyclopedic, however, means to be eclectic; thus an adequate grasp of Leibniz's thought implies viewing him as an eclectic, though a systematizing eclectic in the tradition called for by Francis Bacon and imperfectly undertaken by such encyclopedists as Bartholomew Keckermann, John Alsted, and John Amos Comenius.

A German version of this paper was read at the Second International Kant Congress held in Bonn in July 1965 and was subsequently published in the *Kantstudien* 56 (1966):315–328.

Considered as a whole, then, Leibniz's philosophy may be viewed after his own analogy of the universe as a city seen from various perspectives. To borrow Jean Laporte's figure, Leibniz's philosophy is like a *"Thèbes aux cent portes,"* such that *"on peut y pénétrer par tous les côtés."*[1] But unlike Leibniz's city, this one does not have a central tower from which all perspectives can be seen in a single unity. The streets upon which these many gates open—some of them broad avenues which have endured until our time—often converge for long stretches, but they are all in one way or another eccentric, each leading to a different central square. And in the effort to get from one avenue to another, the labyrinthine complexity of the system becomes apparent.

It is not my purpose, in this paper, to examine the faults and gaps in these various perspectives, for these are well known. If you take the gateway of logic, whether with Bertrand Russell or Louis Couturat, Ernst Cassirer or Heinrich Scholz as guide, you end in road blocks or blind alleys—facing, for example, the problems of assimilating to a logic the concepts of force, change, individual existence, and the modes of perception and appetite. If you begin with individual things and the harmony of their acts and passive states, you lose the force of Leibniz's great mathematical and logical visions. There have been recent efforts to understand him as a dialectician, through the principle of sufficient reason, through his theory of truth, through his ethics, and through other viewpoints. Though remarkably successful in bringing all of the data before him into subordination to a few principles, Leibniz himself never reached the end of clarity and unity; and (this makes interpretation even more difficult, yet also more tempting) there is so much which he must have understood, which would have clarified the difficulties and closed the gaps in his thought, but which he never put into words. Like many of his contemporaries, Leibniz seems to have been driven, in the face of the great distractions which coerced him, by an

1. J. Laporte, *Études d'Histoire de la Philosophie Francaise au XVIIe siècle* (Paris: J. Vrin, 1951), p. 251.

eschatological urge to get all of the intellectual tasks possible done within a single lifetime.[2] He was concerned with the major problems of thought and culture; but despite his great mathematical successes and his masterful powers of analysis, it was the little things which so often eluded him.

I find of particular interest two gateways into his thought, both of which he seems to have regarded as essential all of his life, although he developed them carefully only in his later years. Not only do these two approaches bring his thought into close relationship to Kant; they seem also to anticipate and to throw light upon recent issues and points of view. I must add that both, as they develop, seem to me to require some basic—if not radical—changes in Leibniz's system itself. These two approaches are through his scientific empiricism and through his juristically conceived ethics. This paper is concerned only with the former; chapter 11 of this volume examines the latter. Both, however, entail the same fundamental analysis of knowledge.

Leibniz's empiricism centers in the problem of verifying, to the extent that this is possible, truths of fact. Such truths are sharply distinguished from truths of reason, but—and this is his great difference from John Locke—they are not independent of truths of reason. Experience does not mean, for Leibniz, as it does for the English school, simple impressions of sense or of reflection. We do have these, but not distinctly or distinguishably; to appropriate C. I. Lewis's term, they are "given," but not in any way isolatable as merely given. They are not experience, since experience is meaningful. "Sensible qualities," Leibniz writes to Queen Charlotte in his reply to John Toland, "are in fact occult qualities, and there must be other qualities more manifest which could

2. A similar eschatological urgency seems to underlie the philosophical system-building of the golden age of American philosophy at the turn of the century. Charles Sanders Peirce expressed his purpose in the preface of his incompleted *Principles of Philosophy* in terms strikingly like those of Leibniz: "To outline a theory so comprehensive that, for a long time to come, the entire work of human reason, in philosophy of every school and kind, in mathematics, in psychology, in physical science, in history, in sociology, and in whatever other department there may be, shall appear as the filling up of its details. The first step toward this is to find simple concepts applicable to every subject."

render them understandable. Far from understanding sensible things only, it is just these which we understand the least."[3]

It is significant that the terms *experientia* and *experimenta* are usually used interchangeably by Leibniz. His conception of experience comes from a tradition older than British empiricism, one shared by Francis Bacon in England and by men like Luis Vives, Marsilio Ficino, and Paracelsus on the continent. The minimal experience is a perception, and although a perception includes sensory qualities, it involves also a meaningful structure, which in turn implies memory of the past and significance for the future. In short, experience is not "pure" givenness; it is active, imaginative response, and it is always purposeful.[4] It is selective from a continuous field of possibilities of perception, and concepts provide the tools for such purposeful selection and individuation.[5] Such concepts serve as nominal definitions. Memory, imagination and conceptualization are thus progressively the agents of understanding within experience.

Truths of fact differ from truths of reason in that they rest upon experience in this broad sense and are capable of growth with experience. However, truths of fact depend upon the truths of reason, as well; indeed, if we were omniscent, as is God, whose infinite perfections constitute our original natures and the natures of all individuals, and whose knowledge, completely intuitive, depends not at all upon symbols, the truths of fact could be derived completely from truths of reason. For human knowledge, however, the truths of reason which inhere in truths of fact, and which can be arrived at by analysis of them, serve also as the normative formal structures to which truths of fact must conform.

The result is that Leibniz at length recognizes three types of propositions. The first is that of *propositions of reason,* which "are necessary, although the reason also furnishes some which are not absolutely general and only probable, as for example when we presume an idea to be possible until its contrary is dis-

3. Gerhardt, VI:499–500; cf. Loemker, p. 547.

4. *Monadology,* secs. 26, 27; see also "On What is Independent of Sense and of Matter," in Gerhardt, VI:499–508; Loemker, pp. 547–553.

5. Gerhardt, VI:500 ff.; Loemker, pp. 547 ff.

covered by more exact research." Thus truths of reason provide determining forms for both necessary and merely probable truths of fact. Second, there are *propositions of fact,* derived either from the senses (and therefore limited to well-founded phenomena) or from the internal sense or the perception of conscious processes themselves; both of these "also may become general in a way," [Leibniz says], "but this is by induction or observation, so that it is only a multitude of similar facts, as when it is observed that all quicksilver is evaporated by fire."[6] In short, such a generalization is imperfect because we do not see its necessity. It is noteworthy that Leibniz thus distinguishes induction by simple enumeration from a more sophisticated induction, whose synthesis involves necessary truths of reason.

In the third place, there are "mixed propositions" which involve as premises a combination of necessary propositions with propositions of fact, but which can have no higher degree of certainty than the contingent factual propositions built into them, because of the logical rule that "the conclusion follows from the weakest of the premises." Mixed truths are therefore complex truths of fact with "partial" necessities entailed within them; they would not be true without these, though these are not sufficient to establish them.

Thus composite truths of fact of a high degree of generality and probability (such are the physical laws, or what were called "subordinate regulations" in the *Discourse on Metaphysics*) are formed as the conclusions of two kinds of premises: necessary ones (which are *a priori*); and simpler, more particular observations of fact, or what we may rightly call, in the spirit of Leibniz's own distinction between the continuous and possible and the discrete and actual, "empirical abstracts."

Before attempting to probe more deeply into the logical process of this derivation of mixed truths of fact, however, we should point out another helpful distinction of Leibniz's. In the corresponding chapter of his *Essay,* Locke had qualified his early inclination toward nominalism (in Book I) by recognizing a particular type of "general and evident propositions" whose truth

6. *Nouveaux Essais,* bk. IV, chap. 11, sec. 14; Gerhardt, V:427–429.

rests upon some externally existent model and can be discovered by any thoughtful person; uppermost in his thoughts are, obviously, the laws of logic and the first principles of mathematics. In his comment, Leibniz described such eternal truths, admitting their necessity, as "at bottom all conditional and say(ing) in effect: such a thing posited, such another thing is."[7] In this operationally useful form, the eternal truths thus become necessary inferences about all possible empirical truths of a certain class or domain, without having actual existential force. Although analytic and tautological, in the sense that they can be reduced to identities and definitions, such truths are nonetheless useful in imparting form or structure to empirical generalizations.

It is worth commenting that Leibniz and Locke were often in close agreement in their actual conclusions, yet were far apart in the presuppositions which are concealed behind these agreements. Leibniz never lost sight of the requirement of universality and necessity, while Locke ever attempted to reduce necessity to psychological certainty and the *a priori* to the highest generalization—a situation analogous to the relation of C. I. Lewis to the more nominalistic positivists of our own day.

How, then, do mixed or complex truths of fact come into being? Three questions are distinguishable, somewhat unclearly, in Leibniz's answer: the question of the psychological origin (Locke's "original of our ideas"), the question of the logical structure, and that of the verification or justification of the proposition. In one passage in the same chapter of Book IV of the *Nouveaux Essais*, Leibniz suggests answers to all three in answering the third. He writes:

The truth of sensible things is justified by their connection, which depends upon (1) the intellectual truths grounded in reason, and (2) upon constant observations in the sensible things themselves, even when the reasons do not appear. And (3) as these reasons and observations give us the means of judging the future as related to our interest, and as success corresponds with our rational judgment, we could not demand, nor have, indeed, a greater certainty concerning these objects.[8]

7. *Discourse on Metaphysics.*
8. *Nouveaux Essais*, bk. IV, chap. 11, sec. 10; Gerhardt, V:426.

Thus justified truths of fact, particularly those having to do with the physical world, involve three components: deduction from *a priori* necessary truths; generalizations, in which simple induction from empirical observations and their description and conceptual definitions are informed by these *a priori* truths on various levels of generalization; and, finally, by the predictive power of the resulting complex truths of fact, which is confirmed by the predicted future experiences or the success of the predicted acts. The logically concrete proposition of fact is in this way made to fit into a temporal sequence of analysis and synthesis in which the proposition is first formed by a combination of *a priori* forming and *a posteriori* generalizing, and it is then more completely justified by its value in predictive synthesis.

Thus the logical justification of a complex truth of fact involves analysis into the *a priori* principles and more primitive observations out of which it was synthesized, and its further pragmatic verification in terms of the further empirical ends to which it leads.[9]

In describing his method of analysis and synthesis, Leibniz consistently makes the point that it is not only the primary terms or concepts involved in an investigation which must be chosen in relation to the restricted field of the investigation and which need not be more simple than the problem requires, but also the necessary *a priori* principles themselves. Aside from the ultimate first principles from which they are derivative by way of definitions grounded in the discipline involved, therefore, *a priori* principles are relative to the given problem under investigation; if they fail and observation is not at fault, they must be replaced by others. *A priori* principles are always necessary, but never sufficient to justify a truth of fact.

This process, in which the first principles are rendered specific through definitions which make them applicable to the empirical generalizations and conceptual determinations of a particular field, can be exemplified by the special forms assumed by the

9. This application of the methods of analysis and synthesis corresponds closely to the suggestions made by Jacobi Zabarella in his *de Methodis*, and confirms the seminal influence of the Italian on the methodology of the seventeenth century.

principles of identity and sufficient reason in the different regions of Leibniz's scientific concern. Taken most generally, the principle of identity may be taken to mean that, in any empirical relation which has a logically determinate aspect, there must be a component, however abstract, which is identical in its two terms. Thus the principle of identity becomes an identity of the scope of intensional with extensional meanings in any complete or individual concept or in any functional mathematical law applicable in a closed system. In every algebraic equation, the principle of identity becomes the equality of the orders of value on the two sides of the equation. In Leibniz's new qualitative geometry, it becomes the operationally useful relations of similarity or of congruence. In dynamics, it is the principle of the equipollence of the total direction of motion or of the total living force of a system of random moving bodies, with the sum of the directions of motion or the living forces of its component bodies. The universally valid prototype of identity and sufficient reason is Archimedes's balance.

The principle of sufficient reason has already been included in these examples. It can be specified for different fields of investigation along with the principle of identity, but only in situations where the antecedent reasons or causes are sufficient but no more (i.e., not *eminent* reasons, as in the case of God) to explain the consequence. In such cases it becomes a principle of necessary and sufficient reason in mathematics and science. In any case, such *a priori* particularizations serve only as necessary formal principles which are never sufficient (for human intelligences) to determine the empirical generalizations to which they are relevant.

At this point Leibniz anticipates the modern scientific conception of method more adequately than does Kant. He may, indeed, be said to stand midway between Kant's fixed Newtonian apriorism and a Humean empiricism. Like Kant, he holds that our understanding of nature is restricted to *phenomena bene fundata* and that this understanding involves the component roles of *a priori* rationality and *a posteriori* sensibility—the former to assure the universality and necessity of scientific knowledge (to the extent that this contains an element of necessity), the latter to make possible its growth. But unlike Kant, Leibniz does not regard the *a priori* principles underlying science as synthetic or for that matter, as pure, for they cannot be derived solely from the first principles of all knowledge; empirically grounded definitions are needed to make them relevant to the particular fields of investigation. As a consequence, Leibniz makes no effort to set up a closed group of *a priori* principles which restrict the development of science, necessarily, into a single path. The universal principles of logic, whether directed simply at classification or at inferences and explication, do not suffice to assure such a static completion to the scientific task, for after all, these principles apply to all possible worlds. New experiences cannot always be subsumed under the old categories; sometimes they call for new forms of thought. The exhaustive *a priori* formalization of knowledge about this world belongs to God alone; for human thought it can be merely a regulative ideal toward which the analysis of facts always strives but which it never fully attains. It is necessary that judgments involving experience (truths of fact) conform to *a priori* principles, but these are not sufficient to determine the necessity of the judgments themselves; these can have only the degree of certainty which the successful prediction of future experiences, in particular, of designed experiments, assure them.

On this point Kant was overimpressed by the apparent finality of Newtonian science. Leibniz, on the other hand, remained close to Bacon's "mixed" middle axioms, arrived at through experience formed and anticipated by purely logical *a priori* concepts. To this Baconian insight, Leibniz added a sense of the order which science could gain through the analytic procedures of the new mathematics, and the power which this provided for measuring rates of change and other variables arising from the analysis of experience.

For Leibniz, unlike Kant, space and time are not pure forms of intuition; the conceptual constructions of experience in space and time rests upon relations continuous with sensory qualities and their changes themselves—the relations of succession and simultaneity of observed events. But it is only through the application of *a priori* logical concepts and rules to the special fields of knowledge that space and time, these abstractions from experience, can themselves be generalized for scientific purposes.

Thus Leibniz's conception of the *a priori* principles leaves the work of science forever open—a progressive penetration, as observation increases in scope and refinement, and the mathematico-logical orders of existence reveal increasing patterns of necessity in classification or explanation. It was in the interest of this deepening and freeing of the scientific enterprise that Leibniz objected, in Book IV of the *Nouveaux Essais,* to Locke's opinion that science should (but cannot) proceed directly from the connection of ideas (ideas, that is, in Locke's usage as sensory images) to the primary qualities as unknown potentialities ("real essences") of metaphysical substances; in short, that the realm of the empirical sciences should be understood as the immediate action of unknown metaphysical powers. Against this closing of the possibilities of scientific growth, Leibniz's analysis of truths of fact, opening as it does a pragmatic dimension of verification, keeps open the way to a continuing refinement of scientific understanding.

This freeing of experience from a total *a priori* determination places Leibniz in the line of development of scientific thought after Kant, particularly so in the development of American thought in the last century. It is true that the work of Kant, rather than that of Leibniz, was early adopted in America, but it was a Kant whose categorial scheme had been relativized and adapted to the practical ends of man by the idealistic philosophers of Germany and England, so that when Charles Sanders Peirce and his contemporaries read him, it was already in the Leibnizian spirit. It may even be said with some justice that Peirce develops the metaphysics which Leibniz might have developed, had he made his theory of empirical knowledge the dominant concern of his thought, rather than concentrating his concern on the divine justice.

The absoluteness of the Kantian system of categories and principles was early challenged by the German idealists. This challenge was stated sharply, if not always clearly, by Hegel:

> To take up a plurality of categories in any way whatever as a kind of lucky find, for example, from the judgments, and to be thus satisfied with them, must in fact be considered an outrage on science; where

should the understanding be able to demonstrate necessity if it cannot do so about itself, itself being pure necessity?[10]

A similar criticism is stated more dramatically by Josiah Royce in an imaginary dialogue with the great thinker in a famous chapter of *The Religious Aspect of Philosophy*:

Why just these principles and no others? [asks Royce].
"That is inexplicable," replies Kant.
Very well, then, suppose we give up applying to experience those arbitrary principles of ours. Suppose we choose to stop thinking of experience as causally connected. What then?
"But you cannot stop," says Kant, "Your thought, being what it is, must follow this one fashion forever."
Nay, we reply, how knowest thou that, Master? Why may not our thought get a new fashion some day? And then what is now a necessary principle, for example, that every event has a cause, would become unnecessary or even nonsensical. Do we then know *a priori* that our *a priori* principles must always remain the same? If so, how come we by this new knowledge?[11]

One may find the same criticism in Peirce's later metaphysics and in the theory of knowledge of C. I. Lewis, which culminates in a theory of value and an uncompleted ethical theory. It is clear to both that *a priori* truths of relation play a necessary role, but not a completely determining role, in the justification of truths of fact. They agree that empirical judgments are composite syntheses of conceptual determinations and observations, but can be verified or justified only through adequate relations to future goals. Peirce's categories of tychism and synechism have strong similarities to Leibniz's distinction between the two levels of experience: the continuity of possibilities and the conceptually bounded realm of existents. For both Peirce and Lewis, as for Leibniz, the openness of science to future experience is compatible with every established necessity of logical order.

Peirce once wrote of Leibniz that "this great and singular

10. *Phaenomenologie des Geistes*, second edition (Leipzig: Georg Lasson, 1921), p. 159.

11. Josiah Royce, *The Religious Aspect of Philosophy* (Boston: Houghton Mifflin, 1885), p. 387.

genius was as remarkable for what he failed to see as for what he saw."[12] It must be admitted that our interpretation of Leibniz's theory of factual knowledge is not reconcilable with many other aspects of Leibniz's thought, notably with his metaphysical panlogism and his doctrine of the predetermination of every individual through his *notion complète* or the law of his individual nature. Before discussing the modifications in Leibniz's metaphysics which are suggested by his empiricism, however, let me enumerate several fruitful consequences of his empiricism.

This empiricism frees science from the bonds of an immediately superimposed framework of ordering principles which determine its limits and opens the way for progress in the refinement and elaboration of the forms of thought with which science operates, to keep step with a perfection of the physical and logical tools of observation and analysis. In this progress the sciences do not strive toward unity; rather, the field of science consists of an indefinite series of real orders, none of which possesses meaning apart from the experiences on which it is based and the derivative principles by which these are organized. Therefore the sciences develop toward an ever "better founded" phenomenal content (*phenomena bene fundata*) as their principles and primitive concepts move nearer to a metaphysical order of primitive principles and concepts.

According to Leibniz, there are, however, two levels of metaphysics. One contains the truths of reason and the primitive concepts which have validity in all possible worlds. These truths are necessary and completely capable of being analyzed into identities; they depend in no way upon experience and they are insufficient to determine any truth related to this world. They belong to God as intellect, as "region of ideas." The second level of metaphysics, however, is concerned with existence, and hence its truths must have an empirical content. Even for God, a metalogical mode of calculation is necessary in order that the maximal value of every variable quality out of which the world can be made may be predetermined. The empirical content and order of

12. *Collected Papers of Charles Sanders Peirce*, edited by C. Hartshorne and P. Weiss (Cambridge, Mass.: Harvard University Press, 1934), p. 250.

this existing world, insofar as man can know it, is given through two kinds of experience: external perception, limited to phenomena; and inner perception—self-consciousness, which, as Leibniz frequently points out, reveals to us the ground of our own being and therefore the understanding of substance, causality, purpose, and other metaphysical categories, although not in a manner sufficient to reveal the total determination of our own nature or of the world harmony. Here we remain bound to mere concepts and abstract generalizations.

For Leibniz, there are therefore two decisive relationships between metaphysics and scientific knowledge. On the higher level, metaphysics provides the empty and abstract first principles upon which all knowledge rests, but which must be specified through empirically oriented definitions in order to serve as *a priori* principles for particular sciences or, for that matter, for the second level of metaphysics.

This level of the metaphysics of existence, on the other hand, agrees with the sciences in the use of necessary presuppositions in forming and justifying truths of fact, but primarily on the basis of internal experience, not external perception, as do the sciences. This inner experience lacks much of the objectivity and regularity which make possible reliable generalizations, and philosophical method must rely upon a hypothetical use of analysis and synthesis. If we call this method the reflective role of theoretical reason—reflective in the double sense of inner experience and of the mediating role of reason (according to Kant) which undertakes to consider the mechanical order of phenomena and to interpret it through teleology and the principle of unity—then we can say that this second level of metaphysics plays a regulative, direction-giving role in relation to the sciences. We can add that, in their striving to establish the laws of well-grounded phenomena, these sciences stand in a dialectic relation to a concrete metaphysics of existence which operates with the same primitive concepts (for example, power, space, and time) and the same principles (that of the best possible) as do the sciences. This metaphysics of existence is also involved in the same infinite process of knowing, but it is open to a realm of existence through internal experience, which operates regulatively in relation to the sciences.

Thus the metaphysics of possibilities plays a constitutive, but not a completely determinative, role in relation to the sciences, and the metaphysics of existence plays a regulative and reflective role in the same context.

As a consequence, Leibniz's theory of knowledge, which is empirical, phenomenalistic, and pragmatic, can be regarded also as a critical realism. And this is confirmed by his theory of perception. According to this theory, each conscious, rational individual immediately "grasps through" to a real order of harmonious activity. But the rational individual can never perceive or "grasp" this order as it really is, since the individual is shut off from both his own nature and external nature by the labyrinth of the infinite. Through its two-dimensional division into the "giving expression" (*expressio*) to the real, and its explication of it (*ratiocinatio*), the theory of perception establishes a connection between the scientific knowledge and verification of appearances through the given, and the not immediately known but reflectively grounded reality of metaphysics.

What are the implications of this interpretation of Leibniz's empiricism for his metaphysics in general, and particularly for its ethical applications? From the point of view of experience and the knowledge of fact, metaphysics plays a regulative and reflective role. But it must also be admitted that metaphysics is prior to science for Leibniz, as the simple perfections of God are prior to the universe which is their best possible expression. As he wrote in the *Nouveaux Essais*, "Necessary truths contain the determinating ground and the regulative principle of existence itself, and in a word, the laws of the universe."[13] This precedence of meaning over particular occurrence, of essence over existence, of law over its instantification, seemed necessary to Leibniz as it did to many of his contemporaries, since the justification of God in theology and the perfection of mathematics and the sciences depended upon it. But this precedence also endangered ade-

13. *Nouveaux Essais*, bk. IV, chap. 11, sec. 14; Gerhardt, V:429.

quate answers to three pressing ethical questions: the nature of freedom, the relation between the dispositional nature of man and his self-determination, and the reality of a kingdom of grace.

Freedom is, according to Leibniz, self-conscious spontaneity, but spontaneity is merely the determination of events and experiences of the monad through its individual concept of law.

For nearly forty years, Leibniz showed his uneasiness about this conception of freedom and made efforts to explain or modify it, but never in any way which threatened the great chain of essentialistic determinism or admitted a degree of indeterminism. The distinction between *inclinatio* and *determinatio*, and between metaphysical and moral determinism did not help. In the face of challenges by Pierre Bayle and the Cartesians, Leibniz undertook psychological analyses of motivation based on minute unconscious strivings or upon purposive series of perceptions. In a neglected essay of 1679, he outlined such a psychology of motives,[14] interpreting the mind, not as a single series of unified perceptions, but as a complex of conflicting purposive serial processes, each striving for first place in consciousness, and each arising out of a finite affection or appetite determined by the nature of the individual. In this essay, Leibniz concluded that at each moment that particular series which "viewed in itself is the more perfect" takes precedence over the rest. But he does not explain why, in a sequence of events determined by the law of the individual, one trait or disposition should achieve this greater perfection at one time, while giving way to another, more perfect, affection and series at another. On this secondary level, therefore, the issue of determinism remains unexplained.

Only in his commentary on Locke does Leibniz show any inclination to admit a degree of indeterminacy, but even here the absoluteness of the principle of sufficient reason blocks such a conception. In a classical comment,[15] Leibniz follows Locke in distinguishing two meanings of freedom: the power to will as one

14. *De Affectibus: Ubi de Potentia, Actione, Determinatione* in Grua, II:512–537; see especially p. 531.

15. *Nouveaux Essais*, bk. II, chap. 21, sec. 8; Gerhardt, V:160–161.

ought, and the power to do what one wills. What one ought to do is determined by one's understanding, and when one acts according to a will determined by distinct and adequate understanding, one is free in both senses.

Such distinctions, however, in no way remove the ethical difficulties created by the determining role of the law of the individual: for this doctrine demands a priority of the dispositional nature of man over his inclinations and acts and forestalls any attempt to derive new habits or attitudes from his actions. There is no suggestion that the entire nature of the individual is not created by God as a unity. There are many indications in Leibniz's writings after 1695 of the breaking of the Great Chain of Being: there is the turn from logic to history and from the law of the individual series to the dynamic series of experiences themselves; a tendency to separate volition from intellect and regard it as an affective power; the admission that God can at any time create new monads, etc., but there is never an explicit modification of his determinism.

Surely Leibniz needs reinterpretation here, on both ethical and empirical grounds. Psychology must, it is true, recognize both an episodic, temporal side to the mind, consisting of actions and endurings, and also a determinative dispositional side. One can even recognize, as a regulative ideal for theoretical psychology, a "total individual concept" or "law" toward which our experimental models, whether statistical, typological, or in the style of a psychic profile, may strive. But one must also recognize that this dispositional nature, this "persuasive identity of character" (to use Whitehead's phrase) is at least in part the product, the enduring effect, of the conscious and unconscious actions and sufferings of man, and not merely their cause. This was seen by the French spiritualists of the last century, and after them by C. S. Peirce, Josiah Royce, William James, and John Dewey. Peirce in particular considered the process by which our opinions and convictions, when stabilized by experience, become habits which make up the growing order and harmony of life. The question of how far these character habituations are not, themselves, produced by repeated actions but are prior to them, and how far actions are free from established patterns of conduct and may in turn bring new patterns into being, may be unanswerable; but it is not meaningless, and it remains one of those regulative metaphysical issues of which we have spoken.

Leibniz's ethical concerns and ideas, too, point to the need for modifying his theory of the individual at this point. After 1686 his statements of metaphysics usually end with the ideal of the two kingdoms: the kingdom of nature, whose laws must be obeyed by metaphysical necessity, and of which God is the designer and governor; and the kingdom of Grace, of which God is the perfectly just and loving King, nay the Father, whose laws must be obeyed by a "moral necessity." In describing these two states and their relations, Leibniz achieved an exaltation of style and rhetoric which shows this doctrine to be the very heart of his philosophical faith, the ideal which was to give meaning to the *homme honnête* in his efforts to establish a new European order through science, law, and religion. Seen metaphysically, both Kingdoms exist as the best possible ones. As existent, the realm of nature may be perfect in its kind, but that of grace is not. The point of the *Theodicy* is the effort to show that, although the realm of grace is not perfect, it is better that this be so than otherwise. Although justice is defined as the love of the wise and powerful man, the three levels of justice which are held to follow from this definition are needed just because there are crimes and inequities in the world as well as *honestas* and *pietas.* The kingdom of Grace is thus both ideal and real, but the total of Leibniz's great program and efforts presupposes that it should be a possible but not yet realized ideal. If it were at once real and the best possible, such efforts would be either superfluous or inevitable.

This is the dilemma into which Leibniz's shift, in his last two decades, to an emphasis upon the historical and the empirical threw him. His system remained bound to the Great Chain of Being, but his investigations of science and human knowledge in general pointed to a break in that chain, and his ethical thinking demanded it. Seen historically, his thinking stops midway in the modern shift from the Platonic theory in which degrees of perfection are equated with degrees of being and evil and error are but the limitations of the finite, to a metaphysics of the interdependence and the mutuality of a society of substantial entities, bound together in a continuum of possible experience within which minds, self-awareness, purposes, and values have come into being and will, through decisions and efforts, continue to do so.

The import of this paper is that, although this adventuresome philosophy could not have come to be without Kant, Leibniz, seen from one perspective of his thought, was closer to it than was Kant.

9

Logical Difficulties in Leibniz's Metaphysics

Nicholas Rescher

LEIBNIZ NEVER wrote a comprehensive and synoptic treatise setting forth a systematic presentation of his philosophy. He presented his ideas in a myriad of occasional essays, letters, and papers. Notwithstanding the scattered form of its publication, the metaphysical system of Leibniz is, in my opinion, a tightly coordinated structure of conceptions and principles, devised and organized by one of the most informed, powerful, and logically sophisticated minds which the history of philosophy has to offer. In view of this, it is perhaps not surprising that the project—inaugurated in the Anglo-American setting by Bertrand Russell—of seeking to discern inconsistencies and self-contradictions in Leibniz's system has proved relatively barren of positive and tenable results. The great majority of putative objections to Leibniz's system put forward by Russell and his emulators come to be seen as ill-founded on closer inspection. Yet while Leibniz's system is, as I see it, free from the sort of outright inconsistencies attributed to it by the critics of this school, it nevertheless does,

This paper was published originally by Franz Steiner Verlag GmbH, in *Studia Leibniziana Supplementa* I (1968):253–265.

I think, exhibit significant gaps and weak spots. The aim of this paper is to examine the exact nature and the general character of some of these shortcomings.

Incompatible Worlds from Unrelated Substances

Leibniz had a characteristic and seemingly strange doctrine of relations. He taught that relations between substances are never ultimately real: they must invariably be *derivable* from the properties embodied in the defining concepts (the individual notions) of the substances at issue, even as the relational fact that "α is of the same color as β" is embodied in the predicational facts that α and β are both, say, red. One of the cornerstones of Leibniz's theory of substance is the thesis that the only relations which can hold among substances are those that are reducible to and derivable from straightforward *predications* about the respective substances.

But now examine this doctrine of relations in the context of Leibniz's theory of substance. Substances, according to Leibniz, are entirely defined by their "complete individuating notions." These defining concepts of substances are fixed already "prior" to their existence, when they only subsist in God's mind as concepts considered *sub ratione possibilitatis,* as mere possibilities. Thus, let two substances, say α and β, be defined through the enumeration of their predicates:

$$\alpha \ : \ A_1, A_2, A_3, \ldots$$
$$\beta \ : \ B_1, B_2, B_3, \ldots$$

In view of the completeness of its individual notion (which, of course, has a temporal aspect, since it specifies the complete history of the substance at issue) all truths about α—excepting only that regarding its actualization as an existent—must be extractable from the information provided in the A_i list. (The same holds true, of course, for β and for any other substances.) In consequence, whenever α is in some way related to β, say by the relation R, so that "$\alpha \ R \ \beta$" is true, this fact must be extractable from the A_i list and the B_i list. Relations that are not derivable in this way on the basis of predicational data would be *irreducibly* relational. Such irreducible relations cannot possibly characterize *substances,* in Leibniz's view. (This is not to say, of course, that they could not characterize *abstract* entities, such as numbers or colors.)

Now this position, while clearly tenable in itself and free from self-inconsistency, does come into a serious conflict with other Leibnizian doctrines. For as long as this strictly derivational conception of relations is maintained, *no two possible substances can be incompossible.* And this fact would at once lead to a breakdown of the key Leibnizian conception of an infinite diversity of possible substances—considered *sub ratione possibilitatis*—sorting themselves out into alternative possible worlds through mutual relations of compossibility and incompossibility. This feature of the possible substances—that they split apart into mutually exclusive systems of possibilities—is, of course, a crucial feature of Leibniz's metaphysics, for it is just in this realm that the scope for God's exercise of free will comes to be opened up, providing the entire rationale for Leibniz's demarcation between the realms of necessity and of contingence.

Consider again two possible substances as defined through their complete individual notions:

$$\alpha : A_1, A_2, A_3, \ldots$$
$$\beta : B_1, B_2, B_3, \ldots$$

How can an incompatibility possibility arise here: how can α be *logically* incompossible with β? In one way only. We must be able to extract from the conjunction presenting the definitive concept of α, viz.:

$$(1)\ A_1(\alpha)\ \&\ A_2(\alpha)\ \&\ A_3(\alpha)\ \&\ \ldots$$

the deductive conclusion that

(2) there is no substance x such that:

$$B_1(x)\ \&\ B_2(x)\ \&\ B_3(x)\ \&\ \ldots$$

But such a conclusion can follow from the conjunction (1) only if this conjunction gives information about substances distinct from α, this information being of a genuinely relational sort, irreducibly involving an essential reference to substances distinct from α. Consequently the information provided by (1) about α

will, under the circumstances, have to fail to be *genuinely* reducible to a composite of nonrelational predications.

Thus, Leibniz's teaching of the derivative character of substantival relations creates a serious difficulty for his system at another—crucially important—point. Substances characterized solely by purely qualitative predicates which contain no irreducibly relational element can never be incompossible with one another. This result, however, would lead at once to the collapse of Leibniz's conception of possible worlds sorted out into mutually exclusive alternatives on the basis of considerations of mutual compossibility and incompossibility. It is clear that only irreducibly relational properties—properties not specifiable in terms of genuinely qualitative predicates—can underwrite the incompatibility of alternatively possible substances and worlds.

Here, then, we are confronted by a serious logical conflict between two important Leibnizian doctrines. He claims that no two possible substances are related to one another in any nontrivial way. He also teaches that all possible substances fall into mutually exclusive groupings, the alternative possible worlds, on the basis of purely logical compatibility considerations based upon their defining concepts. But clearly, *genuinely* unrelated substances can never be logically incompossible. The logic of the situation is, therefore, such that the two doctrines at issue are seriously at odds with one another.

Process from Atemporal Concepts: The Puzzle of the Present

I turn now to a second logical anomaly in Leibniz's metaphysics. The "complete individual notion" of a possible substance specifies its complete state at every moment throughout its entire history. To use a cinematographic analogy: the complete notion of a possible substance is akin to a reel of film, on which the whole history of what happens on the screen is completely encapsulated, being somehow presented all at once, in a purely synchronous, or more strictly, atemporal manner. Just as the film is "played" across the slit in front of the projector in a temporally sequential way, so an actualized substance moves through its history, impelled by its inherent "appetition" to go onward from moment to successive moment. This analogy is indicative of the sort of picture we are supposed to bear in mind.

But the problem arises "Whence—within the framework of such a conceptual setting—can one arrive at a *now*?" In other words, what plays the role of the projector with its slit to differentiate among successive presents (nows) as the atemporally given monadic history "moves" through its stages? Consider the situation in diagrammatic form, with the complete individual notion of a monad (its "program," as we might call it in up-to-date terminology) displayed before us as follows:

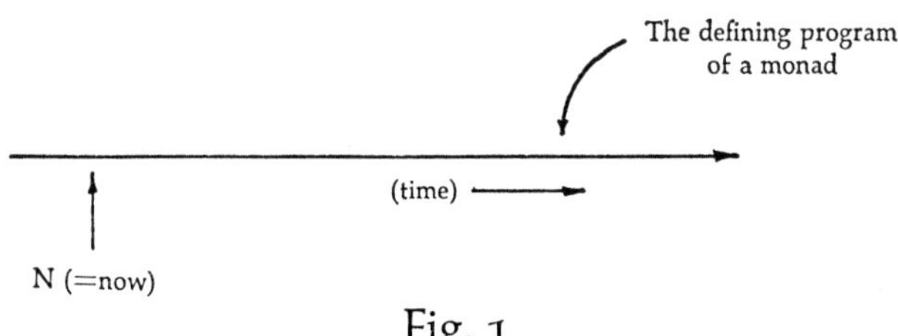

Fig. 1

The problem is: how do we get a now-selector? What makes the monadic history specified in its defining program "go" or "turn over," "move along," or do any thing of this dynamic sort? Leibniz critically needs an account of the transitory "now" as part of the driving force of process in his system. Without such an account, the crucial concepts of force and appetition remain suspended *in vacuo*, and Leibniz's system is not the dynamism he yearns for, but a collage of static elements.

But clearly, we cannot obtain the "now" of the transitory present from the defining concepts of the monads themselves: these are impotent to effect an actual discrimination among potential "nows"—since they are all comprised in a perfectly uniform way within the all-inclusive "complete individual notions."

Nor can we invoke Leibniz's God to help us out of this difficulty, for think here of the recent discussions of the question: "Can God know what is happening *now*"? Clearly he can know what is happening at 3:30 P.M. on Friday, April 22, 1965, or what is happening contemporaneously with my writing of this line. Equally clearly he cannot differentiate one existentially given "now" from another. An extra-temporal being can, of course, know what happens *at any and every instant of time*. But he cannot know what happens *now*, i.e., to know what occurs *in* time from the relational perspective of one positioned *within* the framework. God cannot know temporal facts from the dis-vantage point of one located *within* the framework. He could never entertain the statement: "It is now 3:30 P.M. Friday, April 22, 1965." (This, of course, does not mean that there are any temporal facts —facts about the events or occurrences that go on at various times—that God does not know.)

Nor can Leibniz write the difficulty off as a mere "matter of perception" by monads. For this would not differentiate one stage of their history from another, since they perceive all of the time. His doctrine of the phenomenality of time leaves unresolved—indeed, untouched—the problem of the phenomenal "now"; for it addresses itself to this problem only when it is raised from *within* the temporal framework. What we now seek is a fact about this framework itself, asking the question: When a given juncture is *current* (actual), how does its condition differ from that which it was when it was future and that which it will be when it is past? What denominates it as actual, the way the light of the projector selects the current frame, the phonograph needle the current notes, the reader's sight and attention the current word of the book and so forth? (Note that in all these cases we have an exact analogue of Leibniz's monadic "program"; a *totum simul* whole that is "gone through" sequentially.)

The difficulty is that Leibniz's machinery of monads defined by historically synoptic complete individual notions is not sufficient to give him all that he needs for his theory of time. It is sufficient to give him *B*-series data in terms of before-concurrently-after, but insufficient to give him *A*-series data in terms of past-present-future (to formulate the matter in McTaggart's terminology).

This "puzzle of the present" can be seen as a serious one for Leibniz; he clearly needs "the specious present" in the ontology of his system, as the indispensable prime mover for the wheels of substantival change—that is to say, of monadic appetition. But there is no possible ingredient of his metaphysical system to furnish him with this critical requisite.

Let me cast the problem in somewhat general terms. Any adequate ontology must make room for two sorts of existential contrasts. The first is that between entities or existents, on the one hand, and nonentities or nonexistents, on the other. The second is that between the actual states of existents and their non-actual states in the past or the future. And while dealing brilliantly with the former issue, Leibniz's metaphysics leaves the latter in a sadly unsatisfactory condition. At any point of time there must clearly be *something* to differentiate the then-actual state of a substance from its other (equally real but nonconcurrent) states: some sort of light to illuminate the then-given frame, to revert to our cinematographic analogy. The logic of the situation is such that Leibniz's metaphysical machinery of an atemporal God and transtemporal individual concepts needs to be supplemented by some specifically temporal device for chronology-generation. Not only does Leibniz fail to provide such a device, but he entertains a variety of metaphysical commitments of an entirely static and timeless character which make it dubious that any such device can be provided in his system without generating internal stresses of intolerable proportions. The difficulty here goes to the very root of Leibniz's dynamism. How to extract change from the changeless? The puzzle is the ancient one to which Zeno of Elea had already put his hand: How is one to provide a rationalization of process within the framework of a metaphysic whose stance is fundamentally static and atemporal like the system of Leibniz has to be, since everything is mapped out in God's mind prior to creation *sub ratione possibilitatis*?

The Problem of Creation: Time and Eternity

The problem I am now about to raise is closely related to the just-considered puzzle about the now-of-the-present-moment. It is a problem by no means specific to Leibniz, but generally inherent in the position of a wide group of theological writers of which Leibniz may be regarded as a particularly clear and cogent representative spokesman. The problem is that of introducing process into the fundamentally static ontological situation that obtains "prior" (so to speak) to the creation of a world.

The difficulty arises critically at the juncture where time and eternity come into touch: the creation. Creation *ex nihilo* is to be thought of as a divine action; in fact a *transaction* in which the deity confronts the possible to produce the actual. But all of the actors in this Leibnizian drama—God, the possible worlds, and the possible substances whose features are specified in their complete individual notions—all these are *atemporal.* They subsist only in some mode wholly outside the sphere of the temporal, a static sphere where concepts such as those of process and occurrence and therefore that of *action*—and *a fortiori creative action*—cannot secure a foothold. Leibniz leaves the creation not only in the status of a *miracle,* but even in that of a *mystery.* This position is understandable, perhaps even admirable, as a dogma of theology—but it will clearly not do as a doctrine of a philosophical system.

Given Leibniz's rigidly atemporal, eternalistic picture of the ontological situation "prior" to the creation, it is literally incomprehensible how there could be such a thing as a divine "act of creation." In the final analysis, his answer to the question "How did time (sc. monadic change or appetition) start?" is "God started it going." His answer is thus given in the conceptual setting of *an agent* (viz., God) *doing something* (viz., creating a world). But if the entire setting of the stage here is in no way a temporal one—not even somehow quasi-temporal—then this line of response becomes literally unintelligible. Aristotle's insight appears perfectly valid: in an atemporal, changeless setting, change cannot get a start. The difficulties that lurk here for the concept of creation *ex nihilo* in the context of an omnipresent doctrine of sufficient reason overwhelm Leibniz just as they engulfed the Christianizers of Aristotle who preceded him. Put into a nutshell, the problem is that of "breaking through the time barrier." God, concepts, and *possibilia* all exist in a tenseless, timeless world. Change and process are inextricably temporal; and these two realms are as disparate as different dimensions can and must ever be. To speak of a creation *ex nihilo* is to give the point of transition a name, but this accomplishes nothing in the way of rendering it philosophically intelligible.

Moral Beneficence from Ontological Beneficence

I turn now to my fourth and final Leibnizian puzzle. Suppose that a resolution is somehow effected—I know not how—to our initial problem of sorting *unrelated* substances into mutually incompatible worlds. Contemplating these alternatives *sub ratione possibilitatis,* which of them will God select for actualization? Leibniz bitterly opposed the position of Descartes and Spinoza, whom he took to maintain the indifference and arbitrariness of God's will. He held that possibles are good objectively, by a standing *"règle de bonté"* which operates wholly independently of the will of God. But what is this criterion which a God who seeks to actualize *the best* of possible worlds employs in identifying it? By what criterion of merit does God determine whether one possible world is more or less perfect than another?

On this question, Leibniz is perfectly explicit. His criterion of goodness for possible worlds is very plainly set forth by him in the following terms:

> God has chosen [to create] that world which is the most perfect, that is to say, which is at the same time the simplest in its hypotheses [i.e., its laws] and the richest in phenomena [i.e., its actual contents].[1]

God's way of proceeding in the selection of one of the possible worlds for actualization can thus be represented and illustrated by the sort of infinite-comparison process familiar from the calculus and the calculus of variations.

This procedure can be illustrated in somewhat oversimplified form by minimax-problems in the differential calculus; for example, by considering the choice-situation depicted in a diagram of the following sort:

1. *Discourse on Metaphysics,* sec. 6, Gerhardt, VI:431; Loemker, p. 306. Cf. also, *ibid.,* sec. 5, Gerhardt, IV:430; Loemker, pp. 305–306; *The Principles of Nature and Grace,* sec. 10, Gerhardt, VI:603; Loemker, p. 639; and *Theodicy,* Gerhardt, VI.

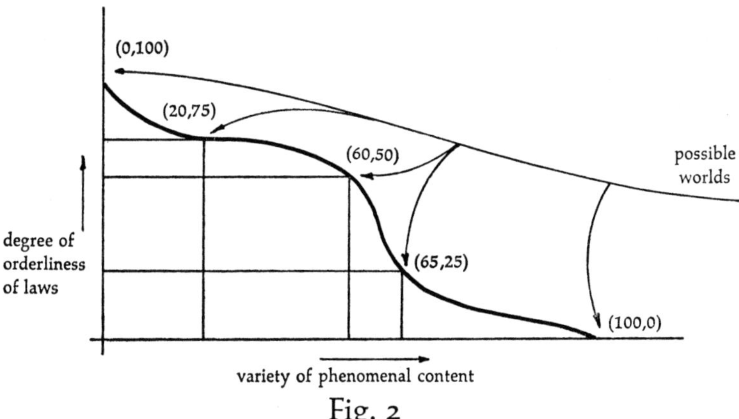

Fig. 2

We suppose here that the merit function is of the simplest additive sort:

merit index = (variety index) + (orderliness).

Our world—the actual world—is the "best possible world" in this somewhat rarefied metaphysical sense of *greatest variety of phenomena consonant with greatest simplicity of laws.* Its being "the best" has (at any rate, in the first instance) little if anything to do with how men—or men and animals—fare in it. The facile optimism of Dr. Pangloss—the butt of Voltaire's parody *Candide*: *Si c'est ici le meilleur des mondes possibles, que sont donc les autres*[2]—misses the mark if Leibniz, and not some rather naive and simpleminded Leibnizian, is intended as its target.

Leibniz is perfectly clear and explicit that this sort of perfection of possible worlds, their ontological perfection—determined on the basis of a two-factor criterion combining variety of contents ("richness of phenomena") with the orderliness of their arrangement ("simplicity of laws")—is at the basis of the metaphysical considerations involved in a choice among alternative possible worlds. But he is not sufficiently tough-mindedly willing to let the matter rest wholly on this cold-blooded metaphysical level: He also insists on bringing *moral* considerations upon the tapis.

2. Voltaire, *Candide*, edited by R. Pomeau (Paris: Nizet, 1959), p. 105.

As is well known, Leibniz sorted substances into three grades: *bare monads,* associated with the inanimate and with lower organisms; *souls,* associated with animals; and *spirits,* associated with beings capable of the exercise of intelligence and reason. The monads of the highest grade, the spirits, alone share with God both in the intellectual capacity for self-consciousness and in the moral capacity for reasoned choice based on a vision of the good. Whereas all monads mirror the created world of other monads, the spirits are a reflection—no doubt a pale one—of God as well. The spirits comprise the "City of God," "this truly universal monarchy, [which] is a moral world within the natural world and is the most exalted and the most divine of all of God's works."[3] The welfare of the spirits is, according to Leibniz, a fundamentally primary consideration in the deity's comparative evaluation of alternative worlds: "There can be no doubt that the happiness of spirits is the principal end of God and that he puts this principle into practice as far as the general harmony permits."[4] This approach, of course, leads to a second and very different criterion of merit in the assessment of possible worlds, viz., not the ontological beneficence that interests itself in such substantially universal considerations as rich phenomena subject to simple laws, but to the specifically moral beneficence of a creator seeking pre-eminently to assure the welfare of the spirits.

His commitments to the conception of the "City of God," with its corresponding emphasis upon the welfare of the spirits, betrayed Leibniz into one of the noteworthy discrepancies of his system. He is, as we have seen, fundamentally committed to the criterion of a "best possible" world as one that exhibits "the simplest laws with the richest phenomena." This highly metaphysical conception of goodness stands in potential conflict with a more emphatically moral criterion, acknowledging God's primary responsibility to the spirits. In one particularly important discussion, however, Leibniz makes it clear that he is prepared

3. *Monadology,* sec. 86, Gerhardt, VI:621–622; Loemker, p. 651. Cf. *Principles of Nature and Grace,* secs. 14–15, Gerhardt, VI:604–605, Loemker, p. 640.

4. *Discourse on Metaphysics,* sec. 5, Gerhardt, IV:430; Loemker, p. 306.

to see the metaphysical considerations prevail over the ethical ones, in the final analysis:

[Objection] *"If there is more evil than good in intelligent creatures, there is more evil than good in all God's Works."* [Reply] I do not admit it because this supposed inference from the part to the whole, from intelligent creatures to all creatures, assumes tacitly and without proof that creatures devoid of reason cannot be compared or taken into account with those that have reason. But why might not the surplus of good in the nonintelligent creatures that fill the world compensate for and even exceed incomparably the surplus of evil in rational creatures? It is true that the value of the latter is greater; but by way of compensation the others are incomparably greater in number; and it may be that the proportion of number and quantity surpasses that of value and quality.[5]

To the extent that this passage is regarded as representing Leibniz's considered and mature position—and I think that, in the final analysis, it probably should be so taken—it must be regarded as a triumph of the cold-blooded metaphysician over the moral philosopher and the Christian theologian.

This gap—or, rather, this tension—between God's universally operative *ontological* beneficence and his specifically *moral* beneficence is never satisfactorily closed by Leibniz. And to invoke at this point the aid of the Pre-Established Harmony would be to *beg* rather than to *answer* the question at issue. In any event, the idea that this tension is resolvable—and, indeed, *resolved* in this "best of all possible worlds"—is, with Leibniz, a fundamental act of philosophic faith and not a systematic part of his system, let alone a logical exigency of its principles.

Conclusion

One could, no doubt, further extend this catalogue of "Logical Difficulties in Leibniz's Metaphysics." Enough has been said, however, to exhibit the nature of these difficulties. Those which we have discerned are certainly not the sorts of outright "self-

5. Gerhardt, VI:377–378.

contradictions" which Bertrand Russell was fond of charging to Leibniz; rather, they have the nature of weak links in the chain linking various parts of a generally coherent system.

In probing for such weak spots within the structure of Leibniz's philosophy, we do not mean to disparage his philosophical powers or to detract from his stature as a philosophical workman of the very first rank. No philosophical fortress is constructed with equal strength at every point. The greatest compliment that can be paid it is to take it seriously enough to put it to the critical test of determining just where the internal weaknesses exist. Even if the critic is wrong, the considerations which point this out cannot but shed significant light upon the thought of the philosopher under discussion; and if the critic is right, his work advances the cause of philosophical understanding. Such an exercise in the critical history of philosophy has always been one of the best training grounds of philosophical work. We learn from the missteps into pitfalls that have trapped the able intellects who have walked the philosophical road before us. The discovery of their missteps cannot, of course, teach us to avoid errors altogether—but it can at least assure that the mistakes we make are original with ourselves, and not the mere rehearsal of faults already committed by others.

10

Individual Identity, Space, and Time in the Leibniz-Clarke Correspondence

N. L. Wilson

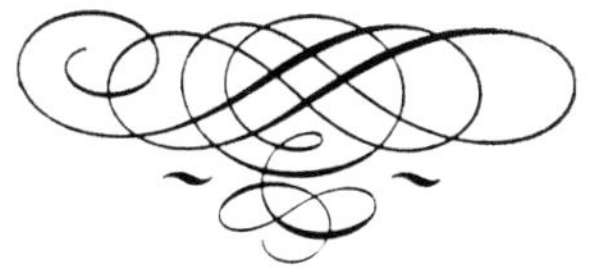

In his fourth letter to Samuel Clarke, the English philosopher, Leibniz writes:

There is no such thing as two individuals indiscernible from each other. An ingenious gentleman of my acquaintance, discoursing with me in the presence of Her Electoral Highness, the Princess Sophia, in the garden of Herrenhausen, thought he could find two leaves perfectly alike. The princess defied him to do it, and he ran [!] all over the garden a long time to look for some; but it was to no purpose.[1]

One thinks: What a delightful way of doing philosophy! Abstract reflection is combined with healthy exercise and social climbing. At the same time, one is more than a little surprised to find Leibniz supporting his *a priori* doctrine of the identity of indiscernibles with the results of a casual inspection of botanical specimens at Herrenhausen.

In reading the Leibniz-Clarke correspondence, one is left with the distinct impression that Leibniz generally gets the best of things. However, it is not all that clear. My purpose in this paper is to show that some of the results of modern technical philoso-

This paper was in part supported by a National Science Foundation grant, GS–572.

1. Gerhardt, VII:372; Loemker, p. 687.

phy can be used to illuminate the controversy. We can see more clearly where Leibniz is right (section III), where he is wrong (section II), and, in both cases, why. I am of course taking it for granted that modern technical philosophy is genuinely *clear,* and you may find this assumption dubious, since I shall have to give a necessarily condensed exposition of the semantical apparatus I propose to invoke (section I).

I

To make a start, let us consider a question that appears in P. W. Bridgman's book, *The Logic of Modern Physics*: "What would the world be like if the whole universe and everything in it were expanding at the same rate?"[2] The answer is that the world would look exactly as it does look. Elsewhere, I have used the term *Bridgman question* to characterize any question beginning, "What would the world be like if . . . ?" where the answer is, "Exactly the same as it is." Meanwhile, however, I have found that similar games are played by R. G. Boscovich[3] and by Berkeley,[4] and so, in order to spread the credits around, I prefer to call them "B"-questions.

Now Bridgman dismisses our specimen question as meaningless, but this move seems a bit speedy. The structure of the question is unobjectionable, the word *everything* is meaningful as is also the word *expands.* It seems to be the combination of the two words which gives rise to a fascinating difficulty, a difficulty which would be expressed by saying that the body of the question appears to be describing a state of affairs different from the actual, but in fact does not succeed in doing so.

Let us now consider another question: What would the world be like if Julius Caesar had all the properties of Mark Anthony and Mark Anthony had all the properties of Julius Caesar? In all

2. P. W. Bridgman, *The Logic of Modern Physics* (New York: Macmillan Co., 1927), p. 28. Bridgman is quoting from Clifford and I have paraphrased.

3. *The Leibniz-Clarke Correspondence,* edited by H. G. Alexander (Manchester: Manchester University Press, 1956), pp. xliv–xlv.

4. George Berkeley, *A Treatise Concerning the Principles of Human Knowledge,* edited by C. M. Turbayne (Indianapolis: Bobbs-Merrill Co., 1957), secs. 18, 20.

this I am assuming that the property of being called "Julius Caesar" and the property of being called "Mark Anthony," together with genealogical properties, are to be included among the properties in question. There is a feature of the present game that is worth pointing out. In phrasing the question, "What would the world be like if . . . ?", we cook it so that we can confidently answer, "Exactly the same as it is." This means that if our purpose were merely to collect "B"-questions, then the enterprise is trivial. In fact the characterization of a certain question as a "B"-question is not a conclusion, but rather a starting point for more philosophy. What I have been doing in a roundabout way is suggesting that, although one may feel inclined to quibble over our alleged "B"-question, all such quibbles can be taken care of by means of sufficiently skillful cookery. We are less interested in debating whether or not a given question is really a "B"-question than we are in actually producing a "B"-question. Then, from the fact that it is a "B"-question—from the fact, that is, that its answer is: the world would be exactly as it is—we draw certain conclusions.

In the present case, if Julius Caesar had all the properties of Mark Anthony, and *vice versa,* the world would be exactly the way it really is. From this circumstance, we conclude, to make a long story too short, that Locke's doctrine of an unknowable substratum is false—a not very exciting result, to be sure. The point is that, if, underlying every concrete individual, there were a substratum, having its own identity, so to speak, then the body of our "B"-question would describe a distinct possible world. But since this is not so, the notion of an underlying substratum is false.

However, this is by no means the end of the matter. It must be confessed that we have not really "refuted" Locke. For in drawing our conclusion, we tacitly invoked an empiricistic premise that might be stated thus: If two possible worlds look alike to their inhabitants and would be described identically by their inhabitants, then those possible worlds are identical. If somebody wanted to raise a *metaphysical* quibble to our claim that the question about Julius Caesar and Mark Anthony is in fact a "B"-question and to insist that there are really two distinct possible worlds, then we would have our work cut out for us to dislodge him.

I do not know whether we shall succeed or not, but we may as well try. The gap in the argument is related to a specific technical puzzle, which we can develop in terms of Rudolph Carnap's state-descriptions. And of course state-descriptions in Carnap's philosophy correspond to possible worlds in Leibniz's. Let us suppose that there is a true state-description couched in some suitable reconstruction of English. From this we get a second state-description by replacing the name "Julius Caesar" in each occurrence in the first by the word "Mark Anthony," and the word "Mark Anthony" in each occurrence by "Julius Caesar." The original "B"-question might now be put as: "What would the world be like if the second state-description were true, rather than the first?" The answer presumably is as before: exactly the same as it is. Yet this is strange; for if that is the correct answer, we should expect the second state-description to be logically derivable from the first. In fact it is not, and we can imagine our Lockean metaphysician saying, "See? I told you so!"

Now the theoretical apparatus behind the notion of a state-description is what I should call primary semantics. Primary semantics is the semantics of designation rules, and in it, a name is thought of as entering into a simple-minded dyadic relation with its nominatum. But primary semantics does not tell us how it manages to enter into this relation, it does not tell us how words link up with things. For that we turn to secondary semantics, which, to put it roughly, is the theory of how names in use function and how that function may be discovered.

Suppose that, in the beginning, I know nothing of Roman history. Now somebody says to me, "Caesar was a Roman general, Caesar conquered Gaul, Caesar declined to be king, Caesar was murdered on the Ides of March." My task is to discover what the name "Caesar" signifies (*not* means!) in the speaker's language, and that is the same as discovering what individual it names. (Obviously, there are some peculiarities in this semantical method, but they need not detain us.) Initially, I know only that "Caesar" is being used as a name, *i.e.*, that just one person, if any, is being talked about. So what is conveyed to me by these four statements is just this: "There exists precisely one x such that x was a Roman general, conquered Gaul, declined to be king and was murdered on the Ides of March." ("E!(ιx) (x was a Roman general, etc.") At this point I shall skip on to the conclusion, even though the situation needs to be (and has been[5]) elaborated. The conclusion is that proper names are really variables. When a person uses a proper name for the first time, that occurrence is tacitly prefixed with an E!-iota operator and the scope of that operator remains open until that person has said his last words.

What I—as field-worker—can do now is to investigate Roman history. I discover that there is just one person, namely Julius Caesar, who fits the characterization given. I conclude that, in the language of my speaker, his name "Caesar" does indeed designate (name, signify) the historical Julius Caesar. At this point I am safely back in primary semantics—if that's where I want to be.[6] It is important to note that primary semantics is *a posteriori,* and not just in the sense that I get empirical knowledge of a person's language behavior, but in the sense that here, at least, it involves knowledge of Roman history. I have to have the knowledge of Roman history before I can write the designation rule. Specifically, it is not just the primary semantics of a used language, but the primary semantics of even an artificial language that is in a clear sense *a posteriori,* and that is of course because the metalanguage we use in either case is a used language. We may conclude that secondary semantics is the "deeper" field, at least in the sense of being more nearly *a priori.*

5. The interested reader is referred to: N. L. Wilson, *The Concept of Language* (Toronto: University of Toronto Press, 1959), and more especially to "Substances without Substrata," *Review of Metaphysics* XII (1959): 521–539, and "The Trouble with Meanings," *Dialogue* III (1964): 52–64.

6. A more perspicuous example might be this: Suppose I go to the University of Outer Siberia to give a paper on Aristocles. I tell my audience that Aristocles was born in 428 B.C., the son of Ariston. He studied with Socrates and after Socrates's death devoted himself to the writing of philosophical dialogues designed to preserve the memory of his teacher. Aristocles gave up the idea of going into politics and founded the Academy in 387. Sooner or later it will dawn on Outer Siberians that by "Aristocles" I intend to signify Plato, and it dawns on them because they already know quite a lot about Plato.

The important thesis is, of course, the thesis that proper names are really variables. The argumentation has perhaps been sketchy, but we may supply it with a kind of confirmation by using it to resolve the puzzle about the two state-descriptions—both describing the actual world but not being inter-derivable. Let us suppose that the proper names in those state-descriptions are variables and that both state-descriptions (which must now be regarded as open) are next prefixed with enough E!-iota operators to close them. Now one state-description is derivable from the other by the simple operation of relettering. They are logically equivalent and must describe the same possible world.

Suppose I am given "$(\exists x)$ $(\exists y)$ (Fx & Gy)" and "$(\exists y)$ $(\exists x)$ (Fy & Gx)." These are logically equivalent, one being derived from the other by successive reletterings. If I deny that they are logically equivalent, then I am guilty of a metalinguistic contradiction.

We may now round things out a bit. In primary semantics we have to say something like this: The two state-descriptions are incompatible. If one is true, then the other is false and must therefore describe a distinct possible, non-actual world. Nevertheless, as empiricists, we claim that the possible worlds are really identical, and that it is absurd, philosophically fruitless, and downright bad manners to maintain otherwise. In secondary semantics we may be more blunt: It is simply self-contradictory to claim that the two state-descriptions describe distinct possible worlds. (See the example in the preceding paragraph.) This, it seems to me, is reasonably close to being a refutation of Locke.

There are two other relevant "B"-questions and these we may treat in summary fashion. "What would the world be like if everything in it were one mile north of its actual location?" and "What would the world be like if every event occurred one year earlier than the date at which it actually occurs?" In both cases the answers are, presumably: Exactly the same. And from the fact that we have "B"-questions, we swiftly conclude that space and time are relative; for if they were absolute, then our two questions would give us distinct possible worlds, not the same actual world all over again. As in the preceding case, we will have the doctrine that place-names and date-names are really variables. Certain complications arise, however, if co-ordinate systems are imposed on space and time. Places and dates now have internal relations, and these must be left intact in any relettering. But all this comes under the heading of advanced cookery and can be by-passed for present purposes.

Let us say that Locke is giving us a doctrine of absolute individuals. Then what Locke, on the one hand, and Newton and Clarke, on the other, are jointly saying is this: Individuals have an absolute identity independent of the properties that happen to characterize them. Places and dates have an absolute identity independent of the way in which individuals and events are actually distributed throughout space and time. All this represents a kind of prototype of logical atomism, and I think it has been shown to be, in some respectable sense, philosophically false. Readers with a taste for the history of ideas will take satisfaction in noting that Locke's *Essay* appeared in 1690, just three years after the publication of Newton's *Principia Mathematica.*

II

It is time now to turn back to the Leibniz-Clarke controversy, and in particular to lend a hand to the Princess Sophia and her house guests in raking up those leaves at Herrenhausen.

Those of us who think of ourselves as Leibnizians in the matter of identity may be buying rather less than Leibniz was actually trying to sell. What we buy is the notion that identity is to be defined in terms of the so-called Leibniz Law: Two things are identical if and only if they have all their properties in common. But it is clear from the extraordinary goings-on in the garden at Herrenhausen that Leibniz, in the doctrine of the identity of indiscernibles, intended something more: Two things are identical if and only if they have all their non-spatio-temporal properties in common. (I shall refer to these latter properties as "intrinsic" properties, because I want to keep away from the word *indiscernible.*) A "contrapositive" phrasing is perhaps more to the point: Two things are distinct if and only if they differ with respect to some *intrinsic* property. In a word, no two things can be exact replicas of each other. This version of the doctrine would appear to be synthetic and empirical. One is tempted to suppose that Leibniz himself thought so, since he appears willing to concede, in the presence of Her Electoral Highness, at least, that his doctrine might be empirically falsified. I think that what he actually has in mind is the possibility of the observable facts serving as a sort of check on his *a priori* reasoning, much as I might check my *a priori* arithmetical reasoning against the observable behavior of an adding machine. But the doctrine, in addition, appears to be almost certainly false. I think it likely that somewhere there exist two electrons that are replicas of each other. It is thus no accident that we find Leibniz continuing the Herrenhausen passage with this observation:

> Two drops of water or milk, viewed with a microscope, will appear distinguishable from each other. This is an argument against atoms, which are confuted, as well as a vacuum, by the principles of true metaphysics.[7]

But we must ask ourselves: What were the considerations that led Leibniz to imagine that he had an *a priori* proof of his strong version of the identity of indiscernibles? First of all, of course, is the principle of sufficient reason. But this, I think, is made to depend on a prior principle, which I shall call the principle of the impossibility of divine embarrassment, which in turn is derived from the principle of God's perfection. We must now examine how these all fit together.

Let us suppose, for the sake of a counter-example, that, on the lowest branch of a large oak tree in the garden at Herrenhausen, there is a leaf, which we shall call *a*; and on the second branch there is an exact replica of *a*, which we shall call *b*. (Incidentally, Leibniz could resist the suggestion that these leaves falsify his doctrine, unless it were stipulated that they are intrinsically identical at every moment of their lives, but we may neglect this complication.) Now, offhand, it would seem that all we can squeeze out of the principle of sufficient reason is the proposition that, if there are two intrinsically identical leaves on this oak tree, there must be a reason for the fact. But it is more complicated than that, as comes out in the rhetorical question: What reason

7. Gerhardt, VII:372; Loemker, p. 687. Leibniz is committed on other grounds to the ancient idea of the world as a plenum. See the *post scriptum* of his fourth letter.

could there be for *a* being on the bottom branch and *b* being on the second branch instead of *a* being on the second branch and *b* being on the bottom branch? The matter may be put in more relevant theological terms: given the alleged actual world with *a* on the bottom and *b* on the second branch, then there is a possible non-actual world in which the positions of *a* and *b* are reversed. What reason could God have had for creating this actual world rather than the possible world? As Leibniz puts it,

> I infer from that principle [the principle of sufficient reason] . . . that there are not in nature two real, absolute beings, indiscernible from each other, because, if there were, God and nature would act without reason in ordering the one otherwise than the other; and that therefore God does not produce two pieces of matter perfectly equal and alike.[8]

In other words, confronted with the option of creating one of these two possible worlds, one with *a* above *b* and the other with *b* above *a,* God would be in the embarrassing position of being unable to make up his mind which one to create. Such embarrassment and the necessity for an arbitrary choice would derogate from the perfection of God. After all, one can hardly avoid thinking at this point of Buridan's Ass.

The march of the argument appears, then, to be this: God is perfect. From this it follows that everything that God does, he does for a sufficient reason, consonant, of course, with his divine nature. In the world that God creates there must be a sufficient reason for everything being as it is, but that is not quite the point. The real point seems to be this: a possible world containing pairs of mutual replicas—and such a possible world comes in a family of at least two—is ruled out as a candidate for actualization for the sufficient reason that it affords God no sufficient reason for choosing *it* rather than some other member of its family. Hence our counter-example involving leaves *a* and *b* is impossible: there could not have been two intrinsically identical leaves in the garden at Herrenhausen.

Now in connection with God's alleged embarrassment, one can, without too much difficulty, imagine God taking particular satisfaction in arbitrarily choosing one of these two equally attractive

8. Gerhardt, VII:393; Loemker, p. 699.

possible worlds and thereby placing two intrinsically identical leaves in the path of that ingenious and energetic acquaintance of Leibniz, for the sufficient reason of giving a lesson in humility to a certain famous German philosopher. This is whimsy, of course, not philosophy; but it points up a fact which never seems to have occurred to Leibniz, the fact that God might have very good reasons for wanting to place one or more replica pairs in the world and that, if such a wish on God's part were somehow thwarted by "the absolute and necessary nature of things," then this equally would be a derogation from God's perfection. This point certainly crossed Clarke's mind.[9] Had Leibniz lived long enough to take Clarke's observation seriously, he might sooner or later have tumbled to the flaw in his argument.

The flaw is that the argument presupposes that leaf *a* and leaf *b* each have an identity apart from their location on their respective branches. In short, we have something like Locke's doctrine of the substratum or what I have been calling the doctrine of absolute individuals.

At this point we naturally turn to Leibniz's *Nouveaux Essais* to see just what Leibniz has to say about what Locke has to say about our complex idea of substance in general.[10] What we find is curious: the notion of substance is something of an embarrassment to Locke. The program of the *Essay* requires him to show how our complex idea of substance is derived from simple ideas of sensation and reflection. And as Hume easily shows, this cannot be done.[11] Yet Locke cannot give up the view that underlying each thing is its substance or substratum, because, as he puts it to Stillingfleet, "*We cannot conceive how qualities should subsist by themselves.*"[12] So he ends up by accepting substance, but calling substance and our idea of it nasty names. He mentions our idea of "the supposed, but unknown, support of . . . quali-

9. Gerhardt, VII:423–424.

10. *Nouveaux Essais*, bk. II, chap. 23, secs. 1, 2; Gerhardt, V:201–210.

11. David Hume, *A Treatise of Human Nature* (Oxford: Clarendon Press, 1888), I, I, sec. vi.

12. John Locke, *An Essay Concerning Human Understanding*, edited by A. C. Fraser (Oxford: Clarendon Press, 1894), I, 108.

ties" and "an obscure and relative idea of substance in general,"[13] and again "the confused idea of something to which [simple ideas] belong."[14]

Leibniz's main quarrel is with this ambivalence. There is no "inadvertence," he says, in attributing several ideas to a simple subject; on the contrary, there are good philosophical reasons for doing so. Nor is there any point in ridiculing philosophers by likening them to the Indian who had the earth resting on an elephant, which rested on a tortoise which rested on something he knew not what. If Leibniz has the advantage over Locke in this passage, it is perhaps because, unlike Locke, he distinguishes between properties in things and ideas in the mind, and also because he is not in the grip of an imagist psychology. Leibniz emerges from the passage as a sort of Locke-without-misgivings. So it is not surprising to find that difficulties charged against Locke also appear in Leibniz.

But all this is too simple; to get a more accurate picture of Leibniz's view, let us go back to those two leaves. It might be thought that the intrinsic identity of *a* and *b* is really a red herring; for even if they are intrinsically different, with intrinsic properties *P* and *Q* respectively, there is still the rhetorical question: What reason would God have had for making *a* exemplify *P* and putting it on the lower branch and making *b* exemplify *Q* and putting it on the second branch, rather than *vice versa*? By parity of reasoning, Leibniz ought to have concluded that God could not have put any leaves at all in the garden at Herrenhausen, in fact could not have put anything anywhere. As stated in this fashion, the problem is formally identical with that presented earlier with Julius Caesar and Mark Anthony and is now in its general form. We might go on to claim that Leibniz has got hold of a very special case of a general puzzle and his principle of the identity of indiscernibles is simply an *ad hoc* device for getting himself off the particular hook.

Leibniz's answer would, I think, be as follows: The identity of

13. *Ibid.*, 392.
14. *Ibid.*, 393.

a thing is bound up with its intrinsic properties, and on this account the supposition that *a* could have intrinsic properties different from what it actually has, and still be *a*, is false. Thus the earlier example with Julius Caesar and Mark Anthony may represent a problem for Locke, but it is no problem for Leibniz.

Before we bid final farewell to Herrenhausen, perhaps we had better tidy up. Let *P* stand for the conjunction of all those intrinsic properties which leaves *a* and *b* have in common. The relevant alleged fact is reported as

a is *P* and *a* is on the bottom branch (of . . .) and *b* is *P* and is on the second branch (of . . .).

What would the world be like if *a* had *all* of *b*'s properties and conversely? Exactly the same—or so, as empiricists, we baldly claim. There is no distinct possible world. In secondary semantics the foregoing becomes rephrased as:

$$E\,!(\iota a)\ [a \text{ is P etc.} \ldots \text{ and } E\,!\,(\iota b)\ (b \text{ is P etc.} \ldots)]$$

Relettering, with *a* for *b* and *b* for *a*, produces a sentence logically equivalent to what we started with. It does not describe a distinct alternative state of affairs. God could, without the embarrassment of having to make an arbitrary choice, have put two intrinsically identical leaves in the garden at Herrenhausen; and there need not have been any violation of the principle of sufficient reason.

Throughout the correspondence Clarke steadfastly refuses to go along with Leibniz in his mistake, but he has all the wrong reasons. On this account we may judge the first match a draw.

III

Let us now turn to the discussion of space and time, which is somewhat complicated by the fact that it takes several exchanges before the disputants flounder through to the heart of the matter. The discussion takes off from the principle of sufficient reason and the identity of indiscernibles. Clarke writes:

'Tis very true that nothing is without a sufficient reason why it is and why it is thus rather than otherwise. And therefore, where there is no cause, there can be no effect. But this sufficient reason is ofttimes no other than the mere will of God. For instance, why this particular system of matter should be created in one particular place, when (all place being absolutely indifferent to all matter) it would have been exactly the same thing vice versa, supposing the two systems (or the particles) of matter to be alike; there can be no other reason but the mere will of God. Which if it could in no case act without a predetermining cause, any more than a balance can move without a preponderating weight, this would tend to take away all power of choosing and to introduce fatality.[15]

What we have here is, in effect, the leaf example. It may be noted in passing that Clarke is inconsistent. He insists that the two alternatives are not really two at all, but really the same. He also says that the alternatives present God with the necessity of making a choice, but that God may nevertheless effect the choice between these two distinct but indifferent alternatives merely from his own will.

Leibniz's reply is worth quoting almost in full:

> The author grants me this important principle, that nothing happens without a sufficient reason why it should be so rather than otherwise. But he grants it only in words and in reality denies it. Which shows that he does not fully perceive the strength of it. And therefore he makes use of an instance which exactly falls in with one of my demonstrations against real absolute space, which is an idol of some modern Englishmen. . . .
>
> As for my own opinion, I have said more than once that I hold space to be something merely relative, as time is: that I hold it to be an order of coexistences as time is an order of successions. For space denotes, in terms of possibility, an order of things which exist at the same time, considered as existing together, without enquiring into their particular manner of existing. And when many things are seen together, one perceives that order of things among themselves.
>
> I have many demonstrations to confute the fancy of those who take space to be a substance or at least an absolute being. But I shall only use, at the present, one demonstration, which the author here gives me occasion to insist upon. I say, then, that if space was an absolute being, there would something happen for which it would be impossible there should be a sufficient reason. Which is against my axiom. And I prove it thus. Space is something absolutely uniform, and, without the

15. Gerhardt, VII:359–360; Loemker, p. 680.

things placed in it, one point of space does not absolutely differ in any respect whatsoever from another point of space. Now from hence it follows (supposing space to be something in itself, besides the order of bodies among themselves) that 'tis impossible there should be a reason why God, preserving the same situations of bodies among themselves, should have placed them in space after one certain particular manner and not otherwise; why everything was not placed the quite contrary way, for instance, by changing east into west.

It would perhaps have made a clearer example if Leibniz had simply suggested the possibility of everything being located one mile north of its actual location.

But [Leibniz continues] if space is nothing else but that order or relation, and is nothing at all without bodies but the possibility of placing them, then those two states, the one such as it now is, the other supposed to be the quite contrary way, would not at all differ from one another. Their difference therefore is only to be found in our chimerical supposition of the reality of space in itself. But in truth the one would exactly be the same thing as the other, they being absolutely indiscernible, and consequently there is no room to enquire after a reason of the preference of the one to the other.[16]

It is worth noting that Leibniz has passed to a different principle of the identity of indiscernibles. The first principle—that two individuals are identical if and only if they have all their intrinsic properties in common—is almost certainly false. The present principle—two *possible worlds* are identical if they are "indiscernible" —amounts to the empiricistic principle mentioned in section I and is, I should think, true. Leibniz goes on:

The case is the same with respect to time. Supposing any one should ask why God did not create everything a year sooner, and the same person should infer from thence that God has done something concerning which 'tis not possible there should be a reason why he did it so and not otherwise; the answer is that his inference would be right if time was any thing distinct from things existing in time. For it would be impossible there should be any reason why things should be applied to such particular instants rather than to others, their succession continuing the same. But then the same argument proves that instants,

16. Secs. 2–5, Gerhardt, VII:363–364; cf. Loemker, p. 682.

considered without the things, are nothing at all and that they consist only in the successive order of things, which order remaining the same, one of the two states, viz., that of a supposed anticipation, would not at all differ, nor could be discerned from the other which now is.[17]

Leibniz's argument appears, offhand, to be this: God must not be confronted with any embarrassing choices. Absolute space and time would in fact do so. Therefore space and time are not absolute. This would appear to be a pretty extraordinary argument. But perhaps a more charitable estimate of Leibniz's mental processes would be this: It is the clash between the principle of sufficient reason and the conception of space and time as absolute that jars Leibniz into a more or less intuitive realization that space and time must be relative. Under pressure from Clarke, he will beef up his arguments.

In his third reply to Leibniz, Clarke begins to apply the pressure:

There is this evident absurdity in supposing space not to be real but to be merely the order of bodies—that, according to that notion, if the earth and sun and moon had been placed where the remotest fixed stars now are, provided they were placed in the same order and distance they now are with regard one to another, it would not only have been (as this learned author rightly says) *la même chose,* the same thing in effect, which is very true; but it would also follow that they would then have been in the same place too as they are now, which is an express contradiction.

Clarke's use of the word *contradiction* suggests that he is still at the level of primary semantics, so to speak. In a later paragraph, he writes:

If space was nothing but the order of things coexisting, it would follow that if God should remove in a straight line the whole material world entire, with any swiftness whatsoever, yet it would still always continue in the same place, and that nothing would receive any shock upon the most sudden stopping of that motion. And if time was noth-

17. Gerhardt, VII:364; Loemker, pp. 682–683. One is reminded at this point of Parmenides's argument against the possibility of being coming to be from nonbeing: "And what need would have driven it [what is] on to grow, starting from nothing, at a later time rather than an earlier" (Fr. 8, as translated in Kirk and Raven).

ing but the order of succession of created things, it would follow, that if God had created the world millions of ages sooner than he did, yet it would not have been created at all the sooner.[18]

Clarke is not saying quite what we want him to say. In the first example (in the third reply), we can at most assume that Clarke intends that if our solar system had been placed where the remotest stars are, then all the fixed stars would have been subjected to a comparable shift. Otherwise we would not have a "B"-question. The second example introduces the red herring of acceleration. We will point out simply that total motion north followed by deceleration is indistinguishable from a state of rest followed by total acceleration southwards, and let it go at that. The third example—that of God creating the world millions of years earlier—does correspond without tinkering to a "B"-question.

Leibniz, who by this time is becoming a trifle waspish, replies:

> But when once it has been shown that the beginning, whenever it was, is always the same thing, the question why it was not otherwise ordered becomes needless and insignificant.

By "insignificant," Leibniz presumably means "meaningless," and here one is reminded of Bridgman's reaction to "B"-questions. Leibniz goes on:

> If space and time were anything absolute, that is, if they were anything else besides certain orders of things, then indeed my assertion would be a contradiction. But since it is not so, the hypothesis (that space and time are anything absolute) is contradictory, that is, 'tis an impossible fiction.[19]

In his reply to all this, Clarke writes:

> If the world be finite in dimensions, it is movable by the power of God, and therefore my argument drawn from that movableness is conclusive. Two places, though exactly alike, are not the same place. Nor is the motion or rest of the universe the same state, any more than the motion or rest of a ship is the same state, because a man shut up in the cabin cannot perceive whether the ship sails or not, so long as it moves uniformly. The motion of the ship, though the man perceives

18. Gerhardt, VII:368–369; cf. Loemker, p. 685.
19. Gerhardt, VII:373–374; Loemker, p. 688.

it not, is a real different state, and has real different effects and upon a sudden stop it would have other real effects; and so likewise would an indiscernible motion of the universe. To this argument no answer has ever been given.[20]

In his fifth paper, Leibniz finally and succinctly hits the nail on the head:

The author replies now that the reality of motion does not depend upon being observed and that a ship may go forward, and yet a man who is in the ship may not perceive it. I answer, motion does not indeed depend upon being observed, but it does depend upon being possible to be observed. There is no motion when there is no change that can be observed. And when there is no change that can be observed, there is no change at all.[21]

I shall expand Leibniz's remarks so as to tie them in more closely with previous interpretations. Leibniz is, in effect, enunciating an empiricist principle: If a change is to be real, it must be observable. We would have a "third" principle of the identity of indiscernibles: Two momentary states of the world (not total possible worlds) are identical in a certain respect (here, location) if there is no discernible difference between them in that respect. I use "scare quotes" around *third* because we have what is really a special case of the identity of indiscernibles for possible words, as comes out in the "B"-question: What would the world be like if there were such and such an unobservable change? (Exactly the same.) Leibniz would certainly assent to the following: A possible world is identical with the actual if it is indiscernible from it, i.e., if there is nothing about the possible world that would compel its inhabitants to describe it differently from the way we describe our actual world.

In the present passage, theology appears to be given up in favor of a purely secular argument. Ironically, Leibniz does not realize that, here, he has his best argument. He continues:

The contrary opinion is grounded upon the supposition of a real absolute space, which I have demonstratively confuted by the principle of the want [besoin] of a sufficient reason of things.

20. Gerhardt, VII:384; cf. Loemker, p. 693.
21. Gerhardt, VII:403–404; cf. Loemker, p. 705.

This passage suggests that Leibniz never really gave up the "extraordinary" argument dealt with earlier.

On the question of time, Leibniz writes:

> As to the question whether God could have created the world sooner, 'tis necessary here to understand each other rightly. Since I have demonstrated that time, without things, is nothing else but a mere ideal possibility, 'tis manifest if any one should say that this same world which has been actually created might have been created sooner without any other change, he would say nothing that is intelligible. For there is no mark or difference whereby it would be possible to know that this world was created sooner.[22]

Leibniz is again saying, rightly, I should think, that a difference which would make no difference to us, is no difference at all—and here it is a difference between two possible worlds, not a difference-in-a-respect between two momentary states of a world.

I think we may stop here. By way of conclusion, I shall simply point out that there is a certain irony in the whole exchange. In the matter of the relativity of space and time, Leibniz was lucky enough to get hold of the right end of the stick. Yet it was Newton's views which were to prevail for the next two hundred years or so. And that was perhaps because in other respects—namely, in the matter of action at a distance, although Newton was not clear on this—it was Newton who had the right end of the stick.

22. Gerhardt, VII:404–405; Loemker, pp. 706–707.

11

The Ethical Import of the Leibnizian System

Leroy E. Loemker

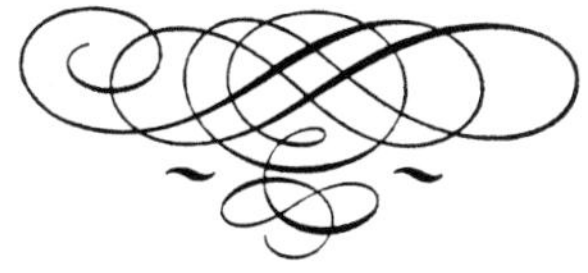

ALTHOUGH LEIBNIZ never prepared a systematic exposition of ethical theory, his frequent comments upon the problems of ethics give evidence, not merely of his concern, but also of his conviction that these problems can be as adequately answered through his system as are the problems of science. It is the argument of this paper that the interpretation of knowledge and of truth, which he developed for the sciences and metaphysics, are directly applicable to the knowledge of the good and the right as well, and that this extension was an essential and explicit aspect of his thought.

Since G. E. Moore's attack on the naturalistic fallacy in his *Principia Ethica* (1904), there exists a radical schism between the discussion of ethical problems and an analytic metaethics which undertakes to investigate the meaning and validity of moral statements. In the center of the discussion are questions like the following: What are the essential ethical predicates? Taken as

A German version of this essay was read at the International Leibniz Congress held in Hanover, November 14–19, 1967, and was subsequently published by Franz Steiner Verlag GmbH in *Studia Leibniziana Supplementa* IV (1969):63–76.

modes of language, what do these predicates mean or intend? Is it meaningful to attribute truth or falsehood to moral statements? If so, how can they be verified or justified, and to what extent? Can the meaning of the good, the right, the obligatory, be determined without committing the naturalistic fallacy? Between a religious ethic which rests upon revelation without rational amplification, and a linguistic-phenomenological analysis of the primary notion, there lies a wide gap in which the living moral issues are ignored or forgotten. In this ethical situation, too, Leibniz can offer instruction.

I

It requires only a superficial reading of Leibniz's writings to see that the ethical considerations are central to his system, and also that they are closely bound to his theoretical thought. Throughout his mature writing, Leibniz never deviated from his early conviction that "when we view the disciplines in and for themselves, they are all theoretical; when we view their application (*usum*), they are all practical."[1] A remark of 1693, to which Erich Hochstetter has recently called attention,[2] shows that Leibniz considered his whole system to be ethically oriented, for he writes that he is contemplating a moral philosopher's stone ("einen Lapidem Philosophicum moralem"), and should like to take this for the *ergon*, everything else for the *parergon*.

In his various discussions of method, Leibniz frequently discussed metaphysics and moral science together.[3] In his judgment, justice and other virtues depend upon metaphysics:

> We must recognize that the true morality is related to metaphysics as practice is to theory, because the knowledge of spirits all together, and particularly of God and the soul, depends upon the nature of sub-

1. *Dissertatio de Arte Combinatoria* (1666), Theses for Disputation, Gerhardt, IV:41, footnote; cf. Loemker, p. 74.

2. E. Hochstetter, *Zu Leibniz Gedächtnis* (Berlin: DeGruyter, 1948), pp. 62–63.

3. For example, the letter to Antoine Arnauld, October 1687 (Gerhardt, II:111–129; Loemker, pp. 338–348); and the *Nouveaux Essais*, bk. IV, chap. 8; Gerhardt, V, especially p. 413.

stances, and this knowledge imparts to justice and virtue their proper scope.[4]

Although his own thought was aimed at a *philosophia perennis* which should preserve what is true in all past systems, he showed no great confidence in the traditional schools of ethics; in them, he sensed the lack of a spirit of joy and of positive well-being; in the *Théodicée,* he wrote:

> The systems of Epicureans and Stoics are as different from true morality as patience is different from joy. For their tranquillity is grounded solely on necessity; our tranquillity, on the other hand, should rest on the beauty of things and on our own felicity.[5]

Thus he wrote to Duke Rudolf August of Brunswick that his ethics "is grounded, not on hope or fear, but solely and alone on the beauty and perfection of God."[6] The goal of ethics was to be regarded as setting up, not a system of thought, but an order of life. As he wrote to the Jesuit Pere Bouvet, a founder of the China mission, "The true practical philosophy—*vera, non simulata,* as our jurisconsults say—consists rather in good orders for education and for conversation and the social relations of men."[7]

Leibniz's motto, *Theoria cum praxi,* therefore, involves no duality in his pattern of thought. Such a unity and action, though implicit in the teaching on method of men like Jacobi Zabarella, is particularly important in a thinker whose work is completed, not in a philosophical system, but in his comprehensive, unified program of projects for the peace and well-being of Europe, indeed, of the entire known world. Leibniz's philosophy was not only an instrument but also a plan for this goal.

Georg Lukács was thus right in describing Leibniz's thought as "a philosophical diplomacy."[8] It was an attempt to give the peoples of Europe a preview of the best of all possible orders of

4. Gerhardt, V:413.

5. *Théodicée,* Gerhardt, VI:268.

6. Onno Klopp, *Correspondance de Leibniz avec l'electrice Sophie de Brunswick-Lunebourg* (Hanover: Klindworth, 1874), II, 65.

7. Dutens, II, i:262–263.

8. Georg Lukács, *Die Zerstörung der Vernunft* (Berlin: H. Luchterhand, 1960), p. 80.

life which an age of new discoveries, new possibilities, but old conflicts, could offer. Indeed, this goal of the best possible is built into Leibniz's thought as the first principle of existence. According to his own reports, he studied mathematics in Paris chiefly to find a new method of certainty in theology. Theology, however, was for him, as was ethics, merely universal jurisprudence. Theology, in turn, was to be not only the keystone of his metaphysical system, but also the ground on which the conversion of nonbelievers and the reunification of Christendom were to be achieved. Furthermore, metaphysics was to serve, *theoretically*, to provide the first principles and primary notions of the sciences and to define the values of science for humanity; *practically*, it was to serve as an apologetic to persuade those important men upon whom Leibniz depended to carry out his great projects for human welfare.

Who were these men? One finds them named as those to whom his letters were addressed, and they are defined in his metaphysics. They were the possessors of power who also showed wisdom and a love for their fellow men. Not only political power was needed. All his life, it is true, Leibniz dreamed of winning the support and influence of "a great monarch"—although Louis XIV of France, the great Sun King, the Emperor Charles VI, and Peter the Great of Russia all disappointed him. But he sought other, less material, powers as well. In general these powers belonged to three classes of men: statesmen and nobility, theologians and ecclesiastics, and scientists, engineers and scholars—members of the Republic of Letters and of Learning. In each man, Leibniz sought the power appropriate to his station—political, ecclesiastical, or intellectual and persuasive. In all men, he presupposed reasonableness and moral responsibility. Thus the ideal to be achieved—the harmonious actualization of the best possibilities for all men—and the human instruments through whom this ideal was to be achieved, both found their significance defined in the Leibnizian metaphysics. For they all expressed, each from his own point of view (or according to the law of his nature) the highest perfections of God: power, wisdom, love, and the combination of these three, justice.

Here one finds the basis for the fundamental concepts and definitions of Leibniz's ethics. Justice is the love of the wise man. Love is one's own joy over the happiness (or the perfection) of another. The good is the affection of joy which arises from the perception of a higher grade of perfection. Behind these definitions, however, is the reality which Leibniz's philosophy is to evoke. This is a unitary and unifying virtue which is grounded in the order and dynamism of the universe. Frequently Leibniz designates this virtue as "honestas," the Stoic virtue, though he gives it a fresh, emotionally deepened, human meaning. The heart of *honestas* (or *honnêteté*) is *generosité*, which might be rendered great-heartedness. Leibniz rejects both the Cartesian physiological interpretation of "generosity" (although he admits that this might serve a purpose in medicine) and the negative, merely external meaning given this virtue toward the turn of the century. (At that time, he says, *honnêteté* was reduced to "doing no baseness."[9] The *homo honestatis* is the man who knows the internal source of his power and his duty in the law of his nature. Therefore he is great-hearted, just, and benevolent. Generosity is the law of his being; joyous obedience is his formal virtue, rooted in the metaphysics of creation and the imperative frame of all moral principles: "Right is the possibility, Obligation is the necessity, of the good man."[10] *Honestas* is thus based upon personal commitment to God, whose perfections are revealed in finite measures in the law of the individual, and therefore also (for human individuals) is a Kingdom of Grace, in which all spirits are involved through those individual traits which they have in common. *Obligatio* is the loyalty of each to the law of his nature, and therefore also to the unity of all men, of which unity each is a part. "We all have a part," Leibniz says, "in the universal Republic whose ruler is God, and the great law of this Republic is this: to attain the greatest state of the good which is possible for us."[11]

9. *Nouveaux Essais*, bk. IV, chap. 16, sec. 4; Gerhardt, V:444. See also the remarks on Shaftesbury's *Characteristics*, Gerhardt, III:423–431; Loemker, pp. 629–635.

10. "Jus est potentia, obligatio est necessitas viri boni" (Dutens, IV, iii:183, 185, *et passim*).

11. Gerhardt, VII:106–107.

II

This close fusion of the theoretical with the practical in Leibniz's philosophy may best be approached through his adaptation of the old doctrine of the transcendentals. The doctrine of the convertibility (or of the logical equivalence) of the transcendental predicates (*unum, verum, bonum,* and sometimes *pulchrum*) with *being* was variously qualified, simplified, and even subjectified in the seventeenth century. However, in Leibniz's metaphysics, they still stand together, their relations qualified by definitions, but their unity justified in the unity of the simple perfections of God and therefore also mirrored in the individual substances of his creation. In the marginal notes which Leibniz as a young student made on John Bisterfeld's *Philosophiae Primae Seminarium,* he added to the discussion of "Being and its Concepts" (*est, debet, potest*) the corresponding fields of human knowledge: *scientia, prudentia,* and *ars.* To Bisterfeld's "Rules of Being," particularly "No being is absolute," "No being is self-sufficient, all being is symbiotic," and "No being is so lowly that it has no commensurate action," Leibniz adds, "and becomes a worthless member of the Republic of Being"—perhaps the earliest reference in his writings to a "Republic of Spirits."[12] In his great *Encyclopedia,* Bisterfeld's teacher, Heinrich Alsted, had added to the *primae modes* of being (*unum, verum,* and *bonum*) a list of *modes ortivae*: *ordo, numerus, perfection,* and *pulchritudo.* Later, Leibniz sometimes threw many or all of these general attributes of being together indiscriminately. For example, in a well-known summary of his ethical views, he subsumes under the two prime determinants of being—power and harmony—a list of interrelated derivative attributes. He writes: "From this, one can see how happiness, pleasure, love, perfection, being, power, freedom, harmony, order, and beauty are all interbound, something which very few have rightly seen."[13]

Leibniz then develops this doctrine analytically through more specific definitions in his metaphysics, though his logical studies

12. Academy Ed., VI, i:151–160, 166.
13. Gerhardt, VII:87.

seem also to suggest approaches to it.[14] The attributes of being are grounded in the unified power of being and are mirrored in every individual creature according to its degree of perfection—though in a moral way only in self-conscious spirits—and are completed in harmony—that is, in the return of plurality to unity.

The unity of being with its two attributes, *verum* and *bonum*, is not only mirrored in every individual, however. It also appears as a unity in every true affirmative proposition. No true proposition is without a reference to being (*res*), and no true proposition of a metaphysical or scientific nature is without ethical significance; this is assured by the principle of the best possible.

Leibniz thus teaches distinctly what ethical thinkers of today are once more beginning to admit: that moral statements or propositions cannot be separated sharply from descriptive ones. Whether imperative or prescriptive or permissive or emotive, all moral propositions have some claim to truth and to descriptive meaning in some sense.

Their factual sense cannot, however, be reduced simply to mere experience. Leibniz made this very clear against what he called John Locke's "arbitrary nominal definitions of virtues and vices." The good and the right cannot be reduced to "that which men praise or condemn"—an opinion which many more recent moralists have shared with Locke. "This interpretation," says Leibniz, "does not conform to usage, nor indeed, is it useful for edification. [It] would sound idle in the ears of many people if anyone should introduce it into practical life and conversation, as this author himself seems to admit in his preface."[15] Moral statements do, it is true, depend upon empirical data, but they are grounded in metaphysics. Leibniz does not commit the naturalistic fallacy as G. E. Moore describes it.

III

It is clear from the *Nouveaux Essais* and related writings that, in his mature period, Leibniz regarded moral truths as *truths of*

14. See the *Inquisitiones Generales*, sec. 151 (*est res*); sec. 144 (*est ens seu res*); sec. 138; sec. 198 (*est verum*); in Couturat, pp. 356–399.

15. *Nouveaux Essais*, bk. 11, chap. 28, sec. 10; Gerhardt, V:233.

fact, not as *truths of reason,* although they are in part determined by truths of reason. Moral truths are therefore to be classed as "mixed truths of fact" which are formed by truths of reason *a priori,* but are derived also from simpler truths of fact as well and must be verified by their predictive success in anticipating future experiences—in this case, future actions.[16]

It is true that, in an early paper on the *Elements of Law,* Leibniz assigned the doctrine of the law to those fields "which rest, not on experience, but on the definitions and demonstrations of reason."[17] And of course, this is as true of the *principles* of the law as it is for principles which are valid in any discipline. As Leibniz frequently and consistently shows, principles are derived from the laws of logic, the principle of sufficient reason, and that of the best possible, rendered applicable to each field in which they are relevant through the definitions which adapt them to that field. The content of the definitions, however, which serve thus to particularize principles and to make them contextually relevant, derive ultimately from experience. Thus, specified principles, though *a priori* and necessary to knowledge in a particular field, always depend to a degree upon previous experience, given a ground of necessity through *first* principles. Leibniz writes in the *Nouveaux Essais* that moral knowledge "is not truth known through reason alone, since it rests upon inner experience or confused knowledge, since there is no adequate knowledge of what pleasure and unpleasantness are."[18] And again: "As concerns morality, a part of it is entirely grounded in reason, but there is also another part which depends upon experiences and refers to the temperaments."[19]

Moral truths, therefore, belong to a particular genus of mixed truths of fact, which contain such predicates as "good," "right," "is just," "is permitted," and "is duty." The empirical content of these truths is derived primarily from the inner perceptions of man, which are also the empirical source of the metaphysical

16. *Ibid.,* bk. IV, chap. 11, sec. 13; Gerhardt, V:427.
17. Academy Ed., VI, i:460; cf. Loemker, p. 133.
18. *Nouveaux Essais,* bk. I, chap. 2, sec. 1; Gerhardt, V:81.
19. *Ibid.,* bk. III, chap. 11, sec. 21; Gerhardt, V:333.

categories, as Leibniz frequently says. These moral predicates, however, cannot be derived from such self-observations; their moral necessity must derive from propositions of reason which are themselves determined by first principles from which they are deduced with the aid of definitions which give these principles moral force. (Some of these definitions have been stated above, in Section II.) It is this derivation which gives them their quality as moral principles, commanding duty or obedience, just as the laws of nature, applying to the simpler monads which constitute the Kingdom of Nature, compel conformity on the level of mechanical necessity. It can thus be said that, according to Leibniz, the principles of logic play a constitutive but not fully determinative role, and the metaphysics of monads plays a regulative role, not only in the natural sciences, but also in ethics. This would be true since the bases of our rational duties are the laws of reason, the perfections of God, and the optimal government of the world, which are mirrored in every spirit monad according to the limited apperceptive and remembering powers which define its point of view (just as the laws of nature become ingredients of the simpler monads without consciousness and memory, as common parts of the laws of their nature). No two individuals are alike, yet all individuals fall into common classes according to the abstract essences which are shared by groups of monads. It therefore follows that the duty of each depends upon his particular point of view or the law of his particular nature; also, that the total configuration of his duties (or the demands of his character, or, in Leibniz's words, his "temperament") contains many duties which bind him to the other members of these various classes. And what is here said about duties applies likewise to rights, since right is the possibility, and duty (or obedience) is the necessity, of the good.

Leibniz's doctrine of the individual's duties and rights thus combines both ethical modes of thought: not only a situation ethics (to use contemporary terms) according to which "my station" determines my duties, as well as a principle of universalizability according to which every common essence or nature which unites a class involves the same law and the same duty or right. In this way the ideal of harmony in the social order of the monads is sustained—a total difference of concrete characters among individuals, but many universalized rights and duties. The Kingdom of Grace, therefore, is a regulative ideal for all historical political groups and all systems of positive law.

IV

This synthesis of experience and reason and of the descriptive and the normative in the formulation of moral laws and the justification of moral judgments can now be explicated in more detail.

First, we may examine the derivation of ethical principles from the first principles through definitions defining the limits of ethics. In each instance, the first principles involved are those of identity, sufficient reason, and the best possible (the ground of the imperative). The principle of identity assumes the more specific form of the contingent relation of commensurability or equipotentiality between two orders of experience—inner experience and the objective, metaphysically based, outer experience. There are five such principles of morality in Leibniz's thought.

1. *There is a best-possible for me (or for each), which is commensurate with my (or one's) point of view, or the law of my (or one's) individual nature.* (Commensurability of the subject with its predicates, of essence with being.) One may read, in place of "point-of-view," either "my station," with F. H. Bradley, or "my situation."

2. *My own (or each person's) joy is commensurable with the degree of the perfection of my (or one's) acts and appetites* (i.e., affections). (Commensurability of unclear perceptions with the acts and appetites of the individual).

3. *My own (or each person's) joy* and therefore *also my (or one's) perfection is commensurate with the perfection of the object of my (or one's) perfection.* (This is the principle of beauty, or the aesthetic principle.)

4. From (2) and (3) it follows that *my joy (or each person's joy) is commensurate with the happiness of others (or with their feeling of perfection).* Thus, rational self-interest (Leibniz uses the term *interest* to express self-interest) is contingent upon par-

ticipation in the perfection, and therefore the happiness, of others. This is the principle of the love of the wise man, or of justice.

5. Justice is commensurable with the love of the wise man, but such love is restricted by three distinct legal situations in which it must operate. Thus there follow from Principle 4 the three stages of justice, which Leibniz formulates as imperatives:

In strict law: *neminem laedere* (principle of retributive justice)

In equity: *suum cuique tribuere* (principle of commutative justice)

Honestas or *pietas: vivere honeste.*

On each level of justice, the principle is determined by the principle of the best possible in an equation—in piety, the honoring of God is equated with the well-being of man;[20] in the lower levels, the equation is between station and right, and between crime and punishment, respectively.

These descriptive and conditional principles[21] become imperatives through the all-inclusive demand of the principle of the best possible as obligatory upon spirit monads. Thus duty requires: thou shalt love, be just, seek thine own joy through the well-being of others, glorify God in this way rather than through fear, etc. Not only moral laws, but juristic laws, as well, should agree with these principles. As natural laws are determined by the best possible to have a metaphysical necessity (though not a merely logical one), so moral imperatives have a moral (but not a purely logical) necessity. On these two kinds of laws, the two Kingdoms of Nature and of Grace are founded.

So much for the derivation of moral principles. Particular moral judgments—what Kant calls maxims—involve a further

20. See, for example, Leibniz's letter to Thomas Burnet, 1699 (Gerhardt, III:261): "You know my principles, and that I prefer the common well-being above all other considerations, even fame and gold. I have no doubt that a man who possesses the powers of Mr. Newton shares this conviction. The solider a man is, the more he has this character *(dispositio)* which is that of the *homme honnête.* For to contribute to the common well-being and to the honor of God are one and the same thing."

21. For an account of the conditional nature of principles, see *Nouveaux Essais,* bk. IV, chap. 11, secs. 13, 14; Gerhardt, V:427–428.

application of the data of inner experience, since the application of the principles and laws requires a consideration of the motives, desires, and temperaments of men. In contrast to other truths of fact, moral maxims involve a reference to the rightness of particular acts and particular habituations, not merely to the rightness of knowledge.

At this empirical level, Leibniz, in his early jurisprudence, resorted to the techniques of casuistry. His mature conception of the way in which motives and acts can be tested by the principles is difficult to determine from his known writings. One must conclude that he probably did not develop his thought at this point to the extent which his criticism of Locke required in the theoretical field. Something can be inferred, however, from certain rather popularly written short discourses about motives and the good life.

It is clear that the nature of the affections—the subjective *materia prima* of the appetitive nature of man—is central in the application of the principles. In determining the goodness of an act, reason must enter to direct the affections toward greater perfection, greater unity of motives, and therefore also greater joy. In the paper entitled *De Affectibus: Ubi de Potentia, Actione, Determinatione* (1679), Leibniz writes, "An affection is a determination of the mind to a certain progression of thoughts through the knowledge of good and bad."[22] Thus the mind is not merely a single series of "thoughts" (or, later, perceptions); a series of perceptions directed toward an apparent good arises from every affection or emotion of man, and these diverse series of purposive thought compete for apperceptive prominence. Leibniz adds that in this rivalry, the more clear and distinct perceptual sequences are victors, and these are also the more perfect. Principles, therefore, must serve to give distinctness and adequacy, and therefore greater perfection, to the goals of our affectively motivated perceptual patterns. To introduce certain terms used later, in other papers, by Leibniz, the affections become sentiments through memory: through repetition they become habits, "talents"; and with the application of reason and more adequate understanding,

22. Grua, p. 531.

they become virtues. The self-knowledge of man, which is of course involved in an infinity of analyses and cannot become perfect, consists of the knowledge of this order of talents and virtues —or vices—which, metaphysically speaking, are expressions of the law of the individual nature.

The final justification of moral judgments, therefore, follows only after action upon the approved maxim. Neither the *a priori* ingredient of moral principles nor the empirical ingredient of clear and distinct affections and purposes is sufficient to establish the rightness of moral judgments. Only through the corresponding action and its effectiveness do they receive the justification of which they are capable. This final justification is provided by the growing unity of the agent's character, the happiness which accompanies it, and the external increase of social harmony according to the law of the best possible.

V

A second short paper on ethics, which might well be designated by its opening line, "On the different kinds of indifference,"[23] contains a simple scale of the instrumental values which further this ultimate ideal of harmony. One may assume that each of these values can be construed as the goal of an affectively motivated series of perceptions, for the paper undertakes to distinguish the goods toward which we should be indifferent or insensible and those which should awaken our highest sensibility. (Leibniz writes in the margin: *"l'indifference òu l'insensibilité."*) These latter are determined by the virtue of *curiosité*, "one of the most beautiful, most harmless, and even the most useful." His table of values follows:

First, riches, fame, and self-esteem are values, but are to be feared, since they can easily be transformed into evils—"as sweets turn into bile when one overindulges in them."

Second, the first concern, the highest sensitivity, should be our duty toward others.

23. E. Bodemann, *Die Leibniz-Handschriften der Königlichen Öffentlichen Bibliothek zu Hannover* (Hanover: Hahn, 1895), IV (Phil.), VII, pp. 53–54.

Third, our sensitivities and sentiments should be expanded through the contemplation of three dimensions of experience:

Art and music, since these arouse unconscious but final harmonies and proportions as feelings.

History, because history reconstructs the past with all of its achievements and failures.

Nature (this interest is most important), because it makes us conversant with the counsels and orders of God.

These value obligations comprise the moral education of our life in time, since they show us the way to greater harmony and perfection in the kingdom of Grace.

VI

The aesthetic character of Leibniz's ethics has already been shown in his principles of the best-possible and his ideal of harmony. All love, that of things as well as that of persons, attests this aesthetic quality, but it is most striking in Leibniz's conception of *grandeur*—greatness in the sense of the sublime. In addition to the light of nature and the light of grace, there is also a light of glory (*gloire*),[24] which we achieve in the hereafter, but which also makes possible a moral sublimity in this life when the soul is moved by and fills its life with sentiments both good and grand.

In a charming short piece, Leibniz describes this beauitful soul.[25] Grandeur of soul requires that inner powers be great even when external goods are small. The poor widow of the parable, who gave her last mite, had this sublime beauty of soul.

Our inner powers, Leibniz goes on to say, are of two kinds. They are either natural or acquired. "Nature forms us, but art perfects us. . . . Those men," he continues, "who want to do everything according to nature in the education of children, have not observed nature closely enough; they should watch sportsmen, riders, those who train horses, dogs and birds; the gardeners who prune and bind trees."[26]

It is true, he concludes, that it is not in our power to increase

24. See *Théodicée*, Discours prelim, sec. 82; Gerhardt, VI:98.
25. Published by Jean Baruzi, *Leibniz* (Paris: Bloud, 1909), pp. 365–368.
26. *Ibid.*

the powers of nature. But art can give us powers which nature has denied us. How combine these two conflicting truths? By seeing that

> art reunites and renders useful powers which nature has scattered or misdirected. . . . By nature we have scattered spirits which have been misguided from childhood through trifles which divide our attention. Only art can reunite our thoughts and give them the right guidance. Most people are children. They take joy in running after trifles. [Leibniz puns on the word *aimant.*] We should have only one single magnet [or love] which draws us and gives us direction. This magnet [love] is the true happiness.[27]

Thus there is a moral art—a self-conscious ordering of talents, of powers of the soul, which makes possible inner harmony of mind and outer harmony of spirits.

It is clear that we come out here with Leibniz's conception of freedom. Freedom is the self-conscious, self-determining, rational ordering of our appetites and therefore of our affections and talents. But how can we reconcile this theory of a moral art which reunifies the motives and talents which nature has given us scattered and misdirected? How can we reconcile this with Leibniz's other metaphysical dictum, that God, out of his own perfections, has determined everything which will happen to us, all our actions and experiences, by determining the law of our individual nature?

This difficulty in his doctrine Leibniz never worked out. He clearly teaches that the law of our nature determines everything that happens to us. He teaches also that by applying the art of moral reason to our disorganized life, we can, ourselves, apply the law of the best-possible by building the unity of talents and sentiments which constitutes part, at least, of the law of our nature (if we may bring Leibniz's thought thus close to C. S. Peirce's doctrine of habits and A. N. Whitehead's "defining characteristics"). Perhaps one can fulfill the promise of freedom which he left unfulfilled by an interpretation. Must it not be that the law of our nature does indeed include all of the possibilities of our life, but does not necessitate and therefore actualize them

27. *Ibid.*

all? That the *a priori* principles of God's creativity are themselves necessary but not sufficient to determine human existence? That the law of our nature itself includes the applicability of the principle of the best possible, *by us,* in further limiting and determining the continuum of possibilities of experience? That therefore our inner life is not merely a strictly determined series of experiences, but in part at least a matter of intentional choices of best possible individual acts out of a continuing range of possibilities implied in the law of our nature? If this interpretation is possible, moral necessity, which Leibniz himself made synonymous with obligation, would include within it a limited metaphysical contingency, and Leibniz's distinction between natural powers and powers bestowed by art, between confused and distinct perceptions, and between apparent and real goods, would have a metaphysical foundation.[28]

VII

I have tried to show that Leibniz succeeds in defining the true good, but only on the basis of principles derived from logical laws which are *a priori* but are rendered synthetic through definitions empirical in scope; that these *a priori* principles and the imperatives corresponding to them are a necessary but not sufficient reason for the determination of right acts; and that these determinations must therefore be confirmed or justified further through the situation of the individual and through the value achievements resulting from his acts. This interpretation of freedom will require an adjustment in Leibniz's metaphysics, but the main logical and metaphysical supports for his ethical theory would, it seems, remain. In his finding the ground of obligation

28. Support for this interpretation is given by Leibniz in the *Théodicée*: "Remarques sur le livre de l'origine du mal, publié depuis peu en Angleterre" (sec. 13). Gerhardt, VI:413: "As for me, I do not require the will to follow always the judgment of the understanding, because I distinguish this judgment from the motives which come from insensible perceptions and inclinations. But I hold that the will always follows the most advantageous representation, distinct or confused, of good and evil, which results from reasons, passions, and inclinations, although it can also find motives for suspending its judgment. But it is always through motives that it acts."

and of moral necessity in the deeper nature of man, Leibniz comes a long way toward Kant. But as in the theoretical side of his analysis, he avoids the unalterable rigidity of the Kantian *a priori* by allowing empirical facts to render old principles no longer necessary and by requiring new principles.

III

Historical Studies

12

A Note on the Origin and Problem of Leibniz's *Discourse* of 1686

Leroy E. Loemker

THE *Discourse on Metaphysics* (as it was named by K. L. Grotefend, its first editor) is the earliest statement of his philosophical opinions with which Leibniz himself expressed some satisfaction. He never published it, however, and never, so far as is known, submitted it to his friends for criticism, as he usually did, and he later considered its position as sound but incomplete. Compared with later summaries of his philosophical views, its emphasis is theological. Whereas the *Principles of Nature and of Grace* and the *Monadology* begin with the conception of individual substance and proceed to the divine harmony, the *Discourse* begins with the divine perfection and, making use of Leibniz's earlier studies in epistemology and logic (from 1679 to 1684) and his contemporary criticism of Cartesian physics (1686), it arrives finally at the conception of man's freedom and his membership in the republic of spirits whose monarch is God. It cannot therefore be considered, as Bertrand Russell and others have held, "the best account he ever wrote" of his philosophy.[1] It is not

First published in the *Journal of the History of Ideas* VIII (October 1947): 449–466.

1. Russell, *A Critical Exposition of the Philosophy of Leibniz*, second edition (London: Allen and Unwin, 1937), p. 7.

even an adequate one; among other things, he had yet to perfect his analysis of *vis viva*, of the gradation of individual substances and their perceptions and appetites, and of the nature of corporeal beings. And he also later changed his argument for the existence and nature of individual substances. The *Discourse* was directed at a more particular problem.

Accounts of Leibniz's purpose in writing the *Discourse* are confused. The best known biographers, G. E. Guhrauer and Kuno Fischer, were unaware of its existence. It is known that Leibniz sent a "summary," consisting of thirty-seven propositions, to Antoine Arnauld for his criticism, and it is generally assumed that he intended the entire *Discourse* for Arnauld, perhaps as a part of his plans for church reunion.[2] The purpose of this paper is to amplify this view and to throw light upon the purpose of the *Discourse* by means of the previously unpublished notes made by Leibniz on the famous controversy between Arnauld and Malebranche on the nature of grace. A supplement following the paper contains a translation of a part of these notes.[3]

I

The *Discourse* is probably a preliminary study for the preface to Leibniz's long projected *Demonstrationes Catholicae*, a Christian apologetic which was to provide the basis, not merely for church reunion, but for the conversion of the world by the force of logical demonstration. It is for this reason that he sought Arnauld's opinion about it.

2. H. Wildon Carr (*Leibniz* [London: E. Benn, 1929], p. 22) asserts, without ground, that since Arnauld was then seventy-five, living in seclusion, and practically excommunicated, Leibniz "could have nothing to gain by his approval or disapproval," but intended the work for Count Ernest of Hesse-Rheinfels. But though Arnauld had been driven from France by Jesuit persecution in 1679, he was in the midst of both controversial and expository writing and was influential both in Paris and in Rome.

3. An excellent critical account of the controversy is found in R. W. Church, *A Study in the Philosophy of Malebranche* (London: Allen and Unwin, 1931), chaps. VI, VII, VIII. A more complete publication of Leibniz's notes on this controversy has since appeared in A. Robinet, *Malebranche et Leibniz* (Paris: J. Vrin, 1955).

Leibniz's plan for the *Catholic Demonstrations* was first developed at Mainz around 1669 or 1670, in connection with the theological discussions with the Baron von Boineburg. Its outline, in brief, was the following:

Preface: The prolegomena will contain the elements of philosophy; as follows: first principles of metaphysics (*de ente*), of logic (*de mente*), of mathematics (*de spatio*), of physics (*de corpore*), of practical philosophy (*de civitate*).
Part I. Demonstration of the Existence of God.
Part II. Demonstration of the Immortality of the Soul.
Part III. Demonstration of the Possibility of the Mysteries of the Christian Faith.
Part IV. Demonstration of the Authority of the Catholic Church.[4]

The plan for securing its acceptance and assuring its influence involved, first, the support of an influential Catholic nobleman, in this case Boineburg; second, Leibniz's submission to the Catholic Church on condition that certain interpretations which he had given of decisions of the Council of Trent be approved by Rome; third, the preparation of the *Catholic Demonstrations*, which involved these interpretations. One of the secondary purposes, at least, of Leibniz's journey to Paris was to secure Arnauld's support for the project, and Boineburg gave him letters to the great controversialist (which Leibniz supplemented with his own prolix letter of November 1671).[5] But Boineburg's death removed the first condition of the plan, support from Catholic nobility, and though Leibniz came to know Arnauld well, he did not present the proposal to him.[6]

In 1679, one of the most creative and fruitful years of his activity, circumstances seemed favorable for the revival of the plan, with the Catholic Duke John Frederick of Hanover as the

4. The complete outline is printed in Academy Ed., VI, i:494 f. It was first described and published, in part, by W. Kabitz, *Die Philosophie des jungen Leibniz* (Heidelberg: Carl Winters, 1909), pp. 110 f., 157 f.

5. Gerhardt, I:71–74.

6. The best summary of the project and of these events is in Leibniz's letter to Duke John Frederick, 1679 (Academy Ed., II, i:487–488; Loemker, pp. 259–262.

noble sponsor, but with the apologetic work itself altered only in minor matters. In his letter to the duke describing the proposal, Leibniz is concerned about the tact and finesse needed in securing the official approval of Rome for his theological interpretations. The Peace of Nymwegen had made Rome more inclined toward winning than censuring the Protestants. Jacques B. Bossuet's exposition of the Catholic faith had received papal approval. That summer the Franciscan priest and imperial legate Spinola arrived at the court in Hanover with a message from Innocent XI, the anti-Jesuit pope who was zealous in his moral reforms and interest in the return of the Protestants to Rome. In August began Leibniz's long correspondence with Bossuet, the friend and supporter of Arnauld, through whom Leibniz also hoped to secure the interest of Louis XIV. Though Arnauld is not named at this time as a judge of Leibniz's doctrinal position, he was certainly strategically connected to serve as one, combining favor both at Paris and at Rome with a searching objectivity and an outstanding ability, not only in philosophy but in mathematics.[7]

The death of John Frederick on December 18, 1679, and the succession of his Protestant brother Ernest August, once more interfered with Leibniz's plan, but this time only briefly. Count Ernest of Hesse-Rheinfels, who had already written in support of church union from the Catholic side, became the new candidate for the position of noble spearhead for the proposal. In 1680 an opportunity was offered for entering into correspondence with the count, and the letters of 1681, 1682, 1683, 1684 reveal the diplomatic adroitness with which Leibniz led up to his plan and drew Arnauld into the discussion of it.[8] It becomes more and more clear, as the correspondence progresses, that Leibniz still has Arnauld in mind as the apologist and thinker whose fairness would lead him to appreciate his views and whose recommen-

7. In 1679 Leibniz insisted, to John Frederick and others, that he had perfected himself in mathematics only to master the methods of demonstration in theology and to create a public confidence in his ability as a logician. See the letter cited in note 6 above.

8. See Academy Ed. II, i:228, 239, 241, 245 for the early letters in the correspondence. In the last letter Leibniz proposes that his work be anonymous and written as if by a Catholic.

dations would carry weight in Paris and Rome. The correspondence with Arnauld was a continuation of this series of letters and was mediated, as is well known, by the count. But the *Catholic Demonstrations* never advanced beyond the preliminary stage; both Count Ernest and Arnauld were concerned about winning so illustrious a convert as Leibniz, but neither became enthusiastic over the prospects of a Christian apology designed to end all apologies.

The contents of the *Discourse* support the opinion that it was intended as a study for the preface of the *Catholic Demonstrations,* in particular, for the metaphysical part in which "true notions of God and the soul, of person, substance, and accidents"[9] were to be presented, and that it was intended for Arnauld's approval or criticism as indicating the position of the greater work from which Leibniz expected so much. Thus the *Discourse* contains no demonstration of God's existence, of immortality, of the eucharist, or of church authority, but is restricted to the crucial problem of God's grace in relation to man's freedom.

II

More interesting is the relation of the *Discourse* to the increasingly bitter controversy which had developed between Arnauld and Malebranche since the publication of the *Des Vraies et des Fausses Idées* by the former in 1683, and which continued until the end of the decade. Leibniz had been a friend to both men in Paris, and his own thought, as worked out in 1679, had undoubtedly been influenced by both. To him, as to both of them, the moral problem of the century appeared in theological garb: the relation of divine grace to human individuality. A revolution threatened Europe; the moral order of the *homme honnête* who found his true freedom in obedience to higher order, political, ecclesiastical, and "natural," was threatened by the *libertin,* whose freedom recognized no higher order than his own thinking.[10] The philosophical problem was to define human freedom

9. Academy Ed. II, i:488.

10. On the European revolution, see Gerhardt, I:26; Loemker, p. 102

without limiting divine wisdom and power, for "Averroism" in its modern forms threatened the former, and Pelagianism, Socinianism, and related trends, the latter. The philosopher of the *homme honnête* was Augustine, but even he was ambiguous, depending on whether he was seen by the Molinist Jesuits, a Cartesian voluntarist like Malebranche, a Jansenist like Arnauld, or a mathematical Platonist like Leibniz. And as John Locke had discovered in England, the broader theological problem involved the narrower epistemological one. So Malebranche and Arnauld argued about the nature of ideas, or more particularly, about the part of God and the part of man in human knowledge. This, however, is but one aspect of their defense of the sovereignty of God and the true freedom of man, against the free thinking which threatened.

Leibniz had probably already been influenced by both men. In the first years after his departure from Paris, he had brought his own metaphysics, logic, and epistemology into harmony with one another. The unifying concept had been the process of expression or representation, a relationship sharply defined in mathematical functions and then applied both to symbolic logic (the *universal characteristic* and *logical calculus*) and to his epistemology.[11] Both Malebranche and Arnauld held that knowledge involves a representation of reality; their disagreement concerned the place of ideas in this representation, Arnauld considering an idea merely the representative aspect of the act of perception itself, while Malebranche made it the divine object of our prception.[12] But Leibniz had extended the notion of representation, or expression, beyond epistemology to the logical and existential structure of being; every individual is a series of actions repre-

(1669); Gerhardt, VII:162 (1679?); *Nouveaux Essais*, bk. IV, chap. 16, sec. 4, Gerhardt, V:444 (after 1700).

11. For example, the "What is an Idea?" (Gerhardt, VII:263–264; Loemker, pp. 207–208) and the *Dialogue* of 1677 (Gerhardt, VII:190 ff.; Loemker, pp. 183 ff., among many other evidences. Leibniz does not use the term *represent* in its epistemological sense, however, until the *Discourse*, sec. 26 (Gerhardt, IV:451; Loemker, p. 320).

12. See the controversy between John Laird and A. O. Lovejoy on Arnauld's alleged new-realism in *Mind* 32 (1923): 449–461; 33 (1924): 176–181.

sentative of the universe according to a limited point of view. Only in the *Discourse,* intended for Arnauld, does he finally adopt the term *represent* for the epistemological relationship, and only in the *Discourse* does he permanently choose the term *perception* rather than *cogitation* for the fundamental act of representation. In this usage he agrees with Arnauld.

One other point Leibniz may have taken from Arnauld. In the *Port Royal Logic* (part IV, chapter VI), Arnauld establishes the rule that, in every axiom, the predicate is included in the subject. This rule Leibniz applies, about 1679, to all propositions, and it is not surprising that the argument for the nature of individual substance which he builds upon it is included in the *Discourse,* though it is paradoxical, perhaps, that it is this very argument which Arnauld later chooses to attack.[13] Leibniz agreed with Arnauld that perception is a representative activity proper to individuals.

To Malebranche, on the other hand, Leibniz wrote in 1679 that he agreed with him on three points: that God always acts in the best possible way, that we see all things in God, and that there can be no direct influence between soul and body.[14] But he had already qualified the second point by working out his own conception of ideas. Ideas are not merely in God as the immediate objects of my perception and the representatives of objects, as Malebranche held; ideas are, rather, the possibilities of my activity in thinking, and therefore the form of my representative perceptions or thoughts.[15] In God, they are the universal harmony out of which the world is made as the best possible choice; in me, they are the law of my individuality, and as this law is expressed in a series of particular events or modifications, an idea is the possibility of each perceptive act in which external order is represented by an internal quality. In his later criticism

13. *Discourse,* secs. 18, 13 (Gerhardt, IV:444, 436; Loemker, pp. 315, 310).

14. Gerhardt, I:328; Loemker, pp. 209–210; Gerhardt, I:330; Loemker, p. 210.

15. See among others, Leibniz's notes to Simon Foucher's reply to Malebranche, 1676 (Felix Rabbe, *L'Abbé Simon Foucher* [Paris: Dijon, 1867], Appendix, xlii f.), and the "What is an Idea?" of 1678 (Loemker, pp. 207–208).

of Malebranche, Leibniz seems above all concerned with his denial that denominations (in the present controversy, modifications) are intrinsic to individuals,[16] or, as Arnauld put it, perceptions are essentially representative modifications of the soul.

Leibniz's own epistemology was thus formulated and well related to his logic before the controversy between Arnauld and Malebranche took place. Moreover, his theory was sharper and more complete than that which either of the men defended in the argument, for both neglected the role of symbols in knowledge. This may explain why Leibniz was rather slow in following the books in which the discussion was carried out, and so far as is known, never read more than the first four works in the series.

In general, he esteemed Arnauld more highly than he did Malebranche as a thinker. To Ernest, he wrote, "Father Malebranche . . . is most ingenious and has some very good and solid thoughts, but he has others which are a little hyperbolic and lightly conceived"; and again, "As for myself, I find [in Malebranche] many beautiful thoughts, but there are still some which have more éclat than soundness." And to E. W. von Tschirnhaus, in a letter in which Malebranche's mathematical attainments are derided, he said, "Father Malebranche has much spirit, but Mr. Arnauld writes with more judgment."[17]

Meanwhile, other friends were asking for Leibniz's opinion about the dispute. Simon Foucher wrote on December 8, 1684:

> I have many things to say and write on this controversy which concern only philosophy—for I leave theology to Mr. Arnauld. But we do not have all the facilities here for publishing that could be desired. . . . Yet I wish with all my heart, Sir, that we might have all that we lack on these matters from you. Your words are dear to us.[18]

But as late as March 4, 1685, Leibniz had not read the controversy, and he seems to have been repelled by the bitterness

16. For example, Gerhardt, IV:506–507, 509 (1698); Loemker, pp. 500–501, 502.

17. Academy Ed. II, i:544 (December 29, 1684) and the letter following, of March 4, 1685.

18. Academy Ed. II, i:248.

which it had developed.[19] The notes here translated must have been written after that time. No information now available provides a date for them, but the fact that they end with the fourth book in the dispute, Malebranche's *Three Letters* of 1685, and the similarity of their problems and some of the comments to ideas in the *Discourse*, suggest a date late in 1685, the *Discourse* having been written in the winter of 1685–1686. During the same year Leibniz also made notes on the *Recherche de la Vérité*;[20] both sets may well have been preparatory for the *Discourse*.

III

We may conclude by summarizing the main points at which Leibniz's reactions to the dispute are reflected in the form and content of his own work. The more direct parallels are indicated in the annotations which we have supplied to his own notes in the supplement to this paper.

The problem of the *Discourse* is the relation of divine grace to man's individuality and to the realm of nature. Leibniz is concerned with two things: to provide a universal order upon which man and nature depend and so to avoid libertinism; and to assure the spontaneous activity of man, not merely in willing, but in perception, and so to avoid a naturalistic pantheism. He shares Malebranche's concern that we recognize God as our light, and agrees that the universal basis of man's knowledge and therefore of his moral duty is in the divine harmony (Supple-

19. Leibniz to Ernest of Hesse-Rheinfels (Academy Ed. II, i:252). However, Leibniz knew the issues in the controversy before he wrote the *Meditations on Knowledge, Truth, and Ideas,* published in November 1684 (see Gerhardt, IV:423, 426; Loemker, pp. 291, 294), and he may have read the *Des Vraies et Fausses Idées* before then.

20. E. Bodemann, *Leibniz-Handschriften,* IV (Phil.), vi, Bl. 6, p. 85. Bodemann did not recognize the work. It can be dated by the watermark of alternate sheets, which contains the date 1685. Cf. W. Kabitz in K. Fischer, *Gottfried Wilhelm Leibniz: Leben, Werke, und Lehre.* 5. Aufl. (Heidelberg: Carl Winters, 1920), p. 754. The watermarks in the notes on the Malebranche-Arnauld controversy do not correspond to these, however.

ment, 1 verso). In short, he approves of Malebranche's starting point in perfection.

But because Malebranche has not understood the nature of ideas, he has not succeeded in establishing man's freedom. When he accuses Arnauld of encouraging libertinism, Leibniz checks his charge with a marginal "N.B." (3 verso), but in a sense it is Malebranche who has encouraged libertinism by defining man's activity entirely in terms of will and making his intellect passive. To make will independent of intellect is to come dangerously close to the libertine's "freedom of indifference" (3 verso). Arnauld is therefore right in stressing perception as a distinctly human activity.

Malebranche's denial that God wills particular events, though intended to establish God's perfect goodness in the face of sin, has a similar effect. Malebranche asserts this because he does not understand the nature of God's will in choosing the best possible world (4 recto). In creating each individual, God's will takes the form of an individual idea, or a law of the individual series, from which the activities of the individual follow. This law includes all the events which will ever befall one, and it is in this sense that Arnauld's rule that the predicate *is in* the subject applies to all propositions having an individual as a subject.[21] God's particular volitions (3 verso) take the form of his approval of every event determined by the individual laws which he has chosen, and since God sees adequately and intuitively all of these events, he wills them in this sense. The subordinate regulations of nature which Leibniz stresses in the *Discourse* (sections 16, 17), along with the laws of individual substances (section 13), are thus expressions of God's will, including his particular volitions. Yet he is absolved from moral responsibility for evil, since the actions of every individual follow from the laws of his own nature. Even miracles are of this nature, rather than direct and particular decisions of God (3 verso). This may explain why Leibniz later considered Malebranche's occasionalism as a continuous miracle,

21. To truths of fact, however, expressing temporal relations within existence, Leibniz always recognized that it applies only implicitly and obliquely.

but his own parallelism as not. Here again Arnauld's individualistic and realistic approach serves to clarify and correct Malebranche's idealism.

Out of the same misunderstanding of the ideas arises Malebranche's theory of an intelligible space, with all of its inconsistencies.[22] This theory is unnecessary, since we do not strictly see things in God; we see things by means of God or the harmony of meaning (2 verso). It is in this sense that God is our light. Arnauld is right in his realism. Ideas are the divinely provided forms of our perceptions (4 recto), but we perceive things, not ideas. If Malebranche had had the right concept of ideas and of their polar nature (involving both activity and passivity in the individual) he might have avoided his tendency to deny reality to creatures (4 verso, 7 recto).

But though perceptions, while representative of external things, are yet essential modifications of the individual, Arnauld is wrong in holding that we do not need to analyze them further (1 verso). To stop with this is to fail to apply logic to our perceptions and to provide a criterion for adequate knowledge. Neither Malebranche nor Arnauld has recognized the passive element in human experience, the *materia prima* of the monad and the symbolic constructions which it makes possible. Thus, though both hold that knowledge involves representation, neither has been clear about the nature of this representation or expression.

Arnauld is also right in defending the activity and essential privacy of the individual's knowledge. A finite individual can have a perception of infinity, but it will be a finite perception, and his own (4 recto). Perceptions are modifications of the soul itself, not of God (4 verso). But though his own logic provides the basis for relating this privacy to God as the universal source of all, Arnauld fails to establish a proper relationship between individual spontaneity and universal order. It is in this sense that he may encourage the libertine.

Leibniz therefore decides that the two views are not irrecon-

22. In 1675–76, before he had worked out his own theory of ideas, Leibniz entertained the notion of an *Immensum* as an aspect of God (Jagodinski, especially VII, 120 f.).

cilable (4 verso), but that Arnauld's realism and individualism is consistent with Malebranche's Platonism and universalism. The synthesis is to be found in the nature of ideas as active principles, in their differentiation into laws of individual substances or series, each with its active and its passive poles, and in the more exact notion of representation as the response of every individual to the entire universe in his own imperfect and inadequate perspective. It is this synthesis that is found, for the first time explicitly, in the *Discourse*. And this is the adequate answer of the dilemma of the *homme honnête*, since it establishes the possibility of spontaneity and freedom under universal law.

But the answer, it is clear, is closer to Arnauld's Jansenism than to Malebranche's voluntarism. It corrects the latter, but merely completes the former. Perhaps this, too, influenced Leibniz to seek the approval of the great controversialist for his new system.

SUPPLEMENT

Bodemann, *Leibniz-Handschriften:* IV (Phil.), vi. 5, p. 85.

This supplement contains my translation of a part of the notes made by Leibniz on the controversy between Arnauld and Malebranche on the nature of grace.

If there is hope of restoring and perfecting a genuine European culture, one of the first imperatives should be the complete critical edition of Leibniz which has been undertaken so often, and, as often, has been interrupted because of war or revolution—first, by the Prussian occupation of Hanover, then by World War I, and, finally, by the fall of the Weimar Republic.

In this translation, I have printed only some of Leibniz's abstracts, but most of his comments. As it was Leibniz's common practice to differentiate between his own incidental comment and his notes by enclosing his comments in parentheses and asterisks, that practice is followed here.

I am indebted to the Director of the Niedersächsische Landesbibliothek and the editors of the Prussian Academy edition of Leibniz for permission to copy and use these manuscripts.

I have given parenthetical references from the abstracts to the corresponding text in Jules Simon, editor, *Oeuvres Philosophiques d'Antoine Arnauld* (Paris: A. Delahays, 1845), the only text of the controversy which was available. (This work is hereafter referred to as Simon.) The footnotes point out the parallels in the *Discourse*. Occasionally I have condensed Leibniz's abstracts in brackets.

1 Recto

ON THE CONTROVERSY BETWEEN M. ARNAULD AND THE REVEREND FATHER MALEBRANCHE ABOUT IDEAS.

The controversy . . . about ideas began with M. Arnauld's book on true and false ideas,[23] published in Cologne by Nicolas Schouten, 1683 (octavo, 339 pp.).

M. Arnauld, wishing to examine the view of Father Malebranche on nature and grace, planned first to examine the principles which he formulated in his book on the *Recherche de la Vérité*. He begins (chap. 1) with the rules which should be kept in view in such an investigation. These are:

1. One should begin with the most simple things.
2. Not to confuse what we know clearly through other confused notions.
3. Not to seek reasons to infinity but to stop with what we know to be of the nature of the thing or to be certainly a quality of it; thus we ought not to seek a reason why extension is divisible, or the mind is capable of thinking.
4. Not to require definitions of terms that are clear in themselves, and which we can only make obscure by trying to define them . . .
5. Not to confuse questions to which one should reply with a formal cause, with those to which one should reply with an efficient cause . . .
6. Not to think of minds as bodies, nor of bodies as minds, in ascribing to either properties which belong only to the other . . .
7. Not to multiply beings beyond necessity, as when the ordinary philosophy asks for the substantial form of stone, gold, etc.[24]

(*In my opinion these rules are good, but they need some restriction or interpretation. Of the third rule, I should say that it is necessary to give a criterion by which to know where to stop, for we cannot go to infinity, but it is also insufficient to know that a quality belongs to something with certainty, since we often seek a reason for the quali-

23. Arnauld's title appears in the *Discourse*, no. 23 (Gerhardt, IV:449).

24. *Discourse*, no. 5 (Gerhardt, IV:431); nos. 10, 11. Cf. Simon, pp. 29 f.

ties of things. This same criterion should also make us understand, in the sixth and seventh rules, what terms are clear in themselves, and when it is unnecessary to seek a formal cause for them.*)

The author says, in chap. 2, that, since we can think of different things without changing their nature, our thoughts are modifications of the soul. He adds, however, that there is perhaps some thought in me which does not change,

1 Verso

and which can be taken for the essence of my soul. . . . I find two of these, the thought of universal being, and that which the soul has of itself; for it seems that both of these are found in all other thoughts: that of universal being because they all include the idea of being, since our soul knows nothing except under the notion of being, possible or existent; and the thought which our soul has of itself because whatever I may know, I know it by a kind of virtual reflection which accompanies all my thoughts. Now since it is the nature of mind to perceive objects, some necessarily and some contingently, it is ridiculous to ask why our mind perceives them. (Simon, pp. 33 f.)

(*I am not of M. Arnauld's opinion in this matter, for since the mind does not see a connection between our soul and most objects, it must seek to inform itself how it perceives them. It is not enough to say that we should seek the efficient cause which makes us think sometimes of one thing and sometimes of another. It is also necessary to know the way in which this efficient cause achieves its effect, and this reduces in part to the formal cause.[25]*)

After this M. Arnauld undertakes to show that it suffices to think of the idea as the perception itself, and that it is useless and vain to assume representative beings as immediate objects of perception. He even believes that it is a vestige of the Scholastic philosophy that has led Father Malebranche to this assumption, since the School assumes that the mind cannot conceive what is at a distance and for this reason has introduced certain species which objects transmit through the air to us; that Father Malebranche has rejected these species leaping through the air, but has retained the principle of such species. This has led him to imagine certain representative beings which the soul sees when it sees the sun. (Chap. 3; Simon, pp. 39, 45–47)

(*To this I should reply that the Scholastics are not as absurd as might be thought in introducing species which are transmitted through the

25. Cf. Leibniz's defense of forms in *Discourse*, nos. 10, 11, 18.

air, since these species are, properly speaking, the propagation of motion by a medium. As for the soul, I admit that there is nothing in it but its qualities and its thoughts, but one can conceive ideas outside of it in God, and God acting immediately on the soul. One can say in a sense that since every perfection or every perfect thing comes from God (as the Apostle says) it is by the divine light[26] that we are illumined, and so God, being our immediate object, communicates to us some relation to the ideas which are in him.[27]*)

2 Recto

[After a series of summaries of Arnauld's criticisms of Malebranche's theory of intelligible space, and its bearing on the question of whether God has particular ideas representative of every object we perceive, which Malebranche denies, the question is raised whether we see God rather than things.]

2 Verso

Father Malebranche had said that since everything that comes from God is for God, we must in some way see God when we see his works, and that if God had given a mind the sun as its immediate object, that mind would be made for the sun. M. Arnauld says that this is a sophism, and points out that Malebranche recognizes that our soul knows itself without seeing itself in God . . . yet it is not necessary that it is made for itself and not for God. He says that we see God in seeing eternal truths, because they are in God. But in the notes he says that we do not properly see God in seeing his creatures. Yet he had said that God is our immediate object, and he says that our soul does not perceive objects outside of us by themselves. M. Arnauld concludes that according to the father it would be necessary to say that we see God rather than objects. (Chap. 17; Simon, pp. 146–151)

(*But it seems to me that if there were connected mirrors so that when we looked through all of them we could not tell whether there were a mirror or not, but could see objects in them, in such a way that we could not perceive by sight whether it was without the mirror or not

26. Leibniz first wrote "les idées" but crossed out these words and substituted "la lumière divine" (*Discourse*, no. 28).

27. This is the first indication of Leibniz's synthesis. *Discourse*, no. 23 (Gerhardt, IV:449) is the closest parallel; nos. 25, 26, 27 modify it in Arnauld's favor.

(though we might know by reasoning or by the relations) then I should say that we were seeing the object without seeing the mirror.[28]*)

3 Recto

[The rest of Arnauld's work Leibniz summarizes without comment. He notes Arnauld's charge that Malebranche's view makes the merely human divine, since a woman admiring her beauty in a mirror is seeing God; Arnauld agrees with Malebranche that we have no clear knowledge of our soul, but holds that knowledge of our body is just as unclear. Leibniz notes Arnauld's criticism of Malebranche's view that only man's will is active and that his understanding is passive.]

The father compares perceptions to figures, and inclinations to movements. But if bodies can give themselves movements they will also give themselves figures. Then the soul in giving itself inclinations will also give itself perceptions.[29] (Simon, p. 239)
[Leibniz has only one comment, on a view of Descartes quoted with approval by Arnauld]:

(*M. Descartes (part 1 of the Principles) says that we know clearly and distinctly color, pain, and other feelings. As for me, I do not agree.*)

3 Verso

Reply of Father Malebranche (Rotterdam: Leers, 1684 [335 pages]). He says in chapter 1 that M. Arnauld was angered at him because he had undeceived certain persons who held the opinions of M. Arnauld about grace.
[Leibniz notes Malebranche's statement that the *Traité de la Nature et de la Grace* was written to refute the libertine, who argues a complete separation of man from God (chap. 2, viii, ix; Simon, p. 280) and checks it with a marginal "*N.B.*"].[30]
Chap. 4. God wills that all men should be saved. It is certain that they are not, and that nothing can resist God; then there must be in God something which prevents him from having a practical will to save all men.
[Malebranche infers that God acts only on the basis of a general will,

28. The analogy of the mirrors is, of course, old in Leibniz. It occurs in *Discourse*, no. 9.

29. The similarity of Leibniz's theory of perception and appetite with Malebranche's parallel of perception and inclination is striking.

30. The strongest implication of libertinism is in chapter 5 of Malebranche's reply.

and not, as do we, by particular volitions. He excepts miracles, "or the effects whose natural or occasional causes are unknown to us."]

(*As for me, I should rather believe that everything that takes place through wisdom takes place through general laws, that is, through rules or principles, and that God always acts wisely. So miracles [are] themselves entirely in the general order, that is, in general laws. But what makes them miracles is that they are not the intelligible notions of subjects and cannot be foreseen by the greatest finite mind that can be imagined. Everything natural can be explained in detail without thinking of God, after we have once established that he is the universal cause of all. Nothing more needs to be said to explain everything that is natural.[31]*)

Father Malebranche believes, in chapter 4 . . . that God is indifferent to acting or not acting externally, but that he is not indifferent in regard to the manner of acting; he always follows the wisest conduct. (Simon, p. 297, xi)

(*As for me, I believe that God is never indifferent to anything. And he follows the wisest conduct also in the question of whether he ought to act or not. Yet he is right in saying that God must not interfere with the simplicity of his ways to prevent a monster, sterility, an injustice.*) (Simon, p. 298, xii)
[Malebranche considers the plan of salvation as based on general volitions only.] (Simon, p. 299, xiv)

(*As for me, I am somewhat doubtful about this discourse of Father Malebranche, for God has a will as to the general as well as the particular. General laws do not dispense with the proportionality of means and ends; on the contrary they rather imply it.[32]*)

4 Recto
He adds, article 15, that if God acts through particular volitions, it follows that it would be a sin to take shelter [from rain], to cure the sick, to help a man who has fallen. (Simon, p. 300)

(*I find this reasoning very strange. It is as if I should say that if a prince rolls a ball, it is a sin for his footman to stop the ball from roll-

31. See *Discourse,* nos. 6, 7 on miracles, and nos. 16, 17 on God's subordinate regulations. Leibniz's distinction of his own view from Malebranche's is not at all clear, but neither is his later charge that occasionalism implies a perpetual miracle.

32. *Discourse,* no. 7 (Gerhardt, IV:432).

ing into a river, since it is the will of the prince for the ball to roll. This does not mean, however, that it should roll forever. One ought always to be content with what God has done in the past, but as for the future, it does not follow that God wills that what he has done should continue or remain, for he himself often wills that we should think of changing it.[33]*)
He says also that if God always acts by particular ways, we ought to cast lots instead of choosing judges; that a duel is the holiest of proceedings. (Simon, p. 301)

(*This reasoning seems weak to me. God acts by particular volitions, but he does not consider one thing by itself. If there were only this in the world, we should have to fear that casting a lot would decide correctly.*)
God has foreseen all the consequences of all possible laws which he could establish; in one eternal and immutable vision he has compared all the possible workings among them, and with regard to the laws of which they are the results. He has retained those which have a greater relation to wisdom, that is, to the simplicity and fruitfulness of their workings, than all other laws and all other works. (Simon, p. 306 f.)

(*This is good.[34]*)
Chap. 6, sec. 4. If ideas are nothing but modifications of the soul, M. Arnauld, in admitting that the soul has an idea of the infinite is forced to maintain that the modifications of the soul are essentially representative of the infinite. (Simon, p. 315)

(*I should say that he is right in maintaining this.[35]*)
Chap. 6, sec. 7. I cannot know the modification of a substance as a being distinct from that substance. So I do not see a modification of my substance when I see some particular being. (Simon, p. 318.) I perceive in myself my perception and that which I perceive.

(*The form of my perception.[36]*)
Sec. 11. The modification of a particular being cannot be general, but the idea of a circle is general. (Simon, p. 319)

33. *Discourse*, no. 4 (Gerhardt, IV:429).

34. Leibniz had approved this concept in Malebranche in 1679 (see note 13, above) and it was, of course, essential in his own thinking from the start. The distinction between possibility and compossibility was worked out in 1678. *Discourse*, no. 19, 22.

35. *Discourse*, no. 26. (Gerhardt, IV:451), no. 27 (452).

36. *Discourse*, no. 26 (Gerhardt, IV:451).

(*It would follow from this that the propositions which we make also cannot be general.*)

4 Verso

Words of M. Arnauld on his seventh definition: What I mean by *representative beings* insofar as I oppose them as superfluous entities applies only to those which are imagined to be really distinct from ideas taken as perceptions. For I am careful not to combat all kinds of representative beings or modifications, since I hold that it is clear to anyone who reflects on what happens in his mind, that all our perceptions are *essentially representative modifications.* (Simon, p. 340.) Father Malebranche says frequently that it is this opinion of M. Arnauld that he is chiefly opposing, namely, that our modifications are essentially representative, because, according to him, they would make us our own light. (Simon, pp. 325, *passim*)

(*But this is like saying that since our paintings are essentially representative things, they are their own light and one can see them by night as well as by day.*)
But Father Malebranche believes that this is M. Arnauld's chief error, for he says (chap. 9) that M. Arnauld writes a book expressly to prove that our modifications are essentially representative, while "I have written only a few pages to defend the honor of universal reason." (Simon, p. 331)

(*So he assumes that the two views are opposed. Still, cannot we say that our thoughts are essentially representative, but that they are also the more perfect the better they are in accord with universal reason?[37]*)
[In the margin]: chap. 9, sec. 2. To what end prove that our modifications are essentially representative, I will not say of creatures, but of the creator? To what end combat in a book of 300 pages my opinion that it is God who illumines us? (Simon, p. 331)

(*It is good to prove this, for we are taught by it that they exist only for the glory of God, being made to represent him.*)
He adds a little later that if a philosopher does not do all he can to render unto God all the honor due his power, by proving that it is he who makes everything and that nature is a chimera, he is either a bad philosopher or a bad man. (Simon, p. 332)

37. See note 27 above.

(*Again he places in opposition what is not opposed. God makes everything, yet it does not follow that nature is a chimera, for it is God who makes it.*)
Likewise, if he [the philosopher] does not do all he can to render unto God all the honor due his wisdom or his Word, by proving that neither the bodies which surround us, nor our modifications, nor even our intelligences can teach us any truth, but only the universal reason which includes them all in its substance, a light always to those who contemplate it attentively, as St. Augustine says, he is either a philosopher of little illumination, or at least a man insensitive to his duties. (Simon, p. 332)

(*In a certain sense we can say that it is only God who illumines us, and that truths come only from him, for truth is a perfection of our thoughts and everything perfect in us ought to be recognized as from God.[38]*)

[There follows an abstract from chap. 13, secs. 3 and 9, without comment.]
Light and evidence should regulate the steps of the mind; instinct and confused feelings are given it only to lead the soul to conserve its body in the shortest and surest way imaginable.

(*Good. I have nothing to say to this.[39]*)

7 Recto
[This sheet contains abstracts, without comments, from chaps. 22, 23, and 26, including Malebranche's argument for immortality, which is similar to Leibniz's own.]
Father Malebranche says a little later, sec. 8: I reject the Koran and I accept the Bible because of the appearances which God, who is no deceiver, has given me by Apostles, miracles, and other grounds for credibility in respect to the Bible. (Simon, p. 447)

(*But these appearances do not prove that there ever was a Jesus Christ, Apostles, Bible—or else the appearances of bodies also prove that there are bodies.*)

7 Verso
Defense of M. Arnauld against the Reply to the Book on True and False Ideas (Cologne: Nic. Schouten, 1684 [octavo, 623 pp.]).

38. *Discourse*, no. 28.
39. *Discourse*, no. 33.

[Leibniz's abstracts are made at random from the first letter, and concern the question whether perceptions are essentially representative modifications of the soul. His only comment, made in the margin, follows]:

(*Perceptions are very lively (trés vivantes) in thoughts, as are motions in bodies. One thought arises from another, and every thought represents the object. This suffices for my system in considering solely how one thing is connected with all the rest.*)

5 Recto

M. Arnauld thinks that to maintain that God is formally our light, as Father Malebranche says, it would be necessary to brutalize our soul, so to speak, and to deprive it of intelligence, and it would follow that it is the divine wisdom which perceives the soul's objects, as Averroes believed of his universal intellect. This gives an air of spirituality to the most bizarre and absurd thoughts, says M. Arnauld; we should have to say then, that the sainthood of saints is not a modification of their own souls. (Simon, pp. 489 f.)

(*But according to this author, the Holy Spirit itself, as the Word, is our light.*)

[The rest of folio 5, front and back, contains further abstracts without comment.]

6 Recto

Three Letters of the Author of the Recherche de la Vérité concerning the Defense of M. Arnauld against the Reply to the Book on True and False Ideas (Rotterdam: Bernier, 1685 [octavo, 280 pp.]).

[Leibniz's notes center on the problem of intelligible extension. They seem to be incomplete, and 6 verso is empty. He makes only one comment.]

p. 98. Intelligible extension is neither a substance nor a modification of substance. It is not divine substance in itself. It is the divine substance only insofar as corporeal creatures can participate in it.

(*Why then say that it is not a substance?*)

13

Boyle and Leibniz

Leroy E. Loemker

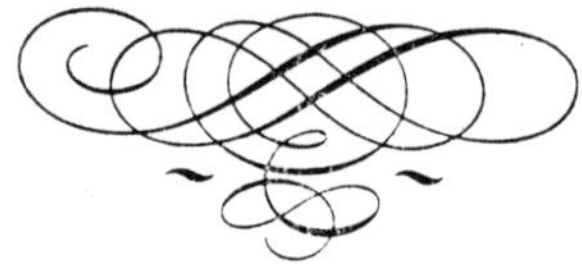

THE PURPOSE of this paper is to examine the influence of the Honorable Robert Boyle, leader of the Royal Society, indefatigable experimenter, and champion both of the new mechanical philosophy and of religious faith, upon the thought of Leibniz, particularly in the decade and a half ending with the first adequate formulations of this thought.[1] The justification for such a study lies not merely in the fact that Boyle influenced Leibniz significantly or that there exist documents recording this influence which are still undiscussed. It follows rather from the common twofold concern of the two men for the expansion of the scientific enterprise as an instrument of the happiness (or the perfection) of mankind, and for the reconciliation of science with religious faith, to the end of strengthening a universal basis for European order. Both had an ideal of "the Christian virtuoso," and both sought recruits for the office. One guided the activities of the Royal Society, the other founded the Berlin Academy, not to

This paper was first published in the *Journal of the History of Ideas* XVI (1955): 22–43.

1. From about 1670 to 1686, when Leibniz's thought had attained at least a provisional synthesis, in such studies as the "General Inquisitions" (1686), the "Meditations on Knowledge, Truth, and Ideas" (1684), the "Discourse on Metaphysics" (1686), and his criticism of Descartes's principles of physics.

mention his other projects for the organized expansion of research and of technology. Furthermore, despite basic differences in their conceptions of both scientific method and religious motives, it is clear that Leibniz was not only spurred on by his reading of the great Irishman's writings, but was also driven to certain important modifications in his thought.

Beyond references to personal contacts between the two men on the occasion of Leibniz's London visit in 1673, the discussion will be based primarily on those works of Boyle which Leibniz is known to have read, particularly *The Origine of Formes and Qualities* and *The Excellency of Theology*.[2]

I

Actual reading notes on *The Origine of Formes and Qualities* have, unfortunately, not been found, but it is clear that Leibniz early became acquainted with its exposition of, and argument for, the new physical science. H. Oldenburg first called his attention to the work in a letter of 10/20 August 1670, a long time after Leibniz had himself accepted the mechanical philosophy.[3]

2. *The Origine of Formes and Qualities (according to the Corpuscular Philosophy) illustrated by Considerations and Experiments* (Oxford: Printed by H. Hall for R. Davis, 1666); *The Excellency of Theology, compar'd with Natural Philosophy (as both are Objects of Man's Study)*, discours'd of in a Letter to a Friend by THRBE . . . to which are annex'd some Occasional Thoughts about the *Excellency and Grounds of the Mechanical Hypothesis* (London: Printed by T. N. for Henry Herringman, 1674). With the exception of *The Origine of Formes and Qualities*, Boyle's works referred to in this paper are cited in the editions used by Leibniz. Extensive reading notes by Leibniz on the last four of Boyle's works, with occasional comments, are to be found on four large sheets in *Die Leibniz-Handschriften der Königlichen Offentlichen Bibliothek zu Hannover*, edited by Eduard Bodemann (Hanover: Hahn, 1895), I (Theol.), xx, Bl. 330–333. The notes on *The Excellency of Theology* have been dated December 1675, from the letter to Oldenburg quoted in this chapter. The other notes are assigned by Albert Rivaud to February 1676, which Leibniz gives as the date when he received *The Possibility of the Resurrection* from his friend Knorr von Rosenroth. Brief descriptions of some of these notes are found in Grua, I:4 f. Many of the notes are scarcely legible. Leibniz's comments are given in the Appendix at the end of this article.

3. Academy Ed. II, i:61. Oldenburg mentioned the work in a list of Boyle's most recent contributions; this list Leibniz passed on to Thomasius

He had been strongly impressed by Boyle's experiments several years before his first London journey, and it must have been this work which fixed in his mind the basic categories in terms of which Boyle worked.[4] Unlike him, Leibniz had been thoroughly trained in scholastic thought as a boy, and the decision to accept the new mechanism instead of the philosophy of forms had been a clear-cut one. Like Boyle, he had learned from Francis Bacon the spirit and the values of the new philosophy, and had appropriated from Pierre Gassendi the mechanistic program of interpreting nature through matter, shape, and motion alone. His teacher at Jena, Erhard Weigel, had stirred Leibniz's interest in adapting Aristotle to the new point of view, and he had already, in 1669, sent to Thomasius his effort to reinterpret "the philosopher" in terms of the corpuscular categories. In the *Confession of Nature against Atheists* (1669), Leibniz sought to base an argument for God upon the fact that cohesion, extension, resistance, and location cannot be explained without motion, and therefore not without God.[5] And in the *New Physical Hypothesis* of 1671, while retaining mechanistic principles, he had moved away from atomism by undertaking to reduce the qualities of bodies to a series of momentary motions, (as he interpreted the conatuses of Hobbes), and had been stirred by some analogies between such

---

on September 23, 1670. On December 8/18, 1670, Oldenburg reported the appearance of the Latin translation published in Oxford.

4. Thus, in communicating with Thomasius, April 20/30, 1669, Leibniz, apparently ignorant of the argument between Boyle and Hobbes about the vacuum, included both men among those who do not commit themselves, either to a vacuum or to a plenum (Academy Ed. II, i:15; cf. *The Origine of Formes and Qualities*). In the early outline for the "Catholic Demonstrations," there is a reference to Boyle's experiments with the weight of growing plants, reported in the *Sceptical Chemist* (Academy Ed. VI, i:496). In the "Confession of Nature against Atheists," Leibniz credits Boyle with the term *corpuscular philosophers*. Later he cites with approval Boyle's theories of color and of elasticity (*New Physical Hypothesis*; Gerhardt, IV:195–208), and his denial of rest (Academy Ed. II, i:66, 167).

5. At this stage in Leibniz's thought, he agreed with Boyle and Descartes that motion must originate in mind. For the early development of Leibniz's physical theories, see W. Kabitz, *Die Philosophie des jungen Leibniz* (Heidelberg: Carl Winters, 1909), pp. 49 ff.

series and the succession of mental events to project a work on the mind, the *Elementa de Mente*, about which he reported with enthusiasm to Antoine Arnauld, Duke John Frederick, and others.[6] Thus he had, by the time of his journey to Paris, firmly adopted the new mechanism, and yet had moved beyond a simple theory of atoms to an analysis of motion, which was to serve him for the understanding of both body and mind.

In the notations which Leibniz made during his visit to London in 1673, memoranda on Boyle's experiments and conversations predominate. He obviously used every opportunity to meet the great man and to learn all that he could from him, not merely about his own chemical discoveries, but also about the studies of the various members of the Royal Society.[7] In his London notes, never fully published, Leibniz appears in the role of a "polyhistor," noting down all information of interest to him under rubrics ranging from algebra and geometry, through the various sciences to biology and medicine, and concluding with a miscellany.[8] Here the name of Boyle appears far more frequently than any other, both in relation to his own experiments and for reports on the work of others.

It was late in 1675, however, that Leibniz became aware of Boyle's theological works, and particularly those which under-

6. Cf. Gerhardt, IV:230; Loemker, p. 141 (prop. 17), Gerhardt, I:61, 67, 72 f. The fullest description of the proposed *Elementa de Mente* is in the treatise "On the Resurrection of Bodies" sent to John Frederick in 1671 (Academy Ed. II, i:133 f., especially secs. 11–15). See, at end of this chapter, Appendix, 331 recto.

7. See J. E. Hofmann, *Die Entwickungsgeschichte der Leibnizschen Mathematik während des Aufenthaltes in Paris* (1672–76) (Munich: Leibniz Verlag, 1949), pp. 13 ff.

8. C. I. Gerhardt's brief report to the Prussian Academy in 1890 entitled "Leibniz in London" is translated in J. M. Child, *The Early Mathematical Manuscripts of Leibniz* (Chicago: Open Court, 1920), pp. 159 ff. There is an additional misplaced sheet in Bodemann, *op. cit.*, XLI, ii:9, which obviously belongs to the London visit. It refers to Charles II's prorogation of Parliament, and contains many notes from a conversation with Boyle, including a long paragraph on Boyle's experience with the Irish healer Valentine Greatrakes.

took a definition of the proper relative roles of faith and the new science. On December 28, 1675, he wrote the following to Oldenburg:

I ask that you commend me to the most Honorable Mr. Boyle, if an occasion offers itself. I esteem him as highly as virtue and wisdom can be esteemed in a man. I recently read his argument that the study of theology is not to be condemned (i.e., *The Excellency of Theology*). It has greatly moved me, and strengthened me in the purpose which as you know I formed long ago, of treating a science of mind through geometrical demonstrations. I have observed many wonderful things in this field which I shall sometime expound. I do not agree with the Cartesians in this matter. They build many things upon ideas which I suspect of being sophisms.[9]

Leibniz's reading notes on *The Excellency of Theology* cover four large closely written folio pages. With them are four even larger sheets with notes on *The Reconcileableness of Reason and Religion, The Possibility of the Resurrection,* and *Some Motives and Incentives to the Love of God,* containing the information that Knorr von Rosenroth had sent him the last-named work in February 1676.

Most significant here is Leibniz's statement that Boyle's discussion of the relative values of theology and the new experimental science, coming at the very time at which he himself was perfecting the algorithms and principles of the calculus, and after he had reread and paraphrased Plato, had studied the unpublished manuscripts of Descartes and Pascal, and had received from Tschirnhaus a first report on the *Ethics* of Spinoza, aroused in him once more the intent of writing the long projected *Elementa de Mente.*

This projected work, which was to be not primarily a psychology but a metaphysical system (though Leibniz proposed to support his conclusions by empirical observations of mental phenomena),[10] was closely related to another project, the *Elementa de Corpore* or the *Elementa Physicae.* Both were intended as sections of two greater and more ambitious projects. One of these

9. Gerhardt Math., I:83; cf. Loemker, p. 165.
10. For example, see the Paris notes in Jagodinski, especially sec. V.

was a rational apology for the Christian faith, the *Catholic Demonstrations,* which was to use the new mathematical method of analysis and synthesis with such convincing force that it would serve as an invincible basis for the reunion of the churches and the conversion of the heathen. The other was the project, variously titled, for a general science and an encyclopedia.[11] Thus the common elements whose serial orderings constitute body and mind alike were to be revealed, to the end that both science and faith could be included in the same general science and be advanced by the same general method of analysis and synthesis. Unfortunately, no papers showing a consistent effort to work out the *Elementa de Mente* have been found, but the existing studies for the *Elementa de Corpore* combine an interest in method with an ordering of scientific content—the former presumably for the work on logic, the latter for that on theology.[12]

This is the extent of Boyle's direct influence upon Leibniz. There is no evidence that the two met when Leibniz again passed through London on his way to his new Hanoverian post in 1676. Nor is there evidence that they ever corresponded, a fact which may seem surprising in view of Boyle's generous graciousness and the very large correspondence of both, but which may be understandable in view of the general impression which the young Leibniz created in England of being a pushing opportunist, ignorant of what had already been achieved and frequently claiming for himself as achievements what were still mere dreams. Years later, after his death in 1691, Boyle's attempt to define nature precipitated a debate in Germany which echoed earlier discussions in England and gave Leibniz an occasion to define precisely in what sense he himself ascribed self-being to nature.[13]

11. For the place of the *Physical Elements* in the general science, see Gerhardt, VII:60, 65; for the place of both in the *Catholic Demonstrations,* Academy Ed. VI, i:494; II, i:489, etc. Cf. note 6 above.

12. The exploratory plan for the *Elementa Physicae* published by E. Gerland, *Leibnizens nachgelassene Schriften physikalischen, mechanischen und technischen Inhalts* (Leipsig: Teubner, 1906), pp. 110–113, is accompanied in the Hanover manuscripts by an extensive discussion of physical method (Bodemann, *op. cit.,* XXXVII, iii, Bl. 1–10.

13. "Concerning Nature itself," Gerhardt, IV:504 ff.; Loemker, pp. 498 ff.

Meanwhile, Leibniz's eagerness to learn everything he could from the older man was early qualified by a critical reserve. To Hermann Conring's staunch defense of Aristotle he answered, completely in the Boylean vein (3/13 January 1678), that an experimental determination of causes is never certain except when crucial instances are offered. But he insisted, too, that

> what [Boyle] stressed continuously, and strove to prove with such great preparation, this I hold to be demonstrated. I believe that no prudent man will doubt that the apparatus of forms and faculties is useless in giving the reasons for things.[14]

But there is a slightly disdainful note in his choice of the words *inculcat* and *tanto apparatu probare nititur*. In 1681, he wrote to Friedrich Schraeder that, while he had great admiration for Boyle's experimental ingenuity and industry, he often marveled that, from so many outstanding observations, Boyle had elicited no conclusions of any importance, almost always ending with the worn-out remark that everything must be explained by magnitude, figure, and motion. "To me," Leibniz adds, "it seems high time we undertake to say by what magnitude, by what figures and motions phenomena are to be explained."[15] And this is his final judgment, repeated much later in the *New Essays*, where he again points to the need of making Boyle's ingenuity fruitful by supplementing it with a logical art.[16]

II

In the realm of science itself, and of logic, Leibniz's greatest debt to Boyle was for the exhibition of experimental procedures and for clues as to their logical nature and limitations. It is true that, as his notes on the English visit and on his reading show, he acquired from Boyle a mass of scientific and chemical detail

---

The work of Boyle which stimulated the debate between G. C. Schelhammer and John Christopher Sturm was *A Free Enquiry into the Vulgarly Received Notion of Nature*, 1685.

14. Academy Ed. II, i:386.

15. *Ibid.*, p. 519.

16. *Nouveaux Essais*, bk. IV, chap. 12, sec. 13. See Appendix below, 33 verso, in the notes on *The Excellency of Theology*.

of which his later writing frequently made use.[17] Boyle himself discussed his method scarcely at all; he seems to have experimented by intuition and curiosity rather than by conscious rule. Yet, he did demonstrate effectively the importance of controlled correlation between observed effects and their causes and made use of a set of physical categories—matter and motion, qualities, and forms—in terms of which he could describe method. He also described the role of hypothesis in the devising of such experiments. Furthermore, using these principles, he drew important conclusions about method, notably about the uncertain nature of physical truth and the value of excluding from consideration any assumptions (for example, about the void, about the ultimacy of the atoms themselves as particles of nature, and about the universality and inclusiveness of the mechanical hypothesis) which were not required to make the hypothesis fruitful. In spite of his failure to state the specific results of his experiments, his view of the importance of his method was itself of great significance, however unsystematic and wavering his various accounts may have been.

The problem which Boyle's experiments presented to Leibniz was that of incorporating their truth into a rationalistic conception of scientific method. He had already recognized the role of sense experience in knowledge. But now the differences between judgments of fact and of reason became explicit,[18] and Boyle gave him a new appreciation of the empirical basis for knowledge at a time when his old concept of a universal science of combina-

17. Beyond this, Leibniz obviously owed to Boyle a large number of chemical illustrations, figures of speech, and historical and literary allusions. A few examples are the title "corpuscular philosophy" itself (Gerhardt, VII:272, etc.; Loemker, p. 478); the theory that atomism originated with Moschus the Phoenician (in "The Sceptical Chemist," in *The Excellency of Theology*, and elsewhere. Cf. Academy Ed. II, i:251; Gerhardt, VII:146, etc.); the hymn of Galen (*The Usefulness of Natural Philosophy*), in *The Works of the Honorable Robert Boyle*, edited by T. Birch (London: Printed for J. & F. Rivington and others, 1772), III, 52; cf. Couturat, pp. 5, 95; Gerhardt, VII:71, 273, etc.; Loemker, pp. 478–479; and illustrations drawn from mining, watchmaking, chemistry, and biology.

18. Cf. the letters to Simon Foucher and Edmond Mariotte in 1675, 1676 (Academy Ed. II, i:245 ff., 269 f.; Loemker, pp. 151–154).

tions was being elaborated into a general method of logical analysis and synthesis, a method which required, therefore, an inclusion of the exploratory function of hypothesis, and a logic of temporal causal analysis and of imperfect verification.[19] That this was involved in experiment, Boyle always showed clearly.

As we have already seen, Leibniz accepted Boyle's estimate of the barrenness of the Scholastic doctrine of forms for a scientific understanding of qualities. It is true that each man redefined and retained a concept of forms consistent with his own scientific theory, Boyle accepting a pragmatic interpretation[20] of form as an organized unity of those qualities which constitute an individual body, Leibniz (much later) re-establishing the term to signify the "individual concept" from which the properties and accidents of the monad follow as values of a variable. But the hypostatized forms of the Scholastics have no value, and in his criticism of them, Leibniz adopted the very figures of Boyle:

> It would be but little satisfaction to one that desires to understand the causes of what occurs to observation in a watch, and how it comes to point at, and strike the hours, to be told that it was such a watchmaker that contrived it.[21]

19. That Leibniz was considering the logical problem in Boyle's experiments is shown by the concluding paragraph in Leibniz's letter to Oldenburg, 28 December 1675, quoted above: "So men will always philosophize in the manner of Boyle, and sometimes carry our way through to the end, except insofar as the nature of things can, to the degree that it is known, be subjected to a calculus, and newly discovered qualities can be reduced to a mechanism"; cf. Loemker, p. 166.

20. *The Origine of Formes and Qualities*, p. 66: "Why may we not say that the form of a body, being made up of those qualities united in one subject doth likewise consist in such a convention of those newly nam'd mechanical affections of matter, as is necessary to constitute a body of that determinate kind? And so, though I shall for brevities sake retain the word *form*, yet I would be understood to mean by it, not a real substance distinct from matter, but only the matter itself of a natural body, consider'd with its peculiar manner of existence."

21. "Supplementary Essay on the Excellency of the Mechanical Hypothesis," in *The Excellency of Theology*, p. 16. Cf. Gerhardt, VII:265; Loemker, p. 173 (1677); *Discourse on Metaphysics*, sec. 10 (1686), (Loemker, p. 308); and frequently elsewhere.

On the positive side, moreover, Boyle showed, however unclearly, that the experimental philosophy offered a method of discovering causes of qualities by means of analysis and synthesis. This, indeed, is the point at which he advanced beyond Francis Bacon's vagueness regarding forms and their dependencies. Made explicit, his rule of method might be stated as a realistic version of Mill's canons. Analyze all of the physical properties upon which a given quality to be investigated may depend; test each for presence, absence, or variation in relation to the presence, absence, or variation of the quality to be explained. Then by experimental or causal explanation, we mean only that the presence of the quality under study depends upon the presence or state of certain analyzed basic properties ("catholic affections," "inseparable accidents")[22] of the body involved. Thus the investigation of qualities involves a correlation of occurrence between two sequences of experienced qualities, the one nearer our subjective experiences, the other nearer to the basic properties of material bodies, i.e., mass, figure, motion, and position; and analysis leads, on the one hand, to the elementary perceptions of sensory qualities which for Leibniz constitute primary elements of truths of fact, and on the other, to the basic principles and concepts of the mechanical hypothesis itself.

This points directly to Leibniz's own integration of the logic of truths of fact into his general science, and in particular to his interpretation of cause and effect as a description of the parallelism of states between two series of individual entities, the more distinctly perceived one being held to be the cause, the less distinctly perceived, the effect.[23] By the principles of sufficient reason and of identity, truths of reason involve a process of analysis and synthesis in which complex concepts are analyzed and synthesized on a basis of the equivalence of their component simple ideas; the ideal of propositional form is an equation, and the basis for advance in knowledge is the definition. In truths of fact this is also true, except that we cannot carry through the

22. *The Origine of Formes and Qualities*, pp. 9 f., 56 f.

23. *Discourse on Metaphysics*, secs. 14, 15, Gerhardt, IV:439 ff.; Loemker, pp. 311–313.

infinity of steps involved, but must stop, pragmatically, with our simplest perceptions. Hence, synthesis now involves succession and time, and the logical principles of identity, sufficient reason, and equivalence reappear as the principle of the equivalence of antecedent and consequent state (if analyzed adequately) in phenomena. Though Leibniz unfortunately never developed his logic to the point of a careful analysis of truths of fact, the methodological papers of the early Hanover period, from 1676 to 1686, point clearly to such a theory.[24]

In an essay dated May 1677, Leibniz attempts a demonstration of how his method of analysis and synthesis would apply to the discovery of causes of chemical qualities.[25] This paper, which must be considered a forestudy for a section of the *Elementa Physicae,* may best be regarded as an effort to systematize Boyle's experimental method within the framework of the old art of combinations. It incorporates many of Boyle's convictions, but adds to them some of Leibniz's own, such, for example, as his argument for the use of concave mirrors in making observations, and his belief in the simplicity of physical explanations. He also repeats Boyle's pragmatic interpretation of the limits of scientific analysis. This is a frequently recurring theme in Boyle. In *The Excellency of Theology,* he admits that chemical analyses are "sometimes the most obvious and ready" but "not the most fundamental and satisfactory."[26] The corpuscles themselves may not be the ultimate indivisible parts of nature, but "made up of the coalition of several . . . *minima naturalia,*" which "are the seeds or immediate principles of many sorts of natural bodies."[27] This vague concept may have suggested to Leibniz the notion of infinite analysis.

Although bodies may be infinitely divisible into other subtler bodies, and it is incredible that there should be any prime element, this should

24. See particularly the *General Inquisitions,* secs. 71–75 (1686); Couturat, pp. 375 ff.

25. "On a Method of Arriving at a True Analysis of Bodies and the Causes of Natural Things," Gerhardt, VII:265–269; Loemker, pp. 173–176.

26. *The Excellency of Theology,* p. 24.

27. *The Origine of Formes and Qualities,* p. 72.

not keep us from seeking causes. He who uses stones in architecture does not object to the bits of earth interposed between them; he who uses water in hydraulic engines pays no attention to the air in it which can nevertheless be extracted by the Guericke pump. . . . It is possible that the effects of very subtle bodies within the bodies which we handle are no more relevant to our experiments than are the small stones in a field or even the insensible corpuscles in contributing to the strength of fortifications.[28]

The practical limitations which Boyle imposed upon the corpuscular hypothesis must in fact have strengthened Leibniz's conviction that scientific knowledge is probable only and cannot claim the absolute certainty of mathematics. Boyle and others in the seventeenth century anticipated the scientific attitude of later centuries when they combined a complete faith in the value and adequacy of a mechanistic science with a frank acknowledgement of the limited certainty of scientific knowledge. Not only does Boyle exempt from his hypothesis the "reasonable soul" and the "origin of qualities in beasts," but he admits that he can give no complete account of "the nature of each several quality explicated,"[29] and he argues that

physical demonstrations can beget but a physical certainty (that is, a certainty upon supposition that the principles of physic be true), not a metaphysical certainty (wherein 'tis absolutely impossible that the thing believed should be other than true).[30]

Many things regarded as physical demonstrations really possess "but a moral certainty."[31] This need not even assume the objective and independent reality of the quality or form which it studies. The nature of body in general and of sensations are not understood, though such understanding would be basic to physical certainty.[32] Indeed, Boyle devotes a section of *The Origine of Formes and Qualities* to a refutation of the scholastic treatment of qualities and accidents as real; sensory qualities in par-

28. "On a Method of Arriving at a True Analysis of Bodies and the Causes of Natural Things," Gerhardt, VII:268; cf. Loemker, p. 175.

29. *The Origine of Formes and Qualities*, p. 5.

30. *The Excellency of Theology*, p. 140.

31. *Ibid.*, p. 142.

32. *Ibid.*, p. 144.

ticular, "are not in the bodies that are endowed by them any real or distinct entities, or differing from the matter itself"; they depend, rather, upon "a certain congruity or incongruity in point of figure or texture (or other mechanical attributes) to our sensories."[33] Thus a degree of phenomenalism is involved in Boyle's conception of his method, and he anticipates the strictures which Leibniz places upon scientific mechanism. Though Leibniz is unwilling to exempt even mind from mechanical analysis, as did both Descartes and Boyle, he agrees with the latter in denying to mechanism an insight into the ultimate nature of existence, assigning to it the important role of describing the order of phenomena involved in our perception of natural processes.

Consistent with his phenomenalism and his growing emphasis upon activity, however, Leibniz is forced to reject the remnant of materialism that Boyle retains. He had in 1671 reduced both body and mind to a series of momentary motions. In 1675, after a period in which he toyed with Cartesian dualism, he noted, in commenting upon Boyle's remark that no philosopher has taught that matter itself is made out of nothing, that it is obvious to him that matter is something far different from what Boyle thinks.[34] Thus, while Boyle, with the fresh openmindedness which seventeenth-century science still retained, accepted an unexplained dualism of mechanism and vital and telic principles, Leibniz conceived a new synthesis by subordinating matter as passive content or state, to the dynamic individualism of his new forms.

The most conspicuous aspect of Boyle's theory of scientific uncertainty is to be found in his conception of hypothesis. Not only did he treat his own theory as a hypothesis, but he improved on Bacon by making explicit the role of conjecture in the investigation of nature, adding to previous discussions the requirement that a hypothesis must "fairly comport not only with all other truths, but with all other phenomena of nature as well as those 'tis framed to explicate."[35]

33. *The Origine of Formes and Qualities*, p. 19.

34. See Appendix below: notes on *The Origine of Formes and Qualities*, 332 recto.

35. *The Excellency of Theology*, pp. 207 f., where the nature of hypothesis is discussed more fully.

In contrast to Pascal,[36] both Boyle and Leibniz regarded hypothesis as an imperfect, preliminary stage in science, to be replaced, ideally at least, by complete proof, though both admitted too that such completion may be both impossible and unnecessary for science.[37] In the "New Method for Teaching and Learning Jurisprudence" (1668), Leibniz had still discussed empirical method in the spirit of Bacon, moving directly from *historia* through *observatio* to *scientia*. In 1671, however, he treated his new physical theory as a hypothesis, and explained its hypothetical character in his preliminary dedication.[38] Much later, after Leibniz's critics closed in upon his first published philosophical position, he treated his system, too, with increasing frequency as a hypothesis.[39]

After 1675, however, it became necessary for Leibniz to find an interpretation for scientific hypothesis within his outline of a method of analysis and synthesis. In his effort to do so, he found an analogy in the algebraic (or "specious") analysis in which the value of an unknown quantity is determined by accepted operations upon a formula embodying the conditions of the problem.[40]

36. Response to Noel, October 29, 1647 (*Oeuvres*, Brunschwig, II, 99 ff.), cited in J. Guitton, *Pascal et Leibniz* (Paris: Aubier, 1951), pp. 45 f.

37. *The Excellency of Theology*, pp. 35 f: "And on this occasion let me observe that it is not always necessary, though it be always desirable, that he that proposes an hypothesis in astronomy, chemistry, anatomy, or other part of physics, be able *a priori* to prove his hypothesis to be true, or demonstratively to show that the other hypotheses proposed about the same subject must be false. For as, if I mistake not, Plato said that the world was God's epistle written to mankind, and might have added, consonantly to another saying of his, it was written in mathematical letters; so, in the physical explications of the parts and system of the world, methinks, there is somewhat like what happens when men conjecturally frame several keys to enable us to understand a letter written in cyphers." (Note Leibniz on the "conjectural method," below.)

38. "New Method for Teaching and Learning Jurisprudence," I, secs. 32, 32a. (Academy Ed. VI, i:284 f.); cf. Gerhardt, IV:180.

39. To Lady Damaris Masham, 30 June 1704. Gerhardt, III:353 f. It was doubtless the discussion of the three alternative theories of the structure of the solar system which revealed the importance of hypotheses for scientific method in the seventeenth century.

40. Leibniz notes the importance of adding the "Initia physicae con-

In the unpublished *Elementa Physicae* of the early Hanover period, his analytic doctrine of hypothesis is explicit.[41] Classifying physical truths into sensual, intellectual, and mixed, and dividing inductions into observations and experiments (which differ from mere observations by the introduction of the scientist's manipulations), he describes a "conjectural method" which, though not certain in its results, is useful in the discovery of causes. The conjectural method may be applied either *a priori* or *a posteriori*. The former is the method of hypothesis, the latter that of analogy.[42] His description:

> The conjectural method *a priori* proceeds by hypothesis assuming certain causes (it may be without proof), and showing that there will result from these assumptions the things which are now happening. Such an hypothesis is like the key to a cryptogram,[43] and the more simple it is and the more numerous the events that can be explained by it, the more probability it has. [But] the same effect can have several causes.[44] Therefore no firm demonstration can be drawn from the success of hypothesis. However I will not deny that the number of phenomena which are happily explained by some hypothesis can be so great that it must be taken as morally certain.

Thus the conjectural method of hypothesis is a valid empirical method, analogous to that of algebra, which involves a special form of the more general method of analysis and synthesis. But it is an auxiliary method, made necessary by the fact that man's understanding is finite while the complexity of the natural order is infinite.

---

jecturalis seu hypothesis" to the Physical Elements in the outline given in Gerhardt, VII:60. See also Couturat 94 (May 1676), where experimental verification is treated briefly after the analogy of algebra, in what may be the first study for the Physical Elements after the reading of *The Excellency of Theology*. (See also Gerhardt, VII:297 f.; Couturat, p. 174.)

41. Bodemann, *op. cit.*, XXXVII, iii, Bl. 1–10. See 8 recto. Since published in Loemker, pp. 277–290.

42. *Ibid.*, 2 verso, 3 recto.

43. Cf. note 37 for Boyle's similar use of the cryptogram.

44. Though not, of course, if causal analysis could be carried through to ultimate simple terms. In this case all divergent formulas or formulations would reduce to the same one. Cf. the dialogue of August 1677 (Gerhardt, VII:192 f.) for this principle of complete analysis.

III

In general, it may be said that Leibniz found it necessary to go beyond the corpuscular hypothesis itself because of an internal inconsistency between Boyle's conception of its adequacy and the strictures which Boyle himself placed upon it. Behind this there was also a difference in religious motive. Boyle had argued that both Aristotelian science and modern materialism threatened the security of religious faith as well as science itself; he therefore urged a corpuscularism in which the origin of motion was still ascribed to mind (as Descartes had done, and, in his early years, Leibniz as well), but which provided an adequate basis for experimental procedures in the region of matter and motion.[45] Leibniz, on the other hand, eventually concluded that the corpuscular hypothesis, while not injurious to religion, could be used by disbelievers to refute it, but that traditional scholastic Aristotelianism, in turn, had been used too widely to discredit the new science. Therefore a new synthesis was needed—a restoration of substantial forms (though the new doctrine resembles the scholastic one not at all, but rather the new Platonic theory of plastic natures), and a reduction of matter to its Aristotelian meaning. The concept of the monad was thus to provide a union of mechanical science with the classical philosophic basis upon which the moral order of Europe had so long rested.[46]

It was therefore not primarily his concern about science and its method which Leibniz found stimulated by the reading of Boyle in late 1675, but, as the letter to Oldenburg shows, his concern was for a rational interpretation of faith; the *Elementa de Mente* was to restore mind to its proper role in the understanding of both the natural and the divine order.[47] How the reading of *The*

45. See, for example, Boyle, *Some Considerations about the Reconcileableness of Reason and Religion*, by T. E., a Layman (London: Printed by T. N. for H. Herringman, 1675), pp. 35 ff. On the roots of infidelism in Aristotle, see *The Reconcileableness of Reason and Religion*, Preface, p. iii f.

46. Gerhardt, VII:324 (ca. 1679); Gerhardt Math. III:134 f. (1687); Gerhardt Math. VI:234 ff. (1695).

47. The need for a theory of mind to complete the *De corpore* is first suggested in a letter to Hobbes, 13/22 July 1670 (Gerhardt, VII:574; Loemker, p. 107).

Excellency of Theology revived his intention to write such a work is made clearer by the detailed sequence of Leibniz's reading notes. As Boyle enumerates the issues upon which revelation speaks more clearly than scientific experiment—our knowledge of angels, good and bad; our knowledge of corporeal things, of the creation of the world *ex nihilo* and the creation of man; our knowledge of the nature of the human soul and Descartes's admission that he cannot prove its immortality but only its difference from the body[48]—the limits in his corpuscular philosophy as the support of a natural theology became clearer and clearer. But a rational theology was to be the purpose of the *Elementa de Mente*. Neither Leibniz nor Boyle made any fundamental distinction between rational and revealed theology, since both were convinced of the reasonableness of Christianity. Leibniz sought, as is well known, a universal instrument of reason which would confirm revelation completely—in the general interpretation accepted by the Council of Trent. Boyle recognized a difference between knowledge by revelation and knowledge by experimental procedure, or between what reason could establish with revelation and without it; he also distinguished between the teaching of "the Christian religion itself," and "that which is taught by this or that church or sect."[49] As the act of endowment of the Boyle Lectures itself attests, his concern was "for proving the Christian religion against notorious infidels, viz., atheists, theists, pagans, Jews and Mahometans, not descending lower to any controversies that are among Christians themselves."

Both men, moreover, accepted the alternative of Christianity or cultural decay; both sought to protect the order of Europe which was now threatened by "the new libertines" who "deny those very principles of natural theology wherein the Christian and those other differing religions agree."[50] Leibniz first expressed his concern about the flood of atheism threatening Europe while at Mainz under the influence of the Elector, John Philipp of Schönborn's and Baron von Boineburg's theological interests,[51]

48. *The Excellency of Theology*, pp. 27 ff.
49. *The Reconcileableness of Reason and Religion*, pp. 6 ff.
50. *Ibid.*, Preface, pp. iv f.
51. Cf. Gerhardt, I:26 ff.; IV:105 ff.; Loemker, pp. 102–103; pp. 109 ff.

but this same concern for the threat of European revolution remained with him throughout his life.[52] Boyle too felt the threat of collapse, and justified his dabbling in theology, as a layman, by pointing to the religious indifference which he believed heralded this collapse.

"Among us here in England," he wrote, "the times to which our memory can reach have been less guilty than the present time is, of a spreading and bold profaneness."[53] "The church militant is threatened by shipwreck." Since the source of the danger was not only "the vicious lives of men, but . . . their licentious discourses," the new science must itself be brought to the support of faith by its more compelling ideal of truth. Indeed, science has an obligation to this religious service, for it has a twofold importance. Both Boyle and Leibniz were convinced of its human utility and worth, but both insisted that it is also an essential part of modern man's glorification of God by revealing the laws of his creation. According to Boyle, man is compelled, by the debt of obedience and gratitude he owes to God, to study not merely theology, but the order of creation as well.[54]

Leibniz, too, urges both grounds for the study of nature. In the *Elementa Physicae* the argument is limited to the knowledge of bodies, which, he says,

> will have two supreme values: one, that we may perfect our mind by understanding the ends and the causes of things; the other, that we may preserve and improve our body, which is the organ of the soul, by achieving satisfaction and avoiding harm. Of these two uses of this science, the former can be sought from rational physics alone, the

---

Leibniz condemns Hobbes and Bodin for their irreligious influence. Boyle's opposition to Hobbes and the "new Somatici" is frequently expressed. Cf. *The Reconcileableness of Reason and Religion*, p. 37: "As for the new Somatici such as Mr. Hobbes (and some few others), by what I have yet seen of his, I am not much tempted to forsake anything that I looked upon as a truth before, even in natural philosophy itself, upon the score of what he (though never so confidently) delivers."

52. *Nouveaux Essais*, bk. IV, chap. 16, sec. 4.

53. *The Reconcileableness of Reason and Religion*, Preface, pp. i, vi.

54. *The Excellency of Theology*, pp. 66 ff.; cf. *The Reconcileableness of Reason and Religion*, pp. 13 f., 17 ff., etc.

latter from empirical physics as well. . . . But what greater master could we serve than the Author of the universe, God? And what more beautiful hymn shall we sing than that in which is expressed his truest praise through the example of things themselves? The more one can give reasons for his love, the more one loves God. For to find joy in the perfection of anyone, this is itself to love.[55]

The last sentence suggests, however, that, in spite of their agreement that there is a Christian motive in the scientific enterprise, the two men differ greatly in their understanding of it. For one, the application of reason to the ways of God is a duty owed him; for the other, it is the fulfillment of Christian love. It is not to be wondered at that Leibniz's notes on Boyle's *Seraphic Love* are casual, desultory, and largely restricted to the noting of scriptural references and literary adornments. It has been plausibly conjectured that Leibniz never loved.[56] Love was for him a cultivated attitude inseparable from reason, binding together the order of goods and the order of men, a far cry from the intense rapture and anguish of the state which Boyle described. Yet the reader of Boyle's strange work will detect a conspicuous disparity between the impassioned account of mystical love (according to an old account, the work grew out of disappointment in human love), and the silence about its social fruits. While Boyle does find certain important values for personal character in the love of God, he does not, like Leibniz, try to subsume under it either scientific endeavors or a just political order.[57]

Leibniz's conception of love is, on the one hand, more intellectualistic and egoistically grounded than Boyle's; but on the other, it is explicitly social in its effects. Leibniz had already anticipated the great religious debates in France and England about the existence of a nonmercenary or disinterested love, by con-

55. *Op. cit.*, 1 recto. On the hymn of Galen, see note 17, above.

56. J. Guitton, *op. cit.*, p. 103.

57. Thus Leibniz asks Burnet de Kemney, if he has opportunity, to persuade Newton to publish his *Optics* from religious grounds, since "to contribute to the public good and to the glory of God is the same thing" (Gerhardt, III:261). And he consistently seeks to relate the three principles of the law given in the Pandects (*Honeste vivere, cuique suum tribuere, nemine laedere*) to the principle of Christian love.

cluding that there is no such love: man is incapable of it. Love is individual joy (and, in this sense, egoistic) in the perfection of the other; on this Leibniz grounds a perfectionist ethics, an idealistic social theory, and an aesthetic theory as well, since perfection involves harmony.

Thus, the implicit dualism of experimental truth and revealed truth in Boyle's theoretical thought is paralleled by his bifurcation of rational duty and irrational love.[58] In spite of the magnificent caution and open-mindedness revealed in his pragmatic treatment of the limits of mechanism, and in his tolerance, on occasion, of alternative nonmechanistic hypotheses, like that of plastic natures and vital forces, Boyle seems to have prepared the way for the deistic separation between creator and creation which was to follow, and which soon involved a forthright repudiation of the very mysticism in which he was so deeply interested. Leibniz, on the other hand, though he extended the mechanistic postulates beyond the areas assigned them by Descartes and Boyle to include the mechanisms of soul itself, ended in an immanent spiritualism according to which, as he put it, "God belongs to me more closely even than my body."[59]

The difference between Leibniz and Boyle thus rests not merely upon a divergence in their conceptions of science; it depends also upon a fundamental disagreement about the relation of reason and faith. Both were at once realists and phenomenalists with regard to nature, and each sought in his own way to resolve the paradox that, though the qualities of bodies depend upon our perception of them, scientific knowledge is nonetheless of real objects. For both, phenomena are "well founded" (to use Leibniz's phrase); there is an underlying "congruity" (Boyle) or "harmony" between the natural order and the order of our analysis and synthesis.[60] Yet Boyle, as we have already seen, was convinced of

58. Note Boyle's general distrust of metaphysics (*Reconcileableness of Reason and Religion*, p. 8) and his emphasis on the failures of philosophy to establish independently the truths of revelation (*The Excellency of Theology*, pp. 23 ff.).

59. "On the True Mystical Theology," Guhrauer, I:410 f.

60. See Boyle's analogy of the relativity of qualities to the congruence of lock and key (*The Origine of Formes and Qualities*, p. 16).

the self-sufficiency of the mechanistic method, and so arrived at a dualism of natural knowledge and divine revelation.

The mediating role of a natural theology (i.e., the theology common to Christianity, Judaism, and Mohammedanism) was thus limited. Reason, for example, cannot prove the resurrection of the body, or, as Descartes admitted, the immortality of the soul.[61] It can prove God's existence but not his moral qualities. All these must be left to scriptural revelation. It is consistent with this that Boyle was deeply committed, all his life, to the cause of Bible translation and the propagation of the gospel in the British colonies. Leibniz, too, was interested in the propagation of Christianity, but his interpretation of scripture already suggested the new criticism, while missionary efforts were to be based, not primarily on scripture, but upon the irrefutable logic of the *Catholic Demonstrations.*

Thus there is a radical difference in the evaluation of reason; for Boyle, it was like the use

> of a watch to estimate time when even the sun is absent or clouded; but when he shines clearly forth, I scruple not to correct and adjust my watch by his beams cast on a dial. So, when no other light is to be had, I estimate truth by my own reason, but where divine revelation can be consulted, I willingly submit my fallible reason to the sure informations afforded by celestial light.[62]

Boyle, in short, was inclined to assign to reason, independent of faith, the field of scientific analysis and explanation, while Leibniz, mathematician and Platonist, believed that the realm of divine order and purpose is itself accessible to it. This in turn involved a difference in the understanding of the divine will. Boyle quoted approvingly Descartes's opinion that God could have made mountains without valleys if he had so willed. But in his notes Leibniz expressed a vigorous dissent. "This does not satisfy me. Whatever implies a contradiction is impossible for this is to say nothing."[63] Without this inclusive concept of rea-

61. *The Excellency of Theology*, pp. 27 f.

62. *The Reconcileableness of Reason and Religion*, Preface, p. xv. An interesting comment on the reliability of seventeenth-century timepieces.

63. *The Reconcileableness of Reason and Religion*, pp. 25 f.; see Appendix, below: 331 recto.

son, Leibniz's proposed completion of logic would be impossible; the same logical principles and operations may serve the realms of both nature and grace, for since the will of God is but his purposive understanding of the best of all possibles, it is not merely scriptural revelation but natural reason that gives us "the knowledge of his will, or positive laws."

IV

It was thus Boyle, rather than Leibniz, whose works encouraged a growing tide of deism, though unintentionally and against his own religious convictions. Three separate teachings led to this result: a belief in the intellectual self-sufficiency of mechanistic science (within its proper limits); a distinction, fundamentally empirical, between reason resting on a general revelation and reason resting on observed fact; and an exclusively religious interpretation of Christian love which excluded from it the social and intellectual virtues.

Leibniz's convictions ran contrary to these divisions, for the regulative principles of his system were harmony, universality, and the mutual "consent" of individual substances. At these points, therefore, Boyle's ideas did not affect him. But there were also contrary trends in Boyle's thought, and it was these which Leibniz used, with his own creative genius, to try to further his attempted syntheses of general science, an ethically grounded legal order, and a Christian theology.

Specifically, Boyle forced him to make place for experiment and hypothesis in his method of analysis and synthesis, and so to develop a logic of truths of fact or empirical and synthetic propositions in which *a priori* and *a posteriori* components are combined. Coming at the very time, too, when Leibniz was becoming conscious of the difficulties in the ontological argument (the keystone of his union of logic and metaphysics), Boyle probably encouraged his shift from this argument to that from an immanent teleology in a mechanistic natural order,[64] and thus

64. In the *Tentamen Anagogicum* (Gerhardt, VII:270–279; Loemker, pp. 477–485), this theory is proposed as an answer to the religious issues raised by the corpuscular philosophy.

from the ideal of philosophic certainty to that of probability.

The fundamental issue between the two modes of thinking seems to have been that of the continuity or discontinuity in human experience itself. Between the claims of scientific evidence and of faith Boyle saw no conflicts, but very little mutual support.[65] It was Leibniz's intention to make each serve the cause of the other, because they shared a common logic and lay close to each other in the realm of human motives. Our own temper is nearer Boyle's (or in more interesting form, Pascal's) than Leibniz's. It seems that intellectual history always decides against the Leibnizes, the Hegels, the Platos (for their harmony is generally achieved too easily and with too great a sacrifice of the self-sufficiency of man's various interests). Yet the striving for unity serves philosophy too. It helped Leibniz to avoid the "misplaced concretions" of Boyle and the eighteenth century and to undertake a new synthesis in the concrete individual instead.

APPENDIX

Bodemann, *Leibniz-Handschriften*: I (Theol.), 332 recto.

Leibniz's comments, interspersed among his reading notes on Boyle, are of secondary importance in the sense that few of them involve any decisive issue in his own thought. They are given here, in English translation, as a supplement to Grua's imperfect description (see note 2 above).

To distinguish his own comments from his brief notes on Boyle, Leibniz followed his common practice of enclosing them in parentheses and stars. The same practice is followed here.

The indicated pages refer to the editions of Boyle used by Leibniz. The notes on *The Excellency of Theology* and *Some Physico-Theological Considerations about the Possibility of Resurrection*[66] are in Latin;

65. Boyle's conception of *miracle* is that of an intermittent irruption of God's will in nature (*The Reconcileableness of Reason and Religion*, pp. 25 ff.).

66. Boyle, *Some Physico-Theological Considerations about the possibility of the Resurrection* (London: Printed by T. N. for H. Herringman, 1675).

those on *Some Considerations about the Reconcileableness of Reason and Religion* and *Some Motives and Incentives to the Love of God*[67] begin in French but are completed in Latin.

I am indebted to the Director of the Niedersächsische Landesbibliothek for access to these manuscripts and for the privilege of photostating them.

I

The Excellency of Theology compared with natural philosophy (as both are objects of men's study) discours'd in a letter to a friend by THRBE. fellow of the Royal Society . . . London by T. N. Henry Herringman at the anchor in the lower walk of the New Exchange, 1674. 8°.

Preface of the editor (*of Oldenburg, I believe*). Written 1665.

(p. 17) They [good angels] refuse to be adored, and [admonish men to worship] God. They worship Christ, and call themselves servants of his disciples.

(*I have often observed that so many different passages of scripture speak of angels in complete agreement, that it would appear that the doctrine was accepted among the Hebrews. The citations from Revelation, i.e., the Apocalypse, are not rightly ascribed to the matters for which they are intended, for the author had not distinctly introduced servant in the margin.*)

(p.20) None of the philosophers ever taught that matter itself is produced out of nothing.

(*N.B. . . . illustrates this neatly with physical reasons. This is obvious to me, for whom matter is a thing far different from what he thinks.*)

(p. 22) But some day this world (or at least this vortex of ours) (*boldly said*) will either be abolished by annihilation or, what is more probable, renewed.

67. Boyle, *Some Motives and Incentives to the Love of God, pathetically discours'd of in a Letter to a Friend*, fifth edition (London: Printed for H. Herringman, 1670). This work is widely known as the Essay on Seraphic Love.

332 verso.

(p. 40) Whether we shall know each other on the Day of Judgment, awakened from this sleep, as Adam, awakened out of his sleep, knew Eve whom he had never seen before.

(*If we should agree with Plato, Eve was separated from Adam; hence he had never felt her nor seen what was taken from him.*)

333 recto

(p. 145) Nor does this notion of his [Descartes's view that body consists of extension] explain the difficulty about the composition of the continuum.

(*The notion of body cannot be expected to explain this, because there is the same difficulty concerning the notion of space or extension.*)

(p. 148 f.) How the soul is affected in such varied ways by the passions of the body is a difficulty as great as any mystery in theology.

(*The difficulty about the union of soul and body is as great as the difficulty about the incarnation; and the difficulty about its action upon itself is as great as that about the incarnation.*)

333 verso.

(p. 166 f.) No great wit is needed to refute certain errors of the ancients, such as that about the torrid zone, about Venus giving off its own light, and about the milky way. Descartes (*doing scant justice to Galileo*) notes that the telescope was invented not by a mathematician but accidentally by a mechanic, a spectacle-maker (*Brillenmacher*).

(p. 170) Verulam confesses that his discovery of nature is *partus temporis potius quam ingenii*. He says his way of philosophizing compensates for genius.

(*The discovery of the true method achieves this.*)

(p.175 f.) Even though the center of the earth is more than 3500 (English) miles away, my inquiries among navigators and miners have not yet instructed us beyond one mile or so at the most, and this not in above three or four places.

(*See Morius on subterranean things.*)

There is appended a treatise about the Excellency and Grounds of the Mechanical Hypothesis.

(p. 15) (*He says he has seen a chain attached to a flea [albo pubici] but this is a deception, for it is done with the aid of a hair.*)

(p. 36 f.) The world is an epistle written by God to mankind (as I believe Plato has said; he could have added, written in mathematical characters.) If two people both claim to have discovered a key to the cryptograph, it is difficult for them to prove *a priori* and without application whether one is to be preferred to the other. Yet there are cases. (*As if someone uses a key in a language which it is certain was unknown to the writer and to his friends.*)

II

330 recto, top

Some Motives and Incentives to the Love of God, pathetically discours'd of in a letter to a friend by the Honorable Robert Boyle. 5th ed. London by Herringman, 1670. 8°. He inscribed it to his sister, Countess of Warwick.

(p. 17) Our beauty is, for the Moors, the livery of the devil.
(*That is, they ascribe white to the devil.*)

III

331 recto, top

Some considerations about the Reconcileableness of Reason and Religion by T. E., a layman, to which is annexed by the publisher a discourse of Mr. Boyle about the possibility of the resurrection.

(p. 14) . . . as the translator of the new thoughts of Galileo into French says.
(*This is Father Mersenne.*)

(p. 26) Descartes, vol. 2, epistle 6. I dare not say that God cannot make a mountain without a valley, or that 1 and 2 might not make 3, but only that he has given me a soul made in such a way that I cannot conceive them otherwise.
(*This does not satisfy me. Whatever implies a contradiction is impossible, for this is to say nothing.*)

(p. 70) Also, Descartes admits somewhere in a letter that he spent six weeks on a problem of Pappus.
(*In my judgment Boyle is the author of this book as well, for he makes the same citation elsewhere in the work on the excellency of theological study, along with many others.*)

IV

331 recto, bottom

Some physico-theological Considerations about the Possibility of the Resurrection by the Honorable Robert Boyle, Esq., fellow of the Royal Society. London by T. N. for H. Herringman, 1674. 8°.

(p. 11) Someone sowed the ashes of a certain plant similar to our English red poppy in my friend's garden, which, sooner than was expected, produced bigger and more beautiful plants. . . .
(*Whether I think the poppy is papaver?*)

(p. 12) God formed Eve from only the rib of Adam; therefore he added other matter. Nonetheless Eve is understood to be taken from Adam.
(*Namely because the flower of substance has come from him.*)

(p. 20) (*He could have added the regeneration of nitre and spirit of wine from vinegar.*)

330 verso

(p. 24) . . . but the form of sparkling metallic substance which needs no further reduction and is taken for gold.
(*A memorable experiment in which it seems copper can be derived from solid silver without it losing its form.*)

V

331 recto, bottom

Six years ago His Most Serene Highness, the Duke of Hanover, who was wont to reflect upon religion, asked Boineburg to find out my opinion on the resurrection of the flesh. I sent this to the Duke at that time in a short paper. Now, in February 1676, I find a work of Boyle, sent me by Knorr, on the possibility of the resurrection. In it a notable agreement with my views. Only he has insisted more upon chemical illustrations; I have rather followed the difficulties concisely. I hold, namely, that the flower of substance is our body; that the flower of substance now persists perpetually in all changes; that this was foreshadowed through the Luz of the Rabbis. Hence it is easy to see why cannibals, in eating a man, have no power at all over the flower of substance. This flower of substance is diffused through the whole body; somehow comprises the whole form. Add to this what Borelli says in his microscopic observations about the figure of the cherry tree in the shell of the seed or nut enclosed by its fruit; also about the tree of the philosophers; also what is found on plastic force in the French journal, from the English. Plastic force is none other than this active substance, of a definite figure, which enlarges itself when it can. This seems already to exist before conception; conception merely gives it the faculty of increasing. Add Scheck on plastic force; Davison and others. I add something which Boyle seems not to have observed—that the soul is firmly implanted in this flower of substance. Add the reasoning of Perrault against Mariotte on the seat of the soul. If it were really necessary to explain also the restitution of eternal mass—which is not necessary, however, since it is for the most part earth—(*See what the Schoolmen have to say about the existence of bodies in body, about the Eucharistic water and wine and bread*) this could perhaps be done in a general dissolution; just as when, in a unique experiment, different salts are dissolved in the same water, several related salts are reformed by a remarkable principle, without any perturbation. But what can be brought about in only four species of salt, can be brought about with greater subtetly in 1,000,000,000, etc., species also; why not assume them? What happens in any species of salt whatever may happen more generally in any human individual whatever, in this solution namely, and all things could be recombined more quickly through crystallization. The argument drawn from cannibals is demonstrative and proves that a flower of substance must be assumed. Add to this what Libavius and Quercetanus say about the resurrection, and what Kirchner and Glauber . . . about the regeneration of nitre.

14

Leibniz and the Herborn Encyclopedists

Leroy E. Loemker

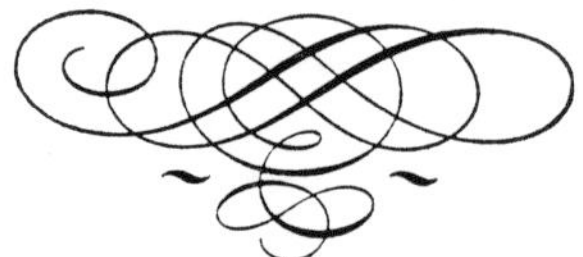

Two intellectual movements in which Leibniz was early interested and which helped him in the formulation of his system have not yet been adequately studied. One was the liberal, activistic, and conciliatory Catholic spirit prevailing in Mainz, where he sojourned from 1667 to 1672. There he not only seems to have defined his ethical thought,[1] he was also clearly stimulated to undertake the vast inclusive projects which were to occupy him for so long.[2]

The second early influence, to which this paper is devoted, began even before Leibniz's move to Frankfurt and Mainz; both his *Dissertation on the Art of Combinations* (1666) and the *New*

First published in the *Journal of the History of Ideas* XXII (1961): 323–338. This article is part of a study of seventeenth-century thought made possible by a John Simon Guggenheim Fellowship and a Fulbright Grant.

1. The influence of the Jesuit Friedrich Spee upon the Elector John Philipp of Schonborn and his circle in establishing a pattern of liberal ethical thought centered on wisdom, justice, and love was pointed out by F. W. C. Lieder, "Fredrick Spee and the Théodicée of Leibniz," *Journal of English and Germanic Philology* 11, no. 3 (July 1912): 1–50.

2. Leibniz's plan for a universal science or art of combinations originated in the pre-Mainz period. But his programs for legal reform, the reunification of the churches, a metaphysical redefinition of theory to support this reunion, a universal encyclopedia, and the founding of scientific societies seem to have begun in the Mainz years.

Method for Learning and Teaching Jurisprudence, which he is believed to have written on the way to Mainz as an introduction to the Bishop Elector, contain many references to it. This is the pansophistic and encyclopedic movement in Reformed Protestantism which flourished in the High Academy of Herborn.

From its foundation in 1584, the old university at Herborn flourished as a center of Reformed theology and philosophy, in close relationship with schools with like convictions in England (particularly Cambridge) and in the Protestant Netherlands. Though its influence endured until the end of what is commonly referred to as "the period of Protestant orthodoxy," the peak was reached, in spite of the perils of plague and war, in the early seventeenth century. This was due largely to the prodigious labor, in teaching and writing, of a half-dozen men who varied greatly in originality and influence but shared a common theological perspective: a moderate Calvinism, the covenant theology and interpretation of history, an ethical casuistry which borrowed much from the Jesuit casuists, a passion for eclecticism, a curiosity for current discoveries and intellectual movements, and a strong millenarian hope. Among these teachers were Kaspar Olevian, John Piscator, and Matthew Martini,[3] founders of the covenant theology; John Althusius, who applied it to political theory; John Henry Alsted, philosopher, theologian, and encyclopedist; and his pupil and son-in-law John Bisterfeld.[4] Among many students who later distinguished themselves, the best known was John Amos Komenski or Comenius, later bishop of the persecuted Brethren of Bohemia and Poland, whose projects in the humanization of education and the unification of learning were clearly inspired by his teacher Alsted. Alsted's massive compilation of knowledge, the final form of which was the *Encyclopaedia* appearing in 1630, assured him a reputation for a century. Some of the writings of Bisterfeld (1605–1655), a philosopher whose pansophic efforts

3. Together with John Alstead, Martini attended the Synod of Dort in 1618; there he was attacked by the Dutch Calvinist leader Gomer for showing moderation for the Remonstrants and some sympathy for the spirit of Arminius.

4. John Clauberg later lectured at Herborn without welcome for his Cartesianism.

were interfered with by diplomatic duties during the later part of the Thirty Years' War, were sent out of Transylvania (where Alsted and he died) in the 1650s, to be published in fragmentary form in the Netherlands. Bisterfeld had been almost completely forgotten, however, until W. Kabitz discovered some enthusiasm for these works[5] on the part of Leibniz even before the Mainz years. The reputation of Comenius, on the other hand, had no need of rescue, since he had attracted a wide following in the years of his wandering through Germany, Holland, Sweden, and England, so that Pierre Bayle saw fit to perpetuate his memory in the *Dictionary*, though it was Johannes Gottfried Herder, much later, who injected something of his spirit into modern pedagogical discussions. It is with Leibniz's interest in these three men, Alsted, Bisterfeld, and Comenius (pre-eminently with the first two), that this paper is concerned.[6]

Their primary influence on Leibniz was the transmission of a philosophical tradition which had moved beyond the sixteenth-century emphasis upon erudition and rhetoric to a new Platonistic metaphysics of universal harmony governing a multitude of interrelated, vitalistically conceived individuals. Through this metaphysics and a corresponding theory of knowledge, they transmitted obvious influences from Raymundus Lullus, Tommaso Campanella, and Giordano Bruno.

The intellectualistic position which the Herborn thinkers shared was frankly eclectic.[7] Eclecticism was a stepping stone

5. John Kvacala has written a brief biography of Bisterfeld in the *Ungarische Revue* (Leipzig, Brockhaus) 3 (1893): 40–59, 171–196. I have been able to consult the following of his works: *Phosphorus Catholicus seu artis meditandi Epitome* (Breda: Joannes á Waesberg, 1649); *Scripturae Sacrae, Divina eminentia et efficientia* . . . in duabus disputationbus . . . proposita (Lugduni Batavorum: Vuyren, 1654); *Bisterfeldus Redivivus*, 2 vols. (Hagae Comitorum: Adrian Vlacq, 1661) contains the major posthumous works.

6. Leibniz's frequent references to Althusius deserve to be mentioned, however; his chief criticism was directed at Althusius's inclusion of positive as well as natural law in the divine covenant.

7. The best-known defense of eclecticism in the seventeenth century is by John Gerard Voss, *De Philosophia et Philosophorum Sectis Libri II* (1659). The literature of eclecticism is large, beginning in the previous century with the efforts to reconcile Plato and Aristotle, Greek and Christian, Aris-

to the great seventeenth-century systems, as an examination of the sources of Descartes, Spinoza, and Leibniz shows. It was supported chiefly by two motives. One was a growing impatience with the philosophical "sectarianism" resulting from the revival of ancient learning, a deploring of "the many . . . names among which the mantle of philosophy [was] being torn to bits," as Leibniz put it in his letter to Jacob Thomasius.[8] The other was the pedagogical motive which characterized philosophy in the sixteenth and early seventeenth centuries. The mission of teaching provided the goal or final cause for philosophy both in the Protestant circles inspired by Melanchthon and in the circles of the Counter Reformation. This pedagogical role must, however, be broadened to include not merely the education of the young and inexperienced "tyros" but also the persuasion of atheists[9] and the conversion of Jews and other nonbelievers. Thus philosophy as education included the aims of Christian apologetics and natural theology.

In the preceding century this educational concern had assured philosophy a central place in the Republic of Letters by assigning it to the realm of *discourse*. Petrus Ramus had defined logic (dialectic) as the *ars bene disserandi*, singling out as its basic unit neither the term nor the proposition but the "theme," and developing a method for the elaboration of this theme by dichotomizing it into subheads determined less by the *"loci,"* which he himself had

---

totle and Euclid, Aristotle and Democritus, Stoics and Platonists, etc. Among influential eclectics were both Francisco Suarez in the new Scholastic tradition and Jacobi Zabarella in the non-Scholastic Aristotelian tradition, as well as Francis Bacon, Bartholomew Keckermann, Pierre Gassendi, the German atomists Daniel Sennert and Johann Sperling, and, later, Robert Boyle and such reconcilers of Descartes and Scholasticism or Aristotelianism as Johann Clauberg, Jean Baptiste Duhamel, and John Christopher Sturm.

8. Leibniz to Jacob Thomasius, 20/30 April 1669 (Gerhardt, I:15; cf. Loemker, p. 93). In his later writings Leibniz frequently complains of the growth of sectarianism, and particularly of the Cartesian sect.

9. Atheism is here used broadly, as it was in the period under discussion, to include skeptics and Libertines or freethinkers. Among the philosophers of the century who aimed explicitly at the overcoming of atheism are Francis Bacon, Descartes, Mersenne, Campanella, Spinoza (in a secularized sense), Henry More, Kenelm Digby, Francis Glisson, and Leibniz.

proposed, then by the Aristotelian distinctions of general and special, formal and material, cause and end. With the turn of the century this Ramist tendency toward the reduction of logic to rhetoric was checked by a Baconian (and a renewed Aristotelian) interest in nature and in the unity of knowledge. The Herborn thinkers, though still Ramist in procedure, shared these newer trends, undertaking as "Philippo-Ramists" to apply Ramus's classification procedure to a modern Aristotelian concern for facts and their metaphysical interpretation. The fresh Aristotelian spirit of Zabarella was mediated by their fellow Reformed philosopher of Danzig, Bartholomew Keckermann. Bacon was known early at Herborn, and Alsted adopted also Luis Vives's empirical psychology of the affections and the *ars magna* of Raymundus Lullus. The result of this eclecticism is a renewed metaphysics which is itself central to, but subordinated to, the final goal of philosophy, the *Encyclopaedia.*

In the foreword to the "candid reader" in his early *Metaphysica tribus libris tractata* (1613), Alsted developed the structure of knowledge as follows:[10] Man is a "divine animal" who, in an uncorrupted state (most of the *Encyclopaedia* is aimed at the uncorrupted nature of man), aims at the two simple ends: not only to live, but to live well. To these ends he is endowed with two powers, contemplation and action. But to these "simple ends" there are so many subordinate ends that there must be found one art which binds together the principles of all the rest. "This art," he wrote, "serving the comprehension of the liberal arts (*Liberalium doctrinarum*) I believe the Greeks would call an *encyclopaedia* or *cyclopaedia,* the Latins, a circle of the universe." The symbolic significance of the circle is that the lines of thought drawn from the circumference of our total knowledge converge upon a center, i.e., the common disciplines of dialectic and metaphysics: "Dialectic is the moon of the sciences. Meta-

10. Alsted discusses the difficulty of defining philosophy (*Encyclopaedia,* I, 67a): "Philosophy, as it were a collective being, cannot be perfectly defined." He explained that a perfect definition is the explication of a single essence, which philosophy lacks, but suggests that the various historical definitions of Plato, the Stoics, Cicero, etc., together approximate a perfect definition.

physics is the sun." The inferior disciplines depend upon both, but logic must be explicated metaphysically, since metaphysics has greater knowledge than has logic by virtue of its amplitude and generality. Logic thus serves for using (*tractans*) the lower disciplines, metaphysics for understanding (*spectans*) them. Metaphysics imparts certitude to them, logic imparts order. Thus, our soul moves downward from the most general principles of "first philosophy" to the particular conclusions of the several disciplines; then it ascends from sense and singular things to universals; the resulting circular motion is perfection. The combination of Baconian and Lullist viewpoints here becomes apparent in these overlapping *a priori* and *a posteriori* perspectives within the total unity of the *Encyclopaedia.*

Alsted's fundamental Neoplatonism becomes more apparent, despite his Aristotelian definition of metaphysics and his treatment of natural theology as a part of metaphysics rather than the end of it, when he moves to the more specific *Praecognita* for the unity and system of the disciplines.[11] These are four in number: *archelogia, hexilogia, technologia,* and *canonica* or *didactica. Archelogia* provides the definition and organization of the sciences; *hexilogia,* the psychology or cognition and action; *technologia,* the nature and differences of the particular arts; and *canonics,* the method of teaching. Taken together, the *praecognita,* which are offered as the introduction to the *Encyclopaedia* (1630) provide the structure of efficient, formal, and final causality for human science and art.

Within this structure, Alsted and Bisterfeld bridge the gap between logic and metaphysics by means of an Ockhamistic theory of significance and supposition.[12] Thus the basic units of speech, and therefore the materials of logic as "the art of discoursing well," are words (*voces*) or terms. These constitute either themes

11. *Philosophia digné restituta: libros quatuor praecognitorum philosophicorum complectens . . .* (Herborn: G. Corvinus, 1612). Zabarella's *Liber de tribus praecognitibus* introduced the consideration of *philosophical praecognita,* which was continued by Keckermann.

12. These correspond in general to representation and ratiocination as the two dimensions of perception in Leibniz.

or arguments. Alsted retains the Scholastic distinction between simple and complex terms, a simple term signifying one thing in its absoluteness, a complex term signifying two things "axiomatically coherent" (i.e., propositions taken as true; Alsted, like Bacon, calls all such propositions axioms). A theme is a term which sets forth the matter proposed for argument. The usefulness of themes in argument is determined by the effectiveness with which they "express" notions or "concepts of the mind." As the fundamental unit of knowledge, the concept has a complex structure: in its *formal* aspect it "represents" the thing known to the mind according to its real attributes; in its *objective* role, it is itself the thing known; and in its "consequently objective" role, it is "that which follows the objective concept as a shadow follows a body." The concept, therefore, serves the knowing process through its role of symbolizing the object, assimilating it to the mind, and preserving it in memory.[13] Bisterfeld calls this process *perception,* and the similitude involved in the representative relation he calls an *idea.*[14] Leibniz too calls the formal structure of an act of knowing an idea; and when he read in Bisterfeld, "Logic is nothing but a mirror of relations," he wrote in the margin, "*Nota bene.*"[15] Like their mentors in logic, Zabarella and Keckermann, and like Francisco Suarez, their guide in metaphysics, the Herborn philosophers are conceptualists, granting ideas a functional status in the divine mind as the formal possibilities of human knowledge.[16]

This logical and epistemological program is developed by the encyclopedists into a metaphysics of harmonious *order* extending, in one dimension, from the most general principles and primary concepts (or *loci*) to concrete particulars, and, in the other dimension, including particulars in an interweaving pattern of

13. Alsted says, "It is the same whether I say that the intellection by which the intellect knows a dog is a conversion of the intellect into the dog, or the dog into the intellect, though the latter seems to be more accurate, since our soul has within it a kind of identifying force by which it assimilates the object to itself or, if you wish, identifies it."

14. *Artificii definiendi catholici Libri III*, 38, in *Bisterfeldus Redivivus*, I.

15. Academy Ed., VI:159.

16. Cf. Suarez, *Disputationes Metaphysicae*, 1, 5; 25, 1.

"congruence" or "consent." Thus the linguistic order, stressed by the Ramists, and the logical methods of analysis and synthesis, as defined by the new Aristotelians, are grounded in an ontological order in which every individual being has two basic properties: *unity* (within itself) and *convening* or *harmony* (with itself and others). It is in their development of the details of this interpenetration of unities or individuals that these thinkers most clearly anticipate the monadology of Leibniz.[17]

Alsted and Bisterfeld interpret metaphysical harmony as fundamentally vitalistic and social, designating the study of it as *symbiotics*.[18] The relation upon which the social harmony rests is *immeation*. Bisterfeld particularly stresses the importance of this concept; it is "a most profound term," regrettably "appropriated by and explicated by few authorities" save by theologians in discussing the mutual containment of the three persons of the trinity. He proposes to rescue it for a much wider ontological use.

> Immeation is real or mental, general or special. Real immeation is the intimate union of things in nature, and an ineffable communion arising from this. This is the basis and norm for mental immeation. Mental immeation is the ineffable and inexplicable penetration of thoughts by which one concept prepares, feeds, and augments another. . . . From this arises the inexhaustible immeation and abundance of words. General immeation is that by which all things, even those at the greatest distance from each other, come together (*convenire*) in at least some things.[19]

This "ineffable and inexplicable" interrelatedness is supported in both Alsted and Bisterfeld by a vitalistic account of existence. This they derive from the Aristotelian definition of nature, in *Physics II*, as that which constitutes an internal source of action, particularly as interpreted by J. C. Scaliger and with further borrowings from Paracelsus.

17. See the *Ars disputandi*, 29–30, in *Bisterfeldus Redivivus*, I.

18. See Alsted, *Encyclopaedia*, bk. 22; Economics; Bisterfeld, *Sciagraphia symbiotica* seu *compendium symbioticae*, in *Bisterfeldus Redivivus*, I. Comenius and his English correspondents also made use of the term.

19. *Logicae libri*, *III*:17–18, in *Bisterfeldus Redivivus*, I.

The "secondary matter" of a natural body is (1) that of the whole, as seed, and (2) partial, as hypostatic principles. Hypostatic principles are what natural bodies consist of as the foundation of their essence; they are three in number: salt, sulphur, and mercury. Everything is seed in a living substance. (But I here understand life broadly, whether it be life properly socalled or considered analogically as in the life of gems, metals, and similar things.)[20]

Thus harmony and dynamic individuality are relative terms. Bisterfeld proceeds a step further and interprets them with the aid of the psychological and epistemological concepts of *perception* and *appetite*.[21] As he points out in discussing the idea of *panharmonia* essential to an encyclopedia, such a harmony may be understood in terms of the processes of knowing and of action.

To *perceive* is to have within oneself, efficaciously, an intrinsic similitude or disposition proportional to the disposition of things, or it is a certain intrinsic conformity or, as it were, a configuration. . . . Thus all perception is necessarily proportional, whether for the perceiver or for what is perceived.

Appetite is the internal voice of substance by which it may be ordered around a fitting thing. . . . Hence it presupposes perception of the unknown, without desire, of course, and is congruent to it merely *ex parte*. The act of desiring is not primary but secondary and, as it were, reflexive. Appetite is commonly love or non-love or hate, these words taken most broadly.[22]

Bisterfeld distinguished two kinds of perception and of appetite: *vital* perception and appetite are cognition and will, respectively, which together involve an internal force of assimilating internal or external order, and of ordering themselves about what is perceived. What is explicitly self-conscious in man is seen obscurely

20. *Encyclopaedia*, I:674. Alsted's hypostatic principles come from Paracelsus.

21. Cf. Bisterfeld's broad use of *perception* which, like that of *immeation*, seems to be borrowed from Bacon: *De Augmentis Scientiarum*, IV:3. There are some indications that Bisterfeld knew Bacon; he may have met him on his first mission to England in 1624–25. See Kvacala, *op. cit.*

22. *Artificii definiendi catholici liber tertius*, secs. 38–57, in *Bisterfeldus Redivivus*, I, contains the entire exposition. Note the recurring figure of the mirror.

in plants and appears as instincts in animals. But there is also a *nonvital* perception and appetite which is a habituation of being to being or the ordering of an inner disposition according to a "perceived" state. It is in appetite that the transcendent quality of goodness inherent in all harmony is actualized in particulars, for goodness is the congruence of a being with its appetite.[23]

The metaphysics of the Hebron philosophers is therefore, one in which pluralism is harmonized with an immanent theistic unity, with the result that transcendentals like *unum, bonum, verum* (and indeed, *pulchrum*)[24] are co-ordinate patterns of being and value for each individual existence. There is evidence in this metaphysics of the influence of Bruno's philosophy of light and shadow; for, like him, both Alsted and Bisterfeld retain the doctrine of a hierarchy of being and of the reality of nonbeing in order to justify a scale of good and evil, of truth and falsity, and of order and confusion.[25]

The similarity of all this to Leibniz's mature metaphysics is apparent, though it required Leibniz's analysis of the degrees of clarity, distinctness, and adequacy of perception to reconcile this doctrine of nonbeing with a monadology. The similarity may be pressed one step further, for in the *Phosphorus Catholicus seu Artis meditandi Epitome,* one of Bisterfeld's works on which Leibniz's marginal comments are preserved, this theory of the proportionality of thought to things and of things to each other is developed into the suggestion of a mathematical mode of logical

23. *Loc. cit.* See also *Alphabetum philosophicum,* sec. 66, *Bisterfeldus Redivivus,* II.

24. The cosmic theory of beauty here is derived from Campanella, and is re-echoed by Leibniz (cf. *De radicali originatione rerum*) and others. Cf. Jonathan Edwards's doctrine of excellence.

25. See the *Phosphorus Catholicus* (1649), sec. 6: "The convenience and difference of being is to be observed most diligently. The convenience of being is that by which all beings whatever—the greatest, the median, and the least—are mutually proportional to each other, by a proportion or convenience not of equality but of similitude. This observation is most useful and efficacious in meditation because it is to be understood not only of positive beings but also of negative and privative beings, and not merely of true beings but also of fictitious ones."

calculation. For the root of multitude in unity, Bisterfeld says, makes possible in meditation a kind of "*mental multiplication,* in which by a congruous and continuous combination of concepts or thoughts resting in being and consentient with being, though dissenting with each other, new terms are produced."[26] In this, too, Bisterfeld, however dimly, certainly anticipated Leibniz.

Space does not permit the discussion of other aspects of the thought of these men which may well have influenced Leibniz. Their moral casuistry, drawn from the Cambridge Puritan moralists William Perkins and William Whittaker, and from such Jesuit works as the *Institutiones Morales* of John Azorius, of which Alsted made extensive use, provides the broad background for the early phase of Leibniz's ethical thought in which, dominated by problems in the logic of the law, he undertook to harmonize legal casuistry through the principle of continuity.

In their conception, the will is derived from the affections[27] and implies spontaneity (as self-determination) in all beings.[28] Both Alsted and Bisterfeld sound like Arminians in their discussion of the will, but both find it necessary to reconcile this with a doctrine of election. In this problem Leibniz is more deterministic than they, for Bisterfeld, though he does not carry the theological problem involved in freedom far beyond Valla, comes

26. See the evidence below that Leibniz had read the *Phosphorus Catholicus* before the appearance of his dissertation on the *Art of Combinations* in 1666. In this work Leibniz introduced the plus and minus symbols (+ and −) for the copula in affirmative and negative propositions. In his earliest papers in the logical calculus, however, he turned to multiplication and division as symbols of logical combination and analysis.

27. Leibniz is more intellectualistic and deterministic in his early thought. "Will does not differ from intellect," he writes in his notes on Jacob Thomasius (Academy Ed., VI, i:45, note 15). The growth of conviction about the importance of self-awareness at the beginning of the seventeenth century deserves more study.

28. Alsted, *Encyclopaedia*, bk. 21 (Ethics), 1336: "If spontaneous action is used widely and generally for any operation whatever which is free from compulsion, and which occurs with a certain appetite, whether it takes place with cognition or without it, then it belongs to all natural beings in the universe. If, however, it is used strictly and specially for action which occurs with reason and will, it applies only to intelligent natures, and thus is nothing but voluntary action, whose opposite is involuntary."

close to Malebranche's radical theory that God wills only general principles, not particular acts.[29]

The fundamental reliance of these men upon reason places them in the tradition of rationalism. Their Platonic answer to the theory of knowledge is drawn from Campanella's conviction that the three sources of knowledge—experience, reason, and revelation—are within limits "proportional" and mutually confirmatory. Thus they can follow Bacon in his doctrine of the natural light and also in his emphasis upon the importance of middle axioms. In the *Triumphus Bibliorum* Alsted undertook to document the sciences with passages from Scripture. In a more thoughtful vein, Bisterfeld says:

> The sources of principles are three—experience, right reason, and revelation. . . . It is not necessary that all three of these criteria of certainty and truth should pronounce conjointly on individual truth; it suffices if either one or two assert something. . . . It is clear from these things that philosophy is the pedagogue to theology, and that Scripture is the principle of philosophy even if it is not philosophy.[30]

The Herborn philosophers, therefore are well on the way to a rationalistic tradition which will seek a universal rational apologetic (the *Demonstrationes Catholices* [Leibniz]) or will attempt to replace revelation with intuition in Campanella's triad (Spinoza, Locke, and others), or to champion a *Philosophia Scripturae Interpres* (Louis Meyer, 1666).

But the times were not obedient to reason, and in the face of destructive warfare, increasing political and religious violence, and the persecution of religious minorities in eastern Europe, the Herborn thinkers were driven to the Scriptural teaching about the end of the age and the approaching millenium. In the *Diatribe de mille annis apocalypticis* (1627), a work widely read on the Continent and in England, Alsted predicted the second coming of Christ in 1694. Comenius, too, was moved by the prophecies

29. *Alphabetum philosophicum*, bk. II, secs. 70–71, 66, *Bisterfeldus Redivivus*, II. The first disputation under Bisterfeld in the Academy at Weissenburg in Transylvania (May 8 and 15, 1630) was on the co-operation between first and second causes and the freedom of the will.

30. *Alphabetum philosophicum*, secs. 8–9.

of Drabicus to proclaim the immanent coming of the new age and to urge efforts to bring about the promised signs of this age. Widely preached, the chiliasm of these men added to the sense of urgency which characterized the mid-century, the urgency in overthrowing Antichrist (the papacy and the empire), in extending education, in mastering nature, in unifying the churches, and in persuading theists and converting the Jews. This chiliastic conviction Leibniz no longer shared, but the sense of urgency it engendered is still apparent in the zeal with which he pursued some of the same goals.

It remains to point out Leibniz's interest in the philosophers of Herborn and to estimate their possible influence upon him.

Leibniz was nurtured educationally in the eclectic tradition, though his teachers were predominantly Protestant Aristotelians.[31] To the extent that eclecticism sought for unifying principles, it assumed the form of Christian Platonism. It is true, of course, that Aristotelianism, whether in its Scholastic or non-Scholastic form, dominated the discussion of particular problems in the seventeenth century, and in this sense the scholars who have pointed out Aristotelian influences, even in Descartes, Spinoza, Leibniz, and Locke, are right. But in the binding principles of the systems there are real differences in emphasis and spirit, if not in letter; for example, in the renewed emphasis upon apriorism and an inborn natural light, in the substitution of harmony for hierarchy as a basis for the logic of being, in shifting emphases in the doctrines of causality and interdependence, in the growing importance of reflection, of inwardness, for metaphysics, and in the dominance of an Augustinian conception of universals and created order. Harmony, selfhood, sympathy, and immanence are some of the new principles. The intricate threads of influence along which Christian Platonism moved from the Franciscans, the Brothers of the Common Life, Nicolas of Cusa, and the Florentine Academy to Bruno, Campanella, and Descartes are still obscure and may remain so; but the Herborn thinkers belong to this tradition, as does Leibniz.

31. Cf. his early reading of Suarez, and the influence of his teachers Jacob Thomasius at Leipzig and Erhard Weigel at Jena, both antisectarians and eclectics in tendency.

Leibniz's reaction to the writing of Alsted, Bisterfeld and Comenius, though never uncritical, was early and enthusiastic. In Comenius he noted primarily the humanizer of education, the pansophist, and the writer of irenic church history. Part I of the *New Method of Learning and Teaching Jurisprudence* (1666) was devoted to the rules of teaching and learning in general, and a part of it which describes principles of effective teaching (sections 17–20) was obviously influenced by the *Analytic Didactic.* Five years later, in response to a request from Magnus Hesenthaler, he wrote a critical opinion of Comenius's work in which he defended his didactics against J. J. Becher, in whose method he found "no light and joy."[32] In the revision notes to the *New Method,* prepared in the last years of the century, he still referred with approval to the *Janua Linguarum,* the *Schola Ludus,* the *Orbis Sensualium pictus,* and the historical writings.[33] And at the further request of Hesenthaler, he wrote a poetic epigram in Comenius's memory, promising that, though the present disordered world had offered only poor soil for the seeds of his *pansophia,* posterity would benefit from them.[34] Yet he criticized Comenius's efforts at a universal science on the grounds of both method and content; they were too general, did not build upon firmly established definitions of "the most powerful terms," and neglected particulars, or empirical details.[35] One may say that it was Leibniz's judgment that Comenius was still committed to the old ideal of erudition neglecting both method and facts.

Leibniz frequently said that when, as a youth, he undertook to categorize propositions, he turned to the Ramists as well as the Aristotelians.[36] It is probable that he was here alluding to his early study of Alsted and perhaps Bisterfeld. In his criticism of the Ramists, Leibniz made exception of Alsted, along with

32. Dutens, V:181–182.

33. See Academy Ed., VI, i:275, 279, 290, 323.

34. G. H. Pertz, *Leibnizens geschichtliche Aufsätze und Gedichte* (Hanover: Hahn, 1847), p. 270.

35. Dutens, *loc. cit.*

36. See for example, Gerhardt, VII:517; Loemker, pp. 463–464 (to Gabriel Wagner).

Theodore Zwinger, John Thomas Fregius, and Keckermann, praising them for "joining method to things," and adding that Alsted's *Encyclopaedia* "seems to me certainly praiseworthy as the summit (*caput*) of those times." He was, however, also early conversant with Alsted's exposition of the Lullian *Ars Magna*, to which he referred in the *De Arte Combinatoria*.[37] But it is the *Encyclopaedia* which, of all of Alsted's works, interested him most. Leibniz's own earliest plan for an encyclopedia, in 1671, involved a revision of Alsted's work. In this proposal, Alsted, who, Leibniz said, "lacked not labor or judgment, but materials and the felicity of our times," was to be brought into the area of the new sciences by drawing upon the physics of Hobbes, completed with the aid of Galileo, Huygens, Aristotle, and Digby; geometry was to be entirely Euclid's; in logic, Joachim Jungius was to be used, with supplementary materials from Clauberg, the Port Royal Logic, and Leibniz's own *De Arte Combinatoria*; for the philosophy of mind, use was to be made of Descartes, Digby, and Thomas Barton; finally, jurisprudence, politics, and medicine were to be treated by Leibniz himself.[38] His mature judgment of Alsted's work is shown in a revision note to the *New Method* written in the late 1690s,[39] in the course of a catalogue of encyclopedists from Pliny on. Here, he still placed him at the top of the tradition (commenting upon Alsted's favorite anagram on his name: Alstedius—Sedulitas); but Leibniz added:

> It must be admitted . . . that he was more versed in the nutshells of distinctions than in the kernels of truth. He treated the arts of speech praiseworthily, historical matters and mathematics in a way average for his time; in the higher faculties he is less satisfactory.

It is noteworthy that Leibniz's proposals to revise Alsted came at a time when he was himself proposing a work, *Elementa de Mente* to supplement Hobbes's *de Corpore*, was trying his hand at the principles of physical motion, and was outlining his own

37. Gerhardt, IV:62; Loemker, p. 82.

38. Academy Ed., VI, i:192, 203, 278. Leibniz also refers to Alsted's work on mnemonics. (Cf. Couturat, *La logique de Leibniz* [Paris: F. Alcan, 1901], note XII, pp. 570–571; Dutens, V:183–185.)

39. Academy Ed., VI, i:288.

encyclopedic projects in letters to Antoine Arnauld, John Frederick of Brunswick, and others, just before the revolutionary intellectual stimulus of the Paris sojourn (1672–1676).

It is clear that, in this early period, when he was himself a complete eclectic and his intellectual ideal was still that of Renaissance erudition, Leibniz reacted against the Ramistic dichotomizing of these men. He was nonetheless affected by their formal method of explicating and analyzing problems through definitions, and he was inspired by their pansophic labors and ideals. His own great projects—formulated under the inspiration of Boineburg—for the reform of the law, the conciliation of conflicting theologies, and the formulation of a universal science were still based on their plans and directions.

It was Bisterfeld's posthumous works which aroused Leibniz's greatest enthusiasm. While describing the metaphysical principles involved in his theory of a combinatorial science in the *De Arte Combinatoria* (1666), Leibniz says:

> In a word, we shall ask that everything be derived from the metaphysical doctrine of the relations of being to being, so that the loci may be formed from the genera of relations, but the highest singulars from theorems. I believe that the most sound John Henry Bisterfeld has seen this in his *Phosphorus Catholicus* or *Epitome of the Art of Meditating,* Leiden, 1657, all of which is founded on the universal *immeation* and *perichoresis,* as he calls it, of all in all, and likewise on the similitude and dissimilitude of all with all, the principles of which are relations. He who reads this little book will see through the use of the complicatory art more and more.[40]

It is significant that this is said in connection with Leibniz's first exposition of the distinction between necessary and contingent propositions. The theorems of the art of combinations are

> propositions which are of eternal truth, resting not on the will of God but on his nature. All singular propositions such as historical ones, e.g., Augustus was Roman emperor, or observations, i.e., universal propositions whose truth is founded not in essences but in existence, insofar as they are true . . . are from the will of God. . . . There is no demonstration of such propositions but only induction, except that

40. *De Arte combinatoria,* sec. 85; Gerhardt, IV:70.

sometimes one observation can be demonstrated from another through the use of a theorem.[41]

Thus Leibniz was led from the fruitful suggestions of a universal harmony and symbiosis to one of his own most important distinctions. Though he did not then see the full significance of this distinction, and it was to be years before he succeeded in fully embodying it in his metaphysics, it appears at the very beginning of his creative work in the effort to adopt his combinatorial analysis to empirical knowledge.

Leibniz's marginal notes on reading Bisterfeld's *Philosophiae Primae Seminarium* and its supplement, *Phosphorus Catholicus*, are enthusiastic and convey the excitement of new and significant discovery, or at least, of new confirmation.[42] On the title page of the former, he writes, "A most brilliant (*praeclarissimum*) little work whose equal in this kind I have not seen," an expression reinforced on the second title page by "A most ingenious little book." Three times he notes similarities to "Verulam": his theory of innate primary notions such as "there cannot be contrary instances"; Bisterfeld's remark that "Whatever is most true in nature is most useful in practice"; and the parallel between Bisterfeld's degrees of being and Bacon's degrees of motion. To Lullus, he refers Bisterfeld's accounts of the proportionality of being and the immeation of terms, saying "These can be adumbrated through the Lullian art."

It is Bisterfeld's conception of the harmony or convening of distinct individuals in the universe, however, which most evokes his consent. When Bisterfeld states his second rule of consistency, "No being is absolute," Leibniz supplements, "No being save only God can be alone. All being, even God, is with another." On Bisterfeld's account of the attributes of being in general ("They are the same thing as being, but have a certain relation and mode themselves"), Leibniz comments, "All resolve themselves into identical propositions." (Bisterfeld's attributes are Leibniz's simple perfections out of which the individual notions or laws of the individuals are compounded.) But Leibniz seems most stirred

41. *Loc. cit.*, secs. 83–85.

42. For Leibniz's annotations and the text of Bisterfeld on which they comment, Academy Ed., VI, i:151–161.

when Bisterfeld describes the *active* nature of the interrelated beings. In his seventh rule of the attributes of being and unity, Bisterfeld defines *active potency* as a fully transcendental attribute of being, adding that no being is so small or insignificant that it does not have its proportional operation. Leibniz adds, "or would be a useless member of the Republic of Beings. Someone could write a book on the Laws of Beings." This project Leibniz was later to undertake. Following Suarez's definition of unity (convertible with *bonum*) as congruence of being with itself, Bisterfeld defines the good as the congruence of being with its own consistency, "or it is such a congruence of being that it can be with other being and other being can be with it." To this, Leibniz, no doubt thinking of the legal basis of his own ethics, first formulated in the *New Method* and never abandoned in his mature thought, adds, "i.e., (congruence) with its duty (*officium*) in the Universal Republic." His differentiation between the Republics of Nature and of Grace would be made later, when Leibniz confronted the challenge of mechanism through his contact with the Cartesians and with Boyle. But his social interpretation of the universe, in which each individual is a dynamic principle operating in proportion to the total harmony, took shape in Mainz while he labored for a metaphysical foundation of a unitary system of law and a conciliating theology. It is also much later that Leibniz himself described the process of individual existence in terms of perception and appetite, as Bisterfeld had already done. This required a long period in which to absorb new mathematical and scientific ideas, and to clarify Leibniz's own logic and epistemology, particularly to arrive at a philosophical synthesis of the act of perceiving with the epistemological relationship of representation or expression. Bisterfeld had recognized the role of representation in knowledge, and his theory of proportionality had provided a metaphysical foundation for it. But Leibniz's own synthesis had to await a more logical analysis of the clearness, distinctness, and adequacy of knowledge, for which he found a beginning in Cartesianism.

Leibniz did, however, respond favorably to Bisterfeld's metaphysics of truth and error, good and evil. To Bisterfeld's suggestion that the primary attribute of unity may serve as a Lydian stone.[43] for the uncovering of impossible and absurd things, Leibniz comments, "The impossible is not one; it is not congruous with itself; even if it were through supposition, it is not. Therefore such supposition is false or does not at all exist, because what is not cannot be." Leibniz's mature idea of error refers to words unfounded on ideas, or in terms of an Ockhamistic logic, terms and sentences without supposition.

The corresponding transcendental attribute of *good,* says Bisterfeld, is the congruence in every way of every mode and degree: "This is absolutely necessary, for unless it were true, there would be nothing more." Transcendental or total evil, on the other hand, is an attribute not of being but of nonbeing, and indeed, of the impossible. All other evil *is* because of the good and is impossible except as it is ordered to the good. So there can be no evil which is not known and invited by the highest Good.

Leibniz's assent to this conception of evil is put in spatial terms: "Thus it (the *summum bonum*) is at once at an infinite distance from all, and in an intimate union with all." This comment suggests the Leibnizian need for a metaphysical as opposed to a physical, phenomenal space, a distinction which he actually makes in a note on Bisterfeld's definition of particular existence: "Entitative space is one thing, corporeal space another." Entitative space is the individuals and the transcending harmony, as a (partly doubtful) reading of another remark of Leibniz's suggests "Entitative space, or the common musical (?) life." Bisterfeld proceeds to derive from his conception of the good a series of axioms regarding appetites, and in particular, the "appetite for communion." This, he says, is an operative appetite, also called the "love or desire for union," and is either primary or secondary. Primary operative appetite is productive, secondary is inspiring.

43. Many of Leibniz's literary figures and allusions are anticipated in Alsted and Bisterfeld. They are probably a part of the common literary store of the time. In addition to the Lydian stone, Alsted uses the figure of the labyrinth and Ariadne's thread, the Hymn of Galen, Ulpian's compact summary of the precepts of the law: "*neminem laedere, suum cuique tribuere, honeste vivere,*" etc. Bisterfeld's title, *Phosphorus Catholicus* (Universal Light Bearer), may be borrowed from Bruno; his use preceded the application of the term to a new chemical by several decades.

Sympathy is the convening (or congruence) of appetites. Leibniz comments, "There is therefore a primary appetite of God toward himself, a secondary one toward creatures."

Bisterfeld's Platonic writings are reflected in more Augustinian shades in Leibniz's first fragmentary formulations of his own metaphysics, imbedded in his legal and theological papers at Mainz. They appear in the context of an Augustinian theory of ideas. For example:

> The substance of things is an idea. Idea is the union of God with creatures, so that the action of agent and patient is one. . . . There are no ideas in God except as there are things outside of him. . . . The ideas of God and the substances of things (substantial forms) are the same in fact, different in relation. . . .[44] In idea is contained ideally both passive and active power (*potentia*), active and passive intellect. Insofar as passive intellect concurs, there is matter in the idea; insofar as active intellect, there is form.[45]

It can be seen that Leibniz was, at this point, well on the way to his own system. From this point of view he corrected Bisterfeld's conception of love as desire for union. In one of the more interesting studies for an *Elementa Juris Naturalis*, Leibniz says, "The appetite for union is not love. . . . In this sense the wolf is said to love the lamb." His own definition follows: "We love him by whose happiness we are delighted."[46]

The notes on Bisterfeld thus show Leibniz giving general assent but often pushing the clarification of his own thought further. His appreciation of the logical and dynamic harmony of the world, its logical order as immanent in God, the quasi-social na-

44. Academy Ed., VI, i:513.

45. Ibid., 512.

46. Ibid., 482; Cf. Loemker, p. 137. At the same time Leibniz had been reading Hobbes, whose political writings Boineburg had discussed in correspondence with Conring. From him, Leibniz took over the notion of *conatus* (cf. Galileo's *impetus*), applying it to his physical theory of motion. In the *Theoria Motus Abstracti*, physical conatus and mental appetite are merged in the proposition that "all body is instantaneous mind, or mind lacking memory," since the conatuses which oppose each other are retained but a moment, and cannot maintain a cumulative direction or end as in consciousness (Gerhardt, IV:230; cf. Loemker, p. 141).

ture of existence, the polarity of action and passion, of being and nonbeing, and his logico-dynamic conception of space of which corporeal space is an appearance, all of these culminating in the vision of a Republic of Being—these are the ideas which are to ripen in his thinking until, in the early Hanover years, refined and clarified by mathematical learning, an appreciation of the mechanical order of nature, and a clear theory of perception, they are reformed into his mature monadology.

The problem of the origin and nature of Leibniz's Platonism and its adaptation to the new scientific dynamism and the new individualism seems to receive new light from this relationship.[47] Similarities to Plotinus, to Augustine, to Nicolas of Cusa, to Bruno, and to Campanella have been pointed out. Surely the Herborn thinkers constitute a neglected but significant link between these thinkers and Leibniz, whose system is the adaptation of Augustinian Platonism to the modern scientific and political mind—a distinctive new synthesis couched in an old tradition.

The achieved synthesis, however, also gives rise to the chief problem of Leibniz, as it is that of the Herborn thinkers. This is the problem of their twofold conception of logic and its role in the order of the world. On the one hand, they receive from Ramus a linguistic logic with an emphasis upon application and use, whether to the ends of teaching and persuasion (erudition) or, later, of scientific discovery. This is analogous to Ockham's earlier correction of Aristotle's logic by freeing it from metaphysics. On the other hand, their metaphysics is itself panlogistic, rooted in the Augustinian and Franciscan traditions. From this perspective, all existence results from a logical process in the mind of God, and the task of philosophy will be adequately completed only when existence is grasped through an incontrovertible necessity of thought.

The goals of the two conceptions may be compatible, or may even coincide, but in philosophical practice the attempt to relate and to reconcile them has always failed. It was so in Leibniz.

47. Cf. Leibniz's comparison of his thought with Locke's in the Preface to the *Nouveaux Essais* (Gerhardt, V:41): "His [Locke's] system has more agreement with Aristotle, mine with Plato, although both of us are far from the doctrine of these two old thinkers in many things."

"When God calculates and exercises his thought the world (with all individuals in it) is made."[48] Yet the universal calculus failed, being able to reproduce neither the simple notions and principles of the order of creation nor the complete notions of concrete individuals. The same dilemma still seems to confront today's logical formalists: whether to abandon the claim of logic to truth, or to continue to extend symbolic formalization until all experience is caught in the net of constructions with a corresponding sacrifice of the possibility of logical operation. The issue is still unclear—can logic be both an art and a science? Is it ontologically neutral or committed?

48. Gerhardt, VII:191.

Index

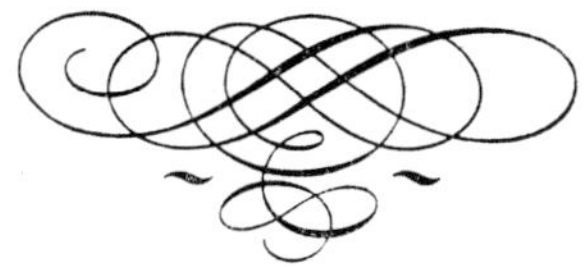